THE ELIMINATION OF MORALITY

The Elimination of Morality strikes at the root of the dominant conception of what medical ethics involves. It addresses the fundamental and timely question of the *kind* of contribution philosophers can make to the discussion of medico-moral issues and the work of health care professionals. It has two main objectives. The first is to establish the futility of bioethics. Anne Maclean challenges the conception of reason in ethics which is integral to the utilitarian tradition and which underlies the whole bioethical enterprise. She argues that the enterprise is philosophically misguided – philosophers do not possess moral expertise and have no special authority to pronounce upon moral issues. In particular, she shows that judgments about the morality of killing cannot be founded on a prior philosophical theory of 'the value of life'. In the final chapter Maclean argues that the primary task for health care ethics is to recover the moral context of medical judgments, and she proposes a role for the philosopher in medical education which deprofessionalises ethical decisions.

The second objective is to expose the inadequacy of a utilitarian account of moral reasoning and moral life. The author rejects the utilitarian claim that reason demands the rejection of special obligations; and argues that the utilitarian drive to reduce rational moral judgment to a single form is ultimately destructive of moral judgment as such. *Pure* utilitarianism eliminates the essential ingredients of moral thinking.

This vital discussion of the nature of medical ethics and moral philosophy will be indispensable reading for students of health care ethics and philosophy.

Anne Maclean has taught philosophy at the Queen's University of Belfast, the University of Newcastle upon Tyne and the University College of Swansea.

THE ELIMINATION
OF MORALITY

Reflections on Utilitarianism and Bioethics

Anne Maclean

London and New York

First published 1993
by Routledge
11 New Fetter Lane, London EC4P 4EE

Simultaneously published in the USA and Canada
by Routledge
29 West 35th Street, New York, NY 10001

© 1993 Anne Maclean

Typeset in 10 on 12 point Garamond by
Witwell Limited, Southport
Printed in Great Britain by
TJ Press (Padstow) Ltd, Cornwall

British Library Cataloguing in Publication Data
A catalogue record for this book is available from the British
Library

Library of Congress Cataloging in Publication Data
Maclean, Anne
The elimination of morality : reflections on utilitarianism and
bioethics/Anne Maclean.
p. cm.
Includes bibliographical references and index.
1. Utilitarianism—Controversial literature. 2. Bioethics—
Controversial literature. I. Title.
B843.M23 1993
171'.5—dc20 93–20281

ISBN 0–415–01081–0   ISBN 0–415–09538–7 (pbk)

To the Memory of

Nelson James Evans
and
Glenys Mary Evans

CONTENTS

PREFACE AND
ACKNOWLEDGEMENTS

In recent years many departments of philosophy in the United Kingdom have acquired students of a novel sort – health care professionals embarked upon courses in medical or health care ethics. A large and ever-expanding body of literature is available for these students; but I believe that they will gain from it an inadequate and one-sided conception of the nature of moral philosophy, of its characteristic concerns, and of the bearing of philosophical enquiry upon their own work. This belief provided one of the impulses behind the writing of this book. Thus, although it is a work of moral philosophy and not of applied ethics, it was written with readers of the above sort in mind. Nevertheless, I hope that other readers too, including students and teachers of philosophy, will find it of value.

The philosophical influence upon me of my former teacher, D. Z. Phillips, will be evident to anyone familiar with his work. As a first year undergraduate at the University College of Swansea I attended his lectures on Plato's *Gorgias*; it was there I first learned of the Socratic condemnation of Sophistry. Many years later, during my brief sojourn in the Centre for the Study of Philosophy and Health Care at Swansea, Professor Phillips was my head of department.

I owe a very considerable debt, both personal and philosophical, to the other members of the original 'Swansea four': Michael Cohen, Geoffrey Hunt and Colwyn Williamson. Michael Cohen in particular has been a constant source of moral support and philosophical enlightenment. I discussed with him, to my benefit, the contents of chapters 2, 8 and 9; and he supplied the title of chapter 8.

Professor John Nelson, of the University of Colorado at Boulder, read and commented extensively upon an earlier version of chapters 3 and 4. He also encouraged me to believe in the value of the book as a whole, although it should not be assumed that the views it expresses are ones with which he would agree.

An earlier version of chapter 2 was read to the Departments of Philosophy at the University of Durham, the University of Leeds, St David's University College Lampeter and University College Cardiff; and to students at University College Swansea and the University of Oxford. An earlier version of chapter 7 was read to a meeting of the Welsh Philosophical Society at Gregynog Hall and delivered as a Francois Bordet Memorial Lecture at the Queen's University of Belfast in 1990. Part of chapter 10 was read to a meeting of the National Centre for Nursing and Midwifery Ethics at Queen Charlotte's College, Hammersmith Hospital. I am grateful to everyone who took part in the discussions on those occasions.

Mr Robert E. Hall (The Queen's University of Belfast) helped in the final revision of the manuscript and saved it from many infelicities and obscurities of expression.

Throughout the book I have followed traditional usage concerning pronouns; none of the devices which authors employ to avoid sexism seemed satisfactory. When an acceptable, genuinely neutral pronoun has been coined I will use it.

Finally, thanks are due to Mrs Lawmary Cohen for typing the whole of the finished manuscript and to Mr Richard Stoneman of Routledge for his patience.

Anne Maclean
Swansea, October 1992

1

INTRODUCTION: UTILITARIANISM AND THE NEW SOPHISTRY

In the opening passage of Plato's *Gorgias* Socrates declares his intention of learning from Gorgias himself 'what the power of the man's craft is, and what it is that he advertises and teaches'.[1] Gorgias, for his part, is only too willing to tell him; he teaches, Gorgias says, the craft of speech, speech in particular about ethical matters – 'the things which are just and unjust'[2] in the wide Greek sense of those terms. He concedes, when pressed, that he does not teach such bodies as juries about these matters, but merely persuades them that what he says is true. However, he also claims that as far as his own pupils are concerned, what he has to offer in exchange for their fees is knowledge – and not mere conviction – about 'the just and the unjust, the fine and the shameful, and the good and the bad';[3] it is not the case that he makes them only *appear* to know about such things as these.[4]

Gorgias, then, claims to possess and teach *moral expertise* – an expertise or craft which stands to matters of right and wrong as, for example, the expertise or craft of the doctor stands to matters of health and illness.[5] If we regard that claim as defining a part, at least, of the Sophistical, then we must also regard a large and influential segment of contemporary philosophical activity as Sophistic. I am referring to *bioethics*; by which I mean medical ethics as conceived and practised by philosophers working in the utilitarian tradition.[6]

This is what one bioethicist, John Harris, has said about the aim of medical ethics in relation to the moral dilemmas posed by medical practice:

> . . . our interest in all these problems and dilemmas will be an interest in their resolution . . . Just as the proper business of medicine is not merely to understand the nature and causes of illness but to try to prevent or cure it, so the proper business of

medical ethics is not merely to understand the nature of the moral problems raised by medical practice but to try to resolve them.[7]

On this view, medical ethics must produce *answers* to the moral questions raised by the practice of medicine; not just any answers, but – as we shall see – the answers it is *rational* to give. The analogy Harris draws in the above passage between medicine on the one hand and medical ethics on the other is a revealing one; let us press it a little further.

The proper business of medicine, Harris says, is the prevention and cure of illness; to which we may add disease and injury as well. These are bad things, things we must eradicate as far as we are able. Something is *wrong* when someone is ill, diseased or injured and it is the business of medicine to put it *right*. Not everyone is qualified to undertake that business; it requires specialised knowledge and specialised training, the kind of knowledge and training that schools of medicine exist to provide. People who have received a medical education – members of the medical and medical-related professions – possess in consequence a unique or special competence in medical matters, one to which the rest of us can lay no claim. Medical practitioners and other health carers are *the experts* when it comes to preventing, treating or curing illness, disease, disability and injury.

What Harris's analogy suggests, if carried far enough, is that similar points apply to the other business he mentions, that of medical ethics. The practice of medicine gives rise to moral dilemmas and disagreements; these, the analogy implies are – like illnesses – bad things, things we must do away with as far as we can. When people differ in their views about a moral issue, something is *wrong* and it is the task of medical ethics to put it *right* – to settle the disagreement by resolving the issue in question. The business of medical ethics, on this account, is to answer the moral questions raised by medical practice. This business, the account implies, like that of medicine itself, is a specialised undertaking. There exists a class of people who, if not uniquely competent to carry it out, are at least especially competent to do so; a class of people who possess *special expertise* in moral matters. These people are not, of course, medical practitioners; they are medical ethicists, who are for the most part professional philosophers.

We saw above that the medical practitioner's title to his special competence in medical matters derives from the fact that he has received the specialised education which is a necessary condition of competence in such matters. He possesses medical expertise because he has been educated or trained in medical science; and it is to his training that he would refer if he were asked why we should attach more weight to his pronouncements on medical matters than to those of anyone else. The question that must now be raised is this: from what is the philosopher supposed to derive his *moral* expertise? What is it that stands to his alleged special competence in moral matters as the doctor's medical training stands to his special competence in medical matters? Why should we attach more weight to the pronouncements of philosophers on moral issues than to those of other people?

There appears to be only one answer to these questions. The special expertise in moral matters that philosophers possess, on the bioethical account, must be the product of an education in philosophy itself; it must be, because there is nothing else which distinguishes philosophers as a group from others. This answer, however, gives rise to a further question: how does an education in *philosophy* make one better at answering *moral* questions than someone who lacks such an education? What connection does the bioethical account draw between philosophical expertise on the one hand and moral expertise on the other? The pursuit of this question will take us to the heart of bioethics; for the answer to it will bring to light the conception of *rational justification* in morality upon which the whole bioethical enterprise is founded. The answer can be summarised in the following way:

If moral questions are genuine questions there must be a procedure for answering them; and that procedure must be a rational one. In the first instance, any answer that is given to such a question must be supported by reasons; as John Harris puts it, '. . . if something is . . . morally right or wrong, there must be some reason why this is so'.[8] If, therefore, someone pronounces an action to be *right* (or *wrong*), he must be able to produce a reason for doing so; he must be able to say what, in his view, makes the action right (or wrong), and in this way provide a justification for the judgement he has made. This is not the end of the matter, however; for he must be able to show in addition that the reason he has produced is an adequate one. 'Reasons' – to quote Harris again – '. . . can always be scrutinised for their adequacy'.[9] If the justification in question is to be truly rational, the reason to which it refers must be capable of withstanding such scrutiny; it must be acceptable from the standpoint of reason or rationality.

The above account of the bioethical position has proceeded in terms of *reasons* for moral judgements and decisions. It could have proceeded in terms of *principles* instead, in the following way: when someone says what makes an action right or wrong, he invokes – explicitly or implicitly – a moral principle; and if the moral justification thus given is to count as a rational one, the principle he invokes must be one which it is rational to employ. Moral principles are no more exempt from rational scrutiny than the judgements and decisions they are used to support; however widely a principle is accepted and however fundamental it may be to our moral outlook, it remains subject to such scrutiny. If it does have a rational foundation, this must be uncovered and set forth; if it does not, the principle is unworthy of the place it holds in our moral life.

On the bioethical account, then, two conditions must be satisfied if a moral judgement or decision is to count as rationally justified. The first is that it must be supported by a reason (or with reference to a principle); the second is that the reason (or principle) in question must be one it is demonstrably rational to accept.

It is in relation to the second of these two conditions that the connection bioethicists perceive between expertise in *philosophy* and expertise in *morality* must be understood. These philosophers would acknowledge that most people can produce reasons of sorts for the moral judgements and decisions they make; but they would insist that those reasons must all be subjected to rational examination or analysis. This examination, they would add, must be conducted by someone who is qualified to do so; and the person who is best qualified, in their eyes, is the philosopher. He and only he is trained in a discipline that takes nothing for granted, a discipline that persists in asking for justifications well beyond the point at which other disciplines have stopped. Philosophy is concerned with the isolation and justification of assumptions, including fundamental assumptions; and it is for those educated in that discipline, therefore – bioethicists would say – to identify the principles on which rational moral judgements and decisions must be based.

We have now arrived at the answer which bioethicists would give to the question posed above: how does an education in *philosophy* make one better at answering *moral* questions than someone who lacks such an education? The answer is: because it enables one to

4

answer these questions *in a rational way*. It does so because it is *philosophical* enquiry which must provide, sanction or underwrite the set of rational principles from which moral judgements should be deduced. The source of the philosopher's special expertise in moral matters is his knowledge of these principles; it is this which gives his pronouncements upon moral issues an authority to which the pronouncements of others can lay no claim.

I have just given a brief account of the conception of rational moral justification which underlies the whole enterprise of bioethics; an enterprise which involves, I have said, the attribution to philosophers (at least by implication) of moral expertise. The account is not yet complete, and it must be admitted that it is something of a caricature – though not, in my view, one which distorts beyond recognition the features of the original. If my understanding of their objectives is correct, bioethicists wish to present the moral conclusions for which they argue as the verdict of philosophy itself upon the issues they discuss.

The objection I wish to make to the bioethical enterprise is a fundamental one. It is that philosophy as such delivers no verdict upon moral issues; there is no unique set of moral principles which philosophy as such underwrites and no question, therefore, of using that set to uncover the answers which philosophy gives to moral questions. When bioethicists deliver a verdict upon the moral issues raised by medical practice, it is their own verdict they deliver and not the verdict of philosophy itself; it is their voice we hear and not the voice of reason or rationality. To say this, it must be emphasised, is not to deny that there can be rational answers to moral questions; it is to deny that, for any moral question, there is a *uniquely* rational answer to it which can be uncovered by philosophical enquiry. My claim is not that rational justification is impossible in morality, but that it is not the sort of thing bioethicists say it is. It is their conception of rational justification I wish to reject and not the concept itself.

Consider the bioethicist's attitude to *moral disagreements*. I said above that bioethicists regard such disagreements as bad things, things we must strive to eradicate. When people disagree about a moral question raised by medical practice, the business of medical ethics, according to bioethicists, is to settle this disagreement by resolving the matter at issue – by discerning which of the competing views, if any, is the rationally justified view. It is not possible, in their eyes, for both of two opposing moral judgements or points of view to have a rational justification; if one is rationally justified, they think, *really* rationally justified, then the other cannot be. Where disagreement exists, the views of one (at least) of the parties to the disagreement must be defective from the standpoint of reason or rationality.

It seems to me that this is not the case. It may in fact be the case, for a given instance of moral disagreement, that only one of the opposing judgements can be given a rational justification; but that is not necessarily the case for all instances. I would contend, then, that opposing moral beliefs, opinions, judgements or attitudes may both – or all – be adequate from the standpoint of reason or rationality; indeed, that there need be in such cases *no* standpoint which is *the* standpoint of reason or rationality. Thus it is possible for there to be moral disagreements which cannot be resolved by an appeal to what it is rational to think about the matters at issue; the reason being that there is *more than one* thing it is rational to think about these matters.[10] The chapters that follow contain several illustrations of this point; let us look briefly at one of these, reserving lengthy discussion of it for a later time.

Two people are trapped in a burning building; one of them is a leading cancer researcher while the other is the charlady in his employ.[11] There comes upon the scene a man who can rescue one, but not both, of these people and who therefore has to choose which of them it should be. This man happens to be the charlady's son. The question is, whom should he save?

If this question were asked of a random sample of people, it would be likely to receive a number of different answers. Some of the people asked would say that the rescuer should save the cancer researcher, others that he should save the charlady, and still others, perhaps, that it would not matter from a moral point of view which of the two he saved.

Why should it not be said that all of these answers would admit of a rational justification? Someone who gave the first could cite the importance for the sick of the work which the cancer researcher's death would bring to a premature end; someone who gave the second could point out that the charlady is the man's *mother*, the woman who gave birth to him and brought him up; and finally, someone who gave the third could remind his listeners that the charlady and her employer are both *human beings*, and that their lives are of equal value or worth.

In the situation described, then, there can be *different* judgements

6

about what the rescuer should do; and all of these judgements can be supported by moral reasons, or with reference to moral notions, standards, values or principles. In other words, all of them admit of a rational justification.

It will be obvious, I think, how the bioethicist would respond to this. He would refuse to allow that all of the judgements just mentioned admit of a rational justification *properly so called*. They can all be supported by reasons, to be sure, the reasons already alluded to; but that, he would say, is neither here nor there. This is because, as we saw above, his view is that it is not sufficient to give reasons for a judgement; one must show in addition that those reasons are acceptable from the standpoint of reason or rationality. It is possible, he would say, that not one of the reasons presently in question is acceptable from that standpoint; and it is surely certain that not all of them can be, at least to the same extent. What must be determined, he would insist, is which (if any) of those reasons (or principles) is the rationally acceptable one. When we know this, and not before, we will know what the rational answer to the question at issue is; we will know whom the rescuer should save.

We have now returned to the place in the bioethical account that we reached on p.14 – the place at which philosophy makes its appearance as the supplier of the principles from which moral judgements must be deduced (or the reasons by which they must be supported) if they are to have a truly rational justification. It is time to complete that account by asking how, according to bioethicists, philosophy can supply these principles; how, according to them, it can pick out from the variety of reasons people give for their moral judgements the ones which are acceptable from the standpoint of reason or rationality. The answer is: by means of a *general theory* of morality. Let us look at how the need for such a theory was expressed by John Stuart Mill, the principal architect of the utilitarian theory which all bioethicists accept in one form or another.

In the 'General Remarks' with which Mill begins his essay on 'Utilitarianism' he writes as follows:

> The truths which are ultimately accepted as the first principles of a science are really the last results of metaphysical analysis . . . and their relation to the science is not that of foundations to an edifice, but of roots to a tree, which may perform their office equally well though they be never dug down and exposed to light. But though in science the particular truths precede the

general theory, the contrary might be expected to be the case with a practical art, such as morals or legislation . . . A test of right and wrong must be the means, one would think, of ascertaining what is right or wrong, and not a consequence of having already ascertained it.[12]

In morality, according to Mill, the general theory must precede the particular truths; the former is the means by which the latter must be established. Note that Mill speaks of *a* test of right and wrong; his point is, not only that moral judgements must be deduced from general principles ('the morality of an individual action is . . . a question . . . of the application of a law to an individual case'[13]), but also that these general principles must be derived from a single common source – a 'first' or 'fundamental' principle which must be brought to light by philosophical enquiry.[14] Once we know what this principle is, he thinks, we can establish, for any 'secondary' principle that is employed or proposed, whether or not it really merits our acceptance.[15] If the principle can be derived from the 'common ground of obligation', we should accept it; otherwise, we should not. It has in the latter case no rational foundation at all, and should not be used to judge the morality of actions.[16] We shall consider in due course what the common ground of obligation is supposed to be.

We now have a full account of the conception of rational moral justification which underlies the bioethical enterprise. As we have seen, it is a conception which assigns to philosophy – and therefore to philosophers – a crucial and indispensable role in identifying the rational answers to moral questions. According to this conception, in morality particular truths (as Mill puts it) must be established by means of general theory; and it is the business of moral philosophy to supply that theory. It is for this reason, bioethicists would say, that philosophers can claim a special competence or expertise in moral matters; they are able to formulate the theory just referred to and use it to identify the principles that must be employed in making rational moral judgements about particular cases. They can distinguish the reasons for judging which are rationally acceptable from the ones which are not, and in this way distinguish the answers to moral questions which are rationally justified from the ones which are not. These answers constitute, therefore, the verdict of philosophy itself upon the matters at issue.

It is high time for my fundamental objection to bioethics to be restated. Philosophy, I maintain, does not deliver a verdict upon moral questions; and it follows that bioethics, conceived of as the search for that verdict, is a futile and misguided enterprise. The moral conclusions to be found in the books and articles written by bioethicists are not ones that philosophy produces or sanctions; they are no more than the opinions bioethicists hold upon the matters they discuss.

It is important, in my view, that this should be said, said loudly and said by philosophers; for if a conclusion is presented as the only rational conclusion which can be reached about a certain matter, the conclusion, indeed, which philosophy itself has shown to be correct, the views of people who think differently on the matter can be dismissed as unworthy of serious attention; and this, in fact, is exactly the attitude that bioethicists themselves seem to take. 'Do we trust arguments, and follow them wherever they lead' asks one bioethicist, James Rachels, 'or do we trust our intuitions and reject argument when it does not lead in the "right" direction?'[17] The insinuation is that bioethicists do the former, whereas those who disagree with them do the latter. I doubt if remarks like the one quoted would cut much ice with Rachels' fellow philosophers. Works on medical ethics, however, are not read only – or even mainly – by philosophers; they are read also by medical practitioners and other health carers, whose acquaintance with philosophy may extend no further than those works themselves, and who may for that reason be more inclined to take them at their own estimation.

I wish to argue, then, for *the futility of bioethics*. It is evident from the account of the bioethical enterprise just given that in order to do so I must take issue with the conception of rational moral justification which the enterprise involves; and in particular with the place that conception assigns to a general philosophical theory of morality. I shall indicate shortly the grounds on which I propose to do this; but before doing so I shall describe as briefly as possible the content of the theory some version of which all bioethicists accept – the theory of utilitarianism.

We saw above that according to Mill the principles from which rational moral judgements should be deduced must all be derived from a first or fundamental principle, or common ground of obligation; and it is the business of moral philosophy, he maintains, to say what this is. Let us look at how Mill himself defines the first principle – the Principle of Utility – in his essay on 'Utilitarianism'.

In chapter 2 of the essay Mill writes as follows:

9

> The creed which accepts as the foundation of morals, utility, or the Greatest Happiness Principle, holds that actions are right in proportion as they tend to promote happiness, wrong as they tend to produce the reverse of happiness. By happiness is intended pleasure, and the absence of pain; by unhappiness, pain and the privation of pleasure.[18]

The moral value of an action, according to the Principle of Utility, depends entirely upon the state of affairs it promotes or produces – upon its *outcome*. Moral action, on this account, has an aim or end, that of maximising happiness and minimising unhappiness. As the passage quoted above makes clear, Mill (like Bentham before him) defined happiness in hedonistic terms; happiness is to be understood as pleasure and the absence of pain, unhappiness as pain and the privation of pleasure. Most contemporary utilitarians, however, speak instead of the satisfaction and frustration of desires or preferences. We must maximise preference satisfaction, they say, if we are to act rightly. Thus *what people want* is the ultimate measure of right and wrong; this is the essence of utilitarianism.

Although all bioethicists are utilitarians, none of them is a *pure* utilitarian; their utilitarianism is invariably of an impure sort. I make a distinction, then, between *pure* utilitarianism on the one hand and *impure* utilitarianism on the other. By impure utilitarianism, I mean any form of utilitarianism that admits standards of conduct independent of (or separate from) utility; by pure utilitarianism, I mean utilitarianism as defined above – a theory of morality that admits only utility as the measure of right and wrong, and that defines utility in terms of the satisfaction of desires or preferences.[19]

It is important not to confuse my distinction between pure and impure utilitarianism with the familiar distinction between act (or extreme) and rule (or restricted) utilitarianism. We have seen that according to Mill the Principle of Utility is the 'first' or 'fundamental' principle of morality. He affirms, however, the practical necessity of 'secondary principles' – derivative moral principles or rules by means of which, for the most part, moral judgements must be made in particular cases.[20] These constitute the rules of rule utilitarianism. The point which must be emphasised is that on Mill's account secondary principles all derive their authority from the Principle of Utility; this principle alone, he insists, is the ultimate standard of right and wrong.

Consider, for example, the rule against lying (or the principle that lying is wrong). On the account Mill gives, this rule (or principle) is justified only because experience has shown that acts of lying are usually detrimental to the general happiness. There is no question, on his account, of such acts being *intrinsically* as opposed to *instrumentally* wrong – wrong 'in themselves', irrespective of what they promote or produce. If lying is wrong, it is wrong because of the bad consequences that acts of lying generally have; and the same goes for any other sort of wrong action. For any moral principle at all, on this view, we can ask if it is really justified; and the only acceptable answer will be one that refers to the utility of having the principle.[21]

The rules of rule utilitarianism, then, do not compromise the essential unity of the utilitarian theory (unless the rule-follower succumbs to rule worship – see p.175); utility remains, in Mill's phrase, the 'common ground of obligation'. This unity is compromised, however, in the case of impure utilitarianism; for impure utilitarianism, as I have said, admits standards of conduct which are independent of utility. Paramount among those standards tend to be *autonomy* (Mill's *'individuality'*) and *equality*. These ideals have been associated with utilitarian thought from the beginning; and both are conspicuously present in the work of bioethicists. I shall comment here upon equality only.

We saw above that according to Mill moral action has an end – the promotion of happiness – and we act rightly only if what we do furthers that end. But it is *people*, of course, who are happy or unhappy, *people* who have desires that can be satisfied or frustrated; and Mill insists that we must not treat the happiness of some people as more important than the happiness of others. He maintains in chapter V of 'Utilitarianism' that this equality of treatment '. . . is involved in the very meaning of Utility, or the Greatest Happiness Principle', which '. . . is a mere form of words . . . unless one person's happiness, supposed equal in degree . . . is counted for exactly as much as another's.'[22]

Thus, in Mill's view, Bentham's oft quoted dictum that 'everybody [is] to count for one, nobody for more than one' does no more than make explicit what is implicit in the Principle of Utility itself. Is he right about this? The answer, I think, is yes and no.

On Mill's account, as we have seen, the Principle of Utility is the only fundamental principle of morality; no other principles are on a level with it. The general happiness – the greatest amount of happiness altogether – is the sole ultimate measure of right and wrong. Actions are right, on this account, if and only if the sum total of the happiness they produce is greater than the sum total of the happiness that would be produced by any of the alternative actions open to the agents in question. Clearly, if what matters from the moral standpoint is the amount of happiness an action produces *and nothing else*, no grounds are available for judging it better that some people rather than others should be happy; no grounds are available for assigning more weight to the happiness of some people than to the happiness of others. The Principle of Utility allows us no moral reason for treating people unequally; to this extent Mill is correct in what he says.

On the other hand, Mill is also incorrect; for the Principle of Utility on its own allows us no moral reason for treating people *equally* either. What I mean is that it allows us no positive moral ground for caring about equality of treatment *as such*. Provided an action produces at least as much happiness as any other that is available, the distribution of the happiness should be a matter of no moral consequence. For example, there should be nothing to choose, morally, between an action productive of happiness in which all share, and one productive of the same amount of happiness more narrowly distributed. Thus anyone who insists that there *is* something to choose between these actions is going beyond what the Principle of Utility implies. He is invoking a positive moral conception of *equal worth or entitlement*; and this conception could actually conflict with utility in certain circumstances – if, for example, the sum total of the happiness in which all shared were less than that of the happiness in which only some shared. In so far as Bentham's dictum involves such a conception, Mill is mistaken in thinking that it is simply an 'explanatory commentary'[23] upon the Principle of Utility.

Equality, as a positive moral conception, value or ideal, is separate from utility and cannot be reduced to it. When utilitarianism admits conceptions of this sort, it becomes – on my account – impure. Pure utilitarianism admits no such conceptions; it recognises utility alone as the standard or measure of moral conduct, and, to repeat, it defines utility in terms of the satisfaction of desires or preferences. This is quite consistent with allowing the necessity for practical purposes of secondary principles or moral rules – those 'intermediate generalisations' compared by Mill to signposts on a road or the contents of a sailor's almanac.[24]

Moral action, according to pure utilitarianism, aims at the maximising of preference-satisfaction; what is right is what is preferred. Mill himself emerges from his writings as a very impure utilitarian indeed; and the philosophers whose work is discussed in chapters 2 to 7 below

– bioethicists like Harris and Singer – are also, as I have said, impure utilitarians. It is not until chapter 8 that a pure utilitarian theory – that of R. M. Hare – makes its appearance. Furthermore, the Principle of Utility tends to appear in bioethical writings *in Kantian disguise*. When Harris, for example, identifies the principle he regards as fundamental to morality, he calls it the principle of *Respect for Persons*;[25] which expression is generally used to refer to the third formulation of Kant's Categorical Imperative.[26] Harris's explanation of what he means by this principle, however, shows that his concerns are essentially those of an impure utilitarian. We show a person respect, he says, by concerning ourselves with his welfare – his well-being or happiness – and respecting his wishes or free choices; and respect understood in this way is owed in equal measure to all persons.[27] Thus the values in terms of which Harris defines respect for persons correspond to *utility*, *autonomy* and *equality*; and it follows that his principle of Respect for Persons is a variation upon the Principle of Utility as understood by Mill.

The same is true of the principle presented by another bioethicist, Peter Singer, as the only rational basis for moral judgements and decisions – the Equality Principle.[28] According to this principle, we must give equal consideration to the interests of all the people affected by our actions; and what people have an interest in, according to Singer, is their well being (understood in terms of 'pleasurable states of consciousness') and their autonomy, or capacity for self determining action.[29] These, he says – apparently in all seriousness – are the 'two main values to which human life gives rise'[30].

We have now identified the essential features of the utilitarian theory of morality which all bioethicists accept. Let us return once more to the conception these philosophers promote of the relationship between this theory and the particular moral conclusions they reach.

Bioethicists set out to resolve specific moral issues; that, as we have seen, is the object or end of the whole bioethical enterprise. The role a general theory is supposed to play in this enterprise is crucial, for it is through the theory that its object is supposed to be achieved. The theory, allegedly, is the means by which moral truths can be established and moral disagreements resolved. In practice, moral justification takes many different forms; people give many different reasons or justifications for the moral judgements and decisions that they make. In consequence moral disagreement can occur, as it does in the example of the burning house. A theory of morality, on the bioethical account, lays down the form that moral justification *should* take; and in this way it enables us to resolve disagreement in the way it is rational to do so. In the case of the rescuer's dilemma, for instance, it enables us to pick out as the rational response to it the first of the ones mentioned on p. 6; the rescuer should save the cancer researcher, because that is the action which would promote the general happiness (or – as Singer would say – the interests of all impartially considered [31]).

According to the view under discussion, then, our moral practice must conform to the utilitarian theory if it is to count as rational; the theory provides the standard or measure by means of which the rationality of practice can and must be assessed.

But there is an obvious question to which this account gives rise: namely, the question of how the theory itself is supposed to be established. As we have seen, the theory is supposed to determine the rationality of practice – the rationality, that is to say, of the way in which people actually make and support moral judgements and decisions. It is supposed to vindicate some ways of making and supporting those judgements and decisions – one way, ultimately – and not others. What is clear, however, is that some account must be given of the theory's own credentials; and furthermore, this account must at no point assume what the theory itself is supposed to establish: the rationality of certain judgements, or certain ways of making judgements, as opposed to others. To speak in Mill's terms, the theory is supposed to 'precede' particular moral truths; it is supposed to be the means by which some moral judgements are shown to be correct and others incorrect. It follows from this that it cannot be constructed by a method which presupposes the correctness of some judgements as opposed to others, or the soundness of some principles of judgement as opposed to others – *not, at least, if those judgements and principles are ones about which people disagree*. It is the object of the whole exercise to resolve moral disagreements by establishing the truth of the matters at issue; it must not assume that the disagreements have already been resolved and the truth established.

In sum: utilitarians, including bioethicists, claim to have identified the form that rational moral thinking must take; and in virtue of having done this, they claim to be able to pick out, from among the multiplicity of ways in which we actually make and justify moral judgements, the way in which we should make and justify those judgements if we are to do so in a rational manner. However, they are required to show that what they say is correct; they are required to show that moral thinking must proceed in the way they say – and, of course, without begging the question. As we shall see, begging the question is just what bioethicists tend to do.

Let me state in brief terms the essence of my opposition to. the claims of utilitarianism in general and bioethics in particular. It is as follows: there is no single form that rational moral thinking must take (either directly or by way of 'intermediate generalisations'); and there are no answers to moral questions that constitute the uniquely rational answers to them. Utilitarians select one of the forms that moral thinking actually does take – the form of which they approve – and label it the only rational form; thus conferring upon it a title to which it has no legitimate claim. At best, utilitarianism embodies an insight into how *some* moral thinking proceeds; it identifies *some* of the considerations we deem morally important. It does not tell us how *all* moral thinking *must* proceed, or identify the *only* considerations we *should* deem morally important.

When we make moral judgements and decisions, we do consider, in very many cases, the impact our actions are likely to have upon the well being, or the happiness, or the interests, of the people who stand to be affected by them – indeed, in some cases there may be nothing else of moral importance to consider. We commonly take into account the sorts of considerations of which utilitarians speak; and utilitarianism derives its plausibility from this fact, and its moral appeal from the importance we attach to those considerations. But that is not the *only* thing we do. We commonly take all sorts of other considerations into account also, depending on the circumstances; and, again depending on the circumstances, we may give these other considerations more weight. Thus the theory utilitarians present as the measure of moral practice is – at best – an aspect of that practice writ large; a particular pattern of moral thinking elevated by *fiat* into a definition of the form that rational moral thinking must take. This is by no means an original point; but the rise of bioethics has made it necessary to state old points anew.

I said above that utilitarian theory is *at best* an aspect of moral practice writ large; and I shall close this introductory chapter by explaining my reason for making this qualification.

I have distinguished between pure utilitarianism on the one hand and impure utilitarianism on the other; the latter, I have said, admits values or ideals which are independent of utility, whereas the former does not. Pure utilitarianism admits only utility as the measure of conduct, and it defines utility in terms of the satisfaction of preferences or desires. According to pure utilitarianism, as we have seen, what is right is what is preferred.

As previously stated, utilitarianism derives its plausibility from the fact that when we make moral judgements and decisions, we do appeal in very many cases to considerations of the sort incorporated into utilitarian theory. We think some of the time, and in certain circumstances, in the way the utilitarian says we should think all of the time, and in all circumstances; *unless, it seems to me, the utilitarian in question is a pure utilitarian.* Pure utilitarianism, in my view, does not give even a partial account of moral reasoning; the procedure it describes does not count as moral thinking at all (despite the title of the book which expounds the pure utilitarian theory I shall discuss, namely, *Moral Thinking*[32]). In order to think morally one must think in moral terms; and pure utilitarianism, I shall argue, contains no moral terms in which to think. Utility, as defined by *pure* utilitarianism, is not a moral conception; and it follows that it cannot serve as the measure or standard of moral conduct.

That point will be developed in chapters 7 and 8. In chapters 2 to 6, we shall be concerned, not with pure utilitarianism, but with the impure utilitarianism of bioethics. We shall begin by examining an argument which brings to the fore a conception that is close to the heart of the bioethical enterprise – the conception of *the value of life*.

2

'PERSONS': THE FUTILITY
OF BIOETHICS

I have described in general terms both the objective of the bioethical enterprise and the means by which that objective is supposed to be attained; and I have stated that bioethics, understood in terms of that objective, is a futile undertaking. Bioethicists set out to discover the answers to moral questions that philosophy itself gives; but philosophy as such, I have said, does not give answers to moral questions; and all these philosophers do is disguise the answers they want to give – that is to say, their own moral opinions – as the verdict of philosophical enquiry. In the present chapter I shall enlarge upon and defend this claim with respect to a specific piece of bioethical reasoning. In form, the argument I shall take is typical of the ones bioethicists construct when they set out to resolve moral issues; and in content, it involves the conception these philosophers present as the basis for almost all of their conclusions – that of the value of life.

It is not possible to read the standard works in applied ethics without encountering one version or another of the argument just referred to; its influence has been such that even its detractors tend to find themselves thinking of certain issues in the terms it lays down. The argument exhibits all the features of which bioethicists approve: logical rigour, a movement from the general to the particular, and a conclusion which the majority of 'ordinary people' are likely to find shocking.[1] What it is supposed to show is that certain issues normally assumed to be moral issues – namely, abortion and infanticide – are not really moral issues at all; or not, at least, moral issues of the sort they are normally taken to be. The lives of foetuses and infants, the argument concludes, are at our disposal. I shall take as the basis for my exposition of this argument the version given by John Harris in his introduction to medical ethics entitled *The Value of Life*.[2]

We saw above that bioethicists themselves perceive their enterprise as a natural and proper extension of moral philosophy. It is the business of moral philosophy, in their view, to provide the general theory they claim to be necessary for the establishment of particular moral truths. In the absence of such a theory, they would say, we have no rational procedure for answering moral questions; we do not know what principles it is rational to use in answering them. As far as questions about abortion and infanticide are concerned, as with all questions about the morality of killing, the theory we need in order to resolve them – according to bioethicists – is one concerning 'the value of life'. We must identify the feature (or set of features) which confers value upon the life of any individual which possesses it; and we must then go on to determine whether or not infants and foetuses actually have that feature. If they do not, it follows that their lives are not valuable lives, or lives that, other things being equal, it would be seriously wrong to end. I shall consider in chapter 3 how the bioethical account of the value of life relates to the utilitarian theory of morality outlined briefly in chapter 1.

So we must begin, according to bioethicists, with the question: what makes life valuable? When we have answered this question, and in their view not before, we shall be able to make rational judgements about the value that attaches to particular lives or sorts of lives, such as those of foetuses and infants. We must know what makes for a valuable life *in general*, they say, before we can know whether or not this or that life is valuable. Harris appropriates the term 'person' to designate the possessor of a valuable life; the term stands, he says, 'for any being who has what it takes to be valuable in the sense described'.[3]

What does it take, according to Harris, to be the possessor of a valuable life – to be a person in the sense he stipulates? The answer is, the capacity to value one's life, or to have the desire to go on living. It follows, he says, that *self-consciousness* is a necessary condition of personhood; for in order to value its life in this sense '. . . a being would have to be aware of itself as an independent centre of consciousness, existing over time with a future that it was capable of envisaging and wishing to experience'.[4] Nothing which lacks con-sciousness of itself, therefore, is a person on Harris's account. This, in brief, is the theory of the value of life which he says we must apply to particular cases; and all that remains, in Harris's view, is the application of the theory to the cases under discussion. We must discover whether or not foetuses and infants are in fact persons according to the criteria it lays down.

The view Harris takes, the bioethical view, is that they are not.

18

Foetuses and infants, he maintains, lack self-consciousness, and it follows from this that their lives are valueless; they are not lives that, other things being equal, it would be seriously wrong to end. On this account, there are no rational grounds for moral qualms about either abortion or infanticide; for we may kill foetuses and infants if it suits us to do so. These are not Harris's words, but they are a fair summary of what his argument implies. I shall elaborate upon this point a little before asking whether Harris's conclusion is really something that reason dictates.

I said above that what the argument in question is supposed to show is that abortion and infanticide are not really moral issues. While not, I think, an incorrect account of the position to which Harris and other bioethicists are committed, it may be a misleading one; for although their position does imply that the lives of foetuses and infants are at our disposal, it allows that moral considerations bound up with the claims of persons can constitute objections to ending those lives in particular cases. What it does not allow is that there can be objections to killing foetuses and infants which turn on some supposed wrong done thereby to foetuses and infants themselves. If I kill an infant, for example, I am killing something which cannot value its own life; I am not, therefore, taking away from it anything it can want to keep, I am frustrating no desire it can have. It follows, on the bioethical view, that I am not *harming* the infant, and if I am not harming it I am not, on this view, *wronging* it. I may, nevertheless, be harming, and therefore wronging, other people – for example, those (if any) who love the infant and would like to bring it up. If there are such people, I will in killing the infant be frustrating desires of which they are the subjects. For this sort of reason, the killing of an infant usually requires a moral justification – but *never*, according to bioethicists, on account of any moral claims possessed by the infant itself.

The point can be put in the sort of terms bioethicists themselves tend to favour by saying that an infant, not being a person, lacks *moral status* in its own right – as, for example, does a piece of furniture or a household pet.[5] As with furniture and pets, however, an infant is likely to be something in which persons have an *interest*; and that is sufficient to give the question of killing the infant a moral dimension. It is also necessary, however; remove the interest of persons and you remove at the same time the moral dimension – it becomes a matter of moral indifference whether or not the infant is killed. Make the interest an interest, on balance, in the *death* of the infant, and its life becomes precarious indeed; for there will then be no good reason for allowing it to live.

The radical character of the bioethicists' position emerges quite clearly when we contrast it with a much more familiar position: the advocacy of infanticide in certain cases on the ground of compassion for the infants concerned. We must all be accustomed to the arguments usually advanced for the latter position; the argument, for example, that in certain circumstances the life an infant could expect would be so appalling that it would be better for the infant if it were spared that life. This is sometimes said in cases of gross physical and/ or mental handicap; the fact of the handicap is cited as providing *a moral argument* for infanticide in this type of instance.

On the bioethical view, in contrast, it is not necessary to offer a moral argument for infanticide, in *any* type of instance; the reason being that on this view an infant is not a person and does not possess a valuable life. In his version of the argument, Michael Tooley makes the point perfectly clear: '. . . if the foetus is not a person', he says, '. . . why would one need to point to special circumstances to justify such an action [destroying it]?'[6] The answer is that one would not. On the bioethical account, a 'normal' infant, being no more a person than a handicapped infant (or a foetus), is in exactly the same position with respect to moral status; though a motive for desiring the death of a normal infant is less likely to be present. An infant without a handicap is much more likely to be wanted than one with.

It would seem, then, that the bioethicists' position puts the lives of infants – as well as of foetuses – entirely at the mercy of the interest which others have in them. As I said before, their position is that we may kill infants if it suits us to do so. That, bioethicists say, is *the rational conclusion*; if it proves repugnant to our *feelings*, it is these we must disregard, and not what reason dictates. What reason dictates, according to them, is that foetuses and infants do not possess valuable lives. We must now consider whether this is really the case.

One thing that can certainly be said in favour of the argument outlined above is that it is *valid*; its conclusion really does follow from the conjunction of its premises. However, as every undergraduate knows, the validity of an argument does not imply that its conclusion must be accepted. The following argument is valid, but its conclusion should be rejected:

All non-Aryans are subhuman

Jews are non-Aryans

∴ Jews are subhuman

No argument can prove its own premisses; and if we are to accept as true the conclusion of Harris's argument, we must first accept as true the premisses from which it is derived.

As we have seen, there are two of these premisses. The first – the major premiss – states the theory of the value of life which Harris and other bioethicists give; the second – the minor premiss – states a fact about foetuses and infants, the fact – if it is a fact – that they lack self-consciousness. We may have no fault to find with the minor premiss; we may be prepared to agree that foetuses and infants lack self-consciousness, and that for this reason they are not persons in the sense Harris stipulates. However, this premiss on its own does not imply that no foetuses and no infants have valuable lives. What gives the required significance to it is the major premiss, the premiss that all and only persons – self-conscious beings – possess valuable lives; and with *this* premiss we may well *not* be prepared to agree. If we do reject it, we can reject the conclusion too; we can continue to insist, without the slightest inconsistency, that the lives of foetuses and infants are *not* valueless, are *not* at our disposal. We need not affirm that foetuses and infants are persons in Harris's sense in order to do that; we need affirm only that their not being persons in his sense is neither here nor there as far as the value of their lives is concerned.

We can reject, then, the major premiss of Harris's argument; we can reject the theory of the value of life from which he derives (or claims to derive) the conclusion that the lives of foetuses and infants are without value. I shall argue in due course that we can deny not only the truth but also the *intelligibility* of this premiss. For the moment, however, I shall stay with the weaker claim, the claim that the major premiss of Harris's argument is false. The reason is that if we consider what grounds might be given for saying this, we can bring out the true relationship of the alleged premiss to what is supposed to be derived from it; and that will take us eventually to the heart of my objections to the bioethical enterprise.

On what ground might the theory of the value of life which Harris shares with other bioethicists be rejected? Well, on the ground, for example, that *the lives of infants have value and that infants are not persons in Harris's sense.* Anyone who thinks that the lives of infants are not at our disposal (as most people do) will have all the reasons he needs for rejecting a general theory which implies that they are; and the same goes for anyone who thinks that the lives of foetuses are not at our disposal. In other words, the unacceptability of Harris's conclusion can be cited as showing that the general theory from which it is said to be derived is similarly unacceptable.

Harris himself, of course, would present this as a thoroughly irrational way of proceeding; moreover, that is the way he would have to present it as someone engaged upon the bioethical enterprise. The reason is that, as we have seen, the enterprise depends upon the claim that in morality general theory must precede particular truths. This conception of moral justification is presupposed by bioethicists when they insist that questions about the value which attaches to particular lives or sorts of lives must be answered by means of a theory about what makes life valuable *in general*. Harris's reply to the above objection – that his account of what makes life valuable must be rejected, because the lives of infants have value and infants are not persons in his sense – would have to be that it puts the cart before the horse; it gives particular judgements precedence or priority over general theory, instead of the other way about. There is, however, a difficulty here, which comes to light as soon as we ask how the theory itself is supposed to be constructed.

Let us look back at the position adopted by Mill in the first chapter of his essay on 'Utilitarianism'. Mill insists that whereas in science the particular truths may precede the general theory, this cannot be the case in morality or any other practical art; for without the theory we do not know on what grounds particular judgements must be made, we do not know what principles of (or reasons for) judgement are adequate from the standpoint of reason or rationality. Strictly speaking, this implies that *in no case* can we proceed rationally without first knowing the theory that determines what is to count as a rational way of proceeding. Thus it would seem that on Mill's account we need a theory about what makes life valuable in general in order to make *any rational judgements at all* about the morality of killing; it is not the case that we need it in order to make only *some* of these judgments (such as those concerning foetuses and infants).

It might look, then, as though the bioethicist should say something like this to his readers: put aside all your views about issues of life and death – your views about abortion, infanticide, euthanasia, suicide, self-defence and murder. You are not entitled to have views about *any* of these issues until you have determined what, in general, makes for a valuable life. So begin by determining this, and *then* look at the issues and make rational judgements about them.

It is clear, I suggest, that if the bioethicist were saying this he would be telling his readers to do something they could not do; not because they would be too stupid to do it, but because they would have absolutely nothing to go on in formulating a theory of the value of life. No one who put aside all his views about issues of life and death could have *anything* to say about what made for a valuable life; and this would include the bioethicist himself. Harris, as we have seen, does formulate a theory of the value of life, or of what it takes to be a person (in his stipulative sense); not, however, after putting aside all his views about issues of life and death. Let us consider the account he gives of the method by which his theory was constructed.

Harris suggests that the question 'what makes life valuable?' can be answered by means of the following strategy:

> . . . we [must] look at creatures we are sure are persons if any are – normal adult human beings – and . . . find features of their lives or capacities which . . . incline us to judge their lives of more significance and value than lives which lack such features . . .[7]

In this way, he says, we might come close to the concept of a person that we need. He proceeds to follow the strategy, identifying the features it uncovers as those of rationality and self-consciousness.

The strategy pursued by Harris, then, approaches the general question 'what makes life valuable?' by way of the more specific question 'what makes *human* life (the life of a normal adult human being) valuable?' The answer to the latter question, it is suggested, will isolate a feature (or set of features) which will confer value upon the existence of any being that possesses it, whether human or not.

It is clear that if Harris's strategy did yield a theory of the value of life, that theory would not be one that preceded all particular beliefs (or judgements) about what lives have value. This is because the strategy takes one such belief (or judgement) – namely, the agreed belief that the lives of 'normal adult human beings' have value – as its starting point. Thus any theory the strategy produced would be derived from moral practice, and would not be prior to it.

It might be argued in reply to this point that the strategy would nevertheless have accomplished its purpose. It may have assumed the rationality of some *central* beliefs about what lives have value, but by bringing out what is implicit in them the strategy would have yielded a method of testing the rationality of other, non-central beliefs of that sort. We do not disagree about *everything*; and where there is agreement, it might be said, there is nothing for bioethics to do. The aim of the bioethical enterprise is to resolve moral disagreements; and the strategy under discussion shows how this aim can be achieved. Bioethicists can identify agreed beliefs and extract from them a theory which can be used to bring about agreement (among *rational* people, at any rate) where there is presently contention and conflict; and this is what Harris does. Thus the enterprise on which he is engaged is certainly not futile or misconceived.

I would concede that it may be possible, on occasion, to follow something like the procedure described in the previous paragraph; this cannot be ruled out. However, moral questions are not intellectual questions, and morality is not a logical system. Scepticism is generally in order when philosophers make claims about what is 'implicit' in ordinary moral beliefs and judgements; indeed, it is generally in order when they make claims about what these beliefs and judgements are. Following Harris, I have spoken about our 'belief' that the lives of people have value; in so far as this is an intelligible thought, however, it is not properly called a *belief*.[8] Even if we set that point aside here and agree to speak of it as something we believe, it will not give Harris the conclusion he wants. The most his strategy could yield, it seems to me, would be an account of the conditions that were *sufficient* to confer value upon a life; it could not yield an account of the conditions that were *necessary* in order to do so. Harris claims that our belief that the lives of 'normal adult human beings' have value implies that value must be attached to the life of any individual which is like a normal human adult in being rational and self-conscious. But even if it does, which I doubt, the conclusion is that the lives of *all* rational, self-conscious creatures have value; it is not that the lives of *only* rational, self-conscious creatures have value. Yet it is the second of these statements, and not the first, which constitutes a summary of Harris's theory.

Thus Harris cannot derive his theory of the value of life from the agreed assumption or belief he identifies as the starting point of the strategy described above – the belief that the lives of normal adult human beings have value. If he wishes to establish this theory, he must assume the truth of certain *other* beliefs as well; and these will be ones that are far from agreed. He must assume, for example, that value does not attach to the lives of foetuses and infants; for if it does it cannot be the case that the lives of *only* those creatures which are rational and self-conscious are valuable. *He must assume, in other words, the truth of the proposition which appears as the conclusion of the argument we have been discussing.* He cannot arrive at the theory he puts forward without doing so.

If this is the case, the whole point of the theory is lost. The bioethicist's reason for constructing a theory in the first place was that it was necessary to do so in order to reach a rational conclusion about the lives of foetuses and infants. The theory was supposed to be the means by which disagreements about the value of these lives could be resolved in a rational way; it was supposed to establish the truth of the matter. What we can see now is that the method by which the theory is constructed assumes that the truth of the matter has *already* been established; and is that foetuses and infants do not possess valuable lives. In these circumstances, people who think the opposite may be forgiven for concluding that the whole exercise has turned out to be a cheat.

I have argued that Harris does not start with a general theory; he starts with the judgements or beliefs he presents as derived from that theory. If this were simply a point about how he proceeds *in fact*, it would be of limited philosophical interest; but it is not. It is a point about how he *must* proceed. Harris, like other bioethicists, sets out to give a general account of what makes life valuable; but how can he begin to give such an account in isolation from the judgements he makes about which lives have value and which do not? As I said before, no-one who sets aside all his particular judgements concerning life and death issues can have anything at all to say about what makes for a valuable life. There is a large measure of agreement in judgements of this kind; but there is a large measure of *dis*agreement too. People differ in all sorts of ways about, for example, the morality of abortion and infanticide; it is precisely differences of this sort that bioethicists see it as their business to resolve. What should be clear by now is that such differences cannot be resolved by means of a general theory or account of the value of life. In so far as such an account is possible at all, it must be constructed with reference to the very judgements at issue; and it follows that no agreed account can be given.

In conclusion: bioethicists present the theory they put forward as showing that their judgements, and theirs alone, are correct. In reality, they have to assume the truth of those judgments in order to construct the theory in the first place. Harris in particular and bioethicists in general *argue backwards*; and they have no alternative but to do so. They depend as much upon their responses to cases –

upon what they like to call 'intuitions' – as the people whose alleged irrationality they deride.

We have been examining the essential features of an argument which can be found in the writings of most bioethicists, the argument for the conclusion that the lives of foetuses and infants are valueless. As we have seen, this argument invokes a certain conception of 'the value of life'. So far, I have been content to speak in terms of that conception, without calling into question its sense or intelligibility. However, I intend to argue now that the bioethical conception of the value of life (which I shall call the *metaphysical* conception) is a meaningless one; the question Harris and other bioethicists claim to answer – the question of what makes life valuable – has no clear sense. This does not mean that talk of valuable and valueless lives *never* has sense; it has many senses, but not one of them is the metaphysical sense (non-sense) the bioethicists try to give it. Their trying to give it this sense, furthermore, is bound up with their very conception of what they are doing, the conception described in chapter 1. Once again, the discussion that follows will be based on John Harris's version of the bioethical position.

One of Harris's strategies for arriving at an account of the value of life has already been considered. There is, however, another, and it will be convenient to begin the present discussion by looking briefly at what it is supposed to involve.

The first strategy, let us recall, was indirect, in that it approached the general question of what makes life valuable through the more specific question of what makes *human* life valuable. The second, in contrast, is as direct as could be; it involves investigating 'just what it is that makes existence valuable'.[9] Harris admits disarmingly that the question 'what makes life valuable?' is 'almost absurd' – not because it has no answer, but because it has 'so many answers':

> There are likely to be, and perhaps are, as many accounts of what makes life valuable as there are valuable lives. Even if we felt confident that we could give a very general account of what makes life valuable for human beings, perhaps by singling out the most important or most frequently occurring features from the list of what they value of a large cross-section of people, we would have no reason to suppose that we had arrived at a satisfactory account.[10]

Nevertheless, the task is not as hopeless as it seems; for what can be said, Harris claims, is this:

... if we allow that the value of life for each individual consists simply in those reasons, *whatever they are*, that each person has for finding their own life valuable and for wanting to go on living, then we do not need to know what the reasons are. All we need to know is that particular individuals have their own reasons, or rather, simply, that they value their own lives.[11]

All beings that value their lives have in common the *capacity* to value their lives; therefore it is this capacity, Harris says, that should be identified as the feature which confers value on the life of any being that has it. Since it can be possessed only by beings which are self-conscious, or aware of themselves, the two strategies Harris employs for answering his question about the value of life converge, he maintains, upon a single concept of a person: any being capable of valuing its own existence.

What are we to make of this argument? The first thing that may strike us is that Harris seems to have conflated two *different* senses of 'the value of life' (or 'existence'). People do sometimes speak of what gives their lives value, and mean by it what aspect or aspects of their lives they find most worthwhile, fulfilling, meaningful, satisfying or enjoyable. As Harris says, there are likely to be as many accounts of what makes life valuable in this sense as there are valuable lives. This sense, however, is surely not the sense with which he is supposed to be concerned. He is supposed to be asking 'what makes life valuable' in some sense crucial to *all* of the moral issues connected with killing; and killing *anything*. It is not implausible to suggest that whether or not a life is valued by its possessor may be relevant in certain ways to *some* of the issues connected with killing *people* – such as suicide, euthanasia and the withdrawal of life-prolonging medical treatment – but that, I think, would be the most that one could say. (It is also clear, of course, that by interpreting his question in the way he does – that is, by effectively identifying it with a different question – Harris has once again begged it against, among other things, foetuses and infants.)

There is one advantage, however, in construing the question 'what makes life valuable' in the way that Harris does here; so construed, the question *makes sense*. It invites whoever is being addressed to talk about what matters most to him in his life – his family, his work, his service to a particular cause, or whatever. I have said that Harris seems to conflate this sense with another; but what exactly is the other sense? If his question 'what makes life valuable?' does not invite each of us to talk about what matters most in his or her life, what does it invite us to do? I, for my part, can attach no clear meaning to the question, and no clear meaning, therefore, to the conception of the value of life which is central to the bioethical outlook.

The oddity of the bioethical conception of the value of life may not at first be clear; for we do speak about the value of life, and we usually succeed in meaning something by what we say. What we mean when we speak in this way depends upon the particular context of utterance; and that context will vary from one case to another. One possible context has just been referred to, and there are many others. For example, if an insurance salesman says in connection with an application for life insurance that the life involved is of no value to his firm, he means that the applicant is a bad risk. This is not what – say – an interrogator means when, having extracted all the information he wants from a hapless captive, he hands him over to the executioner saying that his life is of no further value to his captors. Bioethicists are usually too busy theorising to look at how expressions are actually used; though Harris, for one, claims to have considered the judgements people make in certain circumstances. He maintains that his conception of the value of life is implicit in many of the everyday decisions taken by medical practitioners; these decisions, he says, tacitly presuppose an answer to his question of what makes life valuable. I shall argue that this is not the case; but first, let us try to get clear about what Harris does *not* mean by the value of (a) life.

We saw above that according to Harris a life is valuable in the metaphysical sense for one reason only: because its possessor is capable of valuing it, or of desiring to go on living. However, if its possessor does in fact value it, does in fact desire to go on living, that may be for any number of reasons; and the reasons may well differ from one person to another. What a person values about his life is that person's own affair, and is in that sense a relative matter. As Harris say, 'the value of life for each individual consists simply in those reasons, *whatever they are*, that each person has for finding their own life valuable and for wanting to go on living.'[12]

What makes a person's life valuable in the metaphysical sense, however, is not, according to Harris, his or her own affair. There is supposed to be an *absolute* criterion for this, the one Harris gives. Thus a life can lose the value it has for its possessor without losing its absolute value, without ceasing to be valuable in the metaphysical sense. A person may cease to value his life, but for as long as he remains *capable* of valuing it – as long as he retains self-awareness, therefore – it counts as a valuable life in the sense proper to the argument described above, it remains a life the taking of which requires a moral justification of an appropriate sort. A genuine desire for death on the part of the possessor of the life would provide such a justification in Harris's eyes (see below, p.79). But this desire would not make the life in question *absolutely* valueless; it would make it *relatively* valueless, or valueless to its possessor.

Thus it is not the case that the value of a valuable life, its absolute or metaphysical value, is the same as its value to the person whose life it is. Is it the same as its value *to others*, to persons other than its possessor?

There may be some temptation to think that it is, because Harris is concerned to arrive at conclusions about how living beings may be treated; conclusions specifically about whether or not and under what circumstances they may be killed. However, these are precisely *conclusions*; or at least, as we have seen, that is what they are supposed to be. An account of what makes life valuable figures in the premisses from which these conclusions are said to be derived. As far as a person is concerned, the value of his life in the metaphysical sense is something that should constrain the behaviour of others towards him; it is *because* his life is valuable, according to Harris, that it would not be right – other things being equal – for others to kill him, for example, or allow him to die if they can prevent it. This remains true even if his life is of no value to them in some other sense or senses.

So on Harris's account, just as a person's life can remain valuable in the metaphysical sense even when he himself has ceased to value it, so too it can remain valuable in the metaphysical sense even when others have ceased to value it also. The value, in the metaphysical sense, of a person's life is not – it would seem – its value *to* anybody at all; in which case I must confess that I do not know what sense to make of it.[13]

Harris himself is aware that there is something strange about the question he is trying to ask, the question 'what makes life valuable?' in the metaphysical sense; he says that some of his readers may regard it as too 'abstract' a question to play a role in medical ethics. However, he goes on to maintain that it already plays a role in that sphere, in that 'many of the day-to-day decisions taken in medical practice presuppose particular answers to this question.'[14] Among the decisions he mentions are decisions to abort handicapped foetuses and decisions to allow certain patients (for example, those who are very old, or terminally ill, or permanently comatose) to die. Let us look at the construction Harris places upon these decisions.

Consider first the decision to abort a foetus on the grounds that it is handicapped, physically or mentally or both. For Harris, this decision implies a belief that 'such an individual is, or will become, less valuable than one without such a handicap, less valuable because less *worth saving* or less *entitled to life*.'[15] Is he right? It seems to me that he is not; the decision he mentions does not presuppose or imply any such belief, for it can be understood in quite other terms. Those responsible for it might see themselves (rightly or wrongly) as acting either in the interests of the child that would otherwise be born, or in the interests of the family of which the child would become a member. These concerns may be combined, but it will be convenient here to examine them separately, beginning with the second.

Suppose it is said that the burden of rearing a handicapped child is one which a particular family would be unable to bear. Is there any implication here about the child's 'entitlement to life'? The meaning of this expression is so obscure, in my view, that it is hard to say; but to the extent that the question is intelligible it would seem that it must be answered in the negative. If a doctor, for example, says in these circumstances that he has agreed to carry out an abortion because the family will be unable to cope, then *that* is his reason and there's an end. He is not expressing a view to the effect that people with handicaps are less 'entitled to life' than people without; he is thinking about the family's inability to shoulder the difficulties and responsibilities involved in bringing up a handicapped child. His decision is comparable, I suggest, to that of a colleague who agrees to terminate the pregnancy of a frightened fourteen-year-old who lacks the support of the child's father and of her own family. In both cases, what is held to justify the abortion is an inability to cope; the child's entitlement to life, or lack of it, does not enter into the matter.

An appeal to the interests of the child, rather than the interests of the family, might seem to be more promising from Harris's point of view; because what might be said in the course of such an appeal is that the child's life would not be 'worth living'. Once again, however, this would not be a point about the child's 'entitlement to life'; rather, it would be a point about the *kind* of life the child would have were it to be born – a life of suffering and pain, perhaps, or one devoid of characteristically human activities and devoid, therefore, of character-istically human joys. It is *compassion for the child* that is being urged in these circumstances, not its failure to pass some test which would have secured it the prize of an entitlement to life.

It is important to remember that it is an answer to what I have called the *metaphysical* question about the value of life that the decision in question is supposed to presuppose. As we have seen, Harris is initially careful to make a distinction between the value of a person's life in the metaphysical sense, and the value of a person's life to that person; but his vigilance in the matter is not sustained. If the doctor referred to above asks the question 'would the child's life be *worth living?*' he is attempting to look at its life from the point of view of the person the child would become. His question engages, not with the metaphysical conception of the value of life, but with the conception of the value of a person's life to that person.

It is of course the case that there are reasons other than those just mentioned for deciding to abort a handicapped foetus. The care of handicapped people is costly, and it is in part a desire to cut costs that lies behind programmes which screen for certain handicaps. Where a handicap is detected the mother will be offered an abortion, because that would be cheaper for the National Health Service in the long run. If the offer is accepted, this may not be because the mother believes that she would be unable to *cope* with bringing up the child. Like the National Health Service, she may prefer not to have to cope. This does not mean that she believes people with handicaps to be less 'entitled to life' than people without; there are, after all, gender-related abortions, and while some of these may be bound up with beliefs about the relative worth of men and women, not all of them are. Whatever we may think of someone who opts for an abortion because she is expecting a boy and she doesn't *want* a boy, her doing this does not show that she thinks boys are less 'entitled to life' than girls, or that she has a view about what makes life valuable in the metaphysical sense. No more does the decision of a person who, in Tooley's words, would *prefer* not to raise a handicapped child.[16]

Thus it is not the case, I suggest, that the decision to abort a handicapped foetus implies or presupposes any view about what makes life valuable in the metaphysical sense, the sense (if it is a sense) crucial to the argument discussed above. We must now consider whether Harris fares any better with the other decisions he mentions in this context, ones concerning the giving or withholding of treatment.

Speaking of 'the aged or the terminally ill or those in a permanent coma' Harris says this:

if we decide against resuscitation, or divert resources to more 'worthwhile' cases or types of cases, we are treating these lives as *less valuable, less worthy of preservation* than the others whom we choose to help.[17]

I shall argue once again that Harris distorts these decisions in an effort to make them appear to imply what he says they imply; the fact is that they imply nothing of the sort.

Philosophers who take it upon themselves to say what doctors' decisions imply would be well advised to look at what doctors themselves have to say. This is what one doctor, Richard Lamerton, has written about an experience of his own:

> When I was a junior physician in a hospital we were once called urgently to the bedside of a lady of ninety . . . the old lady's heart had stopped (as hearts are apt to do around ninety!) . . . I and the other houseman launched into a full scale resuscitation. With violent drugs, injected direct into the heart, blasts of electric current through her chest, noise and chaos she had anything but a peaceful death. On reflection we realised that all this had been inappropriate . . .[18]

Why did Lamerton conclude that it had been 'inappropriate' to try to resuscitate this patient? Because her life was 'not worth saving'? Because it was 'without value'? It would be misleading, I suggest, to answer yes to these questions. Lamerton does go on to say that medical teams should consider 'just what *kind* of life they would be restoring the patient to';[19] and we might, I suppose, call this a concern with the value of the patients life. However, once again it would be a concern with its value *to her*, and not its value in the metaphysical sense. Not that the former is an especially happy way of speaking. Consider the words of Eli Khan, a cancer patient who requested his doctors not to treat his condition:

> I am ready to die. The machine is worn out and the mechanic must now give up . . . what is wrong with death? I have lived a very proud life. My children have all been proud of their father and I want them to remember me as a *mensch*, a human being.[20]

It is the *value* of Mr Khan's life – a happy and proud life – not its *lack* of value which explains his refusal of treatment and his readiness to die; together with his view that there is nothing wrong with dying when one has lived such a life. He would have agreed with Lamerton that 'death is not an enemy to be swatted and parried to the last grim moment'.[21]

Decisions to withdraw or withhold treatment, then, can be made, and commonly are made, in the interests of the patient concerned, where these include his interest in dying 'a good death' – one that is as peaceful and as dignified as possible. It is misleading, to say the least, to express the judgements which underlie these decisions in terms suggestive of contempt for the patient involved; this is precisely what Harris does, it seems to me, when he speaks of their lives as 'less valuable, less worthy of preservation' than the lives of other patients.

The last point must be borne in mind when we consider what should be said about people in a prolonged irreversible coma (or a persistent vegetative state). Cases of this sort might be thought to serve Harris's purpose, for there are people with no philosophical axe to grind who are tempted to say of individuals in the conditions mentioned that they are no longer *persons*. Not everyone, however, would say that, and those who would say it would be unlikely to mean by 'person' what Harris means, or to intend the implications he intends. If these people were to say that such individuals should be allowed to die, or even be killed, it would not be because they deemed them no longer 'valuable', or no longer worthy of moral respect. Rather, their view would be that it is precisely because such individuals remain worthy of moral respect that their lives should be brought to a dignified end. To say this is to agree with the bioethicist about the course of action that should be taken; it is emphatically not to agree with him about the reason why it should be taken.[22]

We have now examined the day-to-day decisions which, according to Harris, tacitly presuppose an answer to the metaphysical question of what makes life (or *a* life) valuable. Harris is not claiming that they presuppose his answer; only that they presuppose some answer or other, and show, therefore, that the question he wishes to ask already plays a role in medical practice. I have argued that this is not the case; none of the decisions he mentions implies any assumption about what makes life valuable in the metaphysical sense. Thus I stand by my assertion that the metaphysical conception of the value of life, the conception which is central to Harris's entire discussion, has no clear meaning. We must now consider what, if anything, is left of that discussion.

All that is left, it seems to me, is Harris's own attitude to (or opinions about) certain moral issues – abortion and infanticide, for example. What he thinks, as we have seen, is that the lives of foetuses and infants are at our disposal; we may end these lives if it suits us to do so. I have not argued that *that* judgement lacks sense. If, then, the claim that the lives of foetuses and infants are valueless is taken to *mean* that we may end these lives if it suits us to do so, then *this* judgement does not lack sense either; and I suggest that that is all it should be taken to mean – all it *can* be taken to mean. It is simply the expression of a moral point of view; *one point of view amongst others*.

Bioethicists themselves, when they make claims about the value of life, see those claims as something more than the expression of one point of view amongst others; they see them as expressing the philosophical justification for the only point of view it is rational to hold. The proposition that the lives of foetuses and infants are valueless is presented by them as *the reason why* we may kill foetuses and infants if it suits us to do so; the reason why, moreover, that *philosophy* provides. Their view seems to be that anyone who thinks that we may not do that can be shown by philosophers that he has made a *mistake* about the value which attaches to the lives in question. Thus the bioethical way of construing (or trying to construe) propositions about the value of life is part and parcel of the conception bioethicists have of what they are doing – namely, finding the verdict of philosophy itself upon the moral issues raised by medical practice. They speak as if philosophical enquiry revealed a special metaphysical realm of value or worth, and as if philosophers, in virtue of their insight into that realm, could tell other people *the truth* about the value attaching to lives of a certain sort. Once we know what the truth is, they imply, we will know *the right answers* to questions about how we may treat the possessors of these lives.

But what the above discussion has shown, I suggest, is that talk about the value of a life in this context can be nothing other than talk about how we may treat the possessor of that life; it is not talk about something which *explains* how we may treat the possessor of that life, something it is the philosopher's business to know about. Bioethicists are entitled to their views about abortion and infanticide; but in expressing those views they are not telling us what *philosophy*, as such, says about these issues – philosophy as such is silent about them.

I have argued that the bioethical conception of the value of life, the metaphysical conception, lacks sense. It does not follow from this that there can be *no* intelligible conception of the value of life in a moral context, and in the preceding paragraph I have hinted at the direction in which we should look for one. I shall return to the topic in chapter

7; some remarks are still required here, however, about the question of *justification*.

Is it not the case, it might be asked, that bioethicists give a justification for what they say about infants (for example), whereas people who say the opposite do not? Bioethicists say that the lives of infants are at our disposal; but they offer a *reason* for saying this: that infants cannot value their lives, or have the desire to go on living. If other people believe that the lives of infants are not at our disposal, they too must give a reason for what they say; they must produce a justification for the belief they hold.

One way of responding to this would be to deny the need for a justification or reason in the present case.[23] The proposition in question is not a belief at all, it might be said, but an assumption, a fundamental assumption. Such assumptions are by definition *ungrounded*; they are not supported by reasons or based on any foundation. There have to be such assumptions, furthermore, if the process of justification is not to go on to infinity; if, therefore, justification is to be possible at all. For we could *never* say why if we had *always* to say why — if there were not some point at which we could say, simply, *that's why*.

The trouble with this response, it seems to me, is not that it is wrong, but that it is not right enough – it does not go far enough in its rejection of the bioethical perspective. It concedes too much to that perspective. What the bioethicist presents as a *belief* – a proposition which requires justification – this response presents instead as an *assumption* – a proposition which requires no justification. Thus the difference between the two positions concerns the status of something that both represent as a moral *proposition*; one which can be expressed by saying, for example, that it is generally wrong to kill babies.

This, however, is not something people *think* (in the way they might think, for example, that it is generally wrong to kill wild animals, or that it is generally wrong to leave babies unattended for more than a few minutes). I do not mean that they *assume* it to be true, although it is certainly less misleading to say this than to say that they *believe* it to be true. I mean that it is not something that comes before their minds as a *proposition* at all. To cast it in propositional form, then, is already to misrepresent it, and to do so in a way which tends to serve the bioethical interest. What is misrepresented in this way is neither a belief nor an assumption; the least misleading thing we might call it, perhaps, is an attitude – the sort of attitude that is a matter of the way we instinctively behave. This is the sort of attitude to which Wittgenstein is referring when he says, speaking of what some philosophers call 'the belief in other minds', that 'my attitude towards him is an attitude towards a soul. I am not of the *opinion* that he has a soul'.[24] We are not of the *opinion*, either, that it is generally wrong to kill babies. Our thinking this – our 'valuing their lives' – like our 'belief in other minds', is a matter of what we *do, as of course and without question*. For example, if someone kills an infant, we make him *answer* for it. The question of justification arises *at once* in relation to his deed; it does not arise *at all* in relation to our making him answer for his deed.

The response to what the bioethicist says under discussion is correct, therefore, in rejecting his demand for a justification of what he says we believe; but it errs in representing us instead as assuming the truth of a moral proposition (that infanticide is generally wrong). 'Giving grounds', as Wittgenstein says in a different connection '. . . comes to an end; but the end is not certain propositions striking us immediately as true . . . it is our *acting* which lies at the bottom of the language game'.[25] We treat babies in certain ways and not in others; not, for example, as if their lives were at our disposal. Bioethicists demand *for what reason* we do so, but there is no reason – or, to put the same point differently, their being babies *is* the reason, all the reason in the world.

3

PEOPLE

In the previous chapter we examined John Harris's version of the bioethical argument for the conclusion that the lives of foetuses and infants lack value. Bioethicists are utilitarians; yet at first sight the argument just referred to might not seem to be a utilitarian argument. Harris appeals, not to utility, but to a certain conception of what it is to be a person; and the principle he later presents as fundamental to morality in general and medical ethics in particular is the Kantian sounding principle of *Respect for Persons*. So how, it might be asked, can he be expressing a utilitarian point of view? The answer to this question has already been given. As I said in the first chapter, when we look at what Harris means by respect for persons, we find that although his rhetoric may owe something to Kant, his thinking most certainly does not.

When I discussed utilitarian theory in chapter 1 I distinguished between *pure* utilitarianism on the one hand and *impure* utilitarianism on the other. Pure utilitarianism recognises as the measure or standard of right and wrong only utility, defined in terms of the satisfaction of desires or preferences; whereas impure utilitarianism admits standards of conduct that are independent of utility as so defined, and that can on occasion conflict with it. Foremost among these tend to be *equality* and *autonomy*. It is clear from Harris's account of what respect for persons consists in that his perspective is that of an impure utilitarian. We show a person respect, he says, in two ways: first, by allowing him to do what he wants, and second, by helping him to get what he wants when we can. This is what Harris means by first, respecting the autonomy of a person and second, showing concern for his welfare. Thus what he calls the 'essential elements' of respect for persons correspond to *utility* and *autonomy*; and respect understood in this way is owed *equally*, he insists, to all

37

persons.[1] The principle of respect for persons, then, as Harris understands it, is – as previously stated – a variation upon the Principle of Utility as understood by Mill.

Let us go back for a moment to the way in which Harris defines the term 'person'. We saw in the last chapter that he uses this term to stand for any being who has 'what it takes' to be the possessor of a valuable life; and we saw too that what it does take, according to him, is the capacity to value one's own existence. Something is a person, in Harris's sense, if and only if it is capable of having a certain desire, the desire to go on living. Normally, persons do have this desire, and it is because they do, Harris says, that (other things being equal) they should refrain from killing one another. If I kill someone who has the desire to go on living I frustrate this desire and thus fail to show him respect; what is more, I frustrate at the same time all his other desires.[2] Thus the prohibition on killing rests on the same foundation, for Harris, as all other moral prohibitions; what underlies it is the attitude to a person's desires, preferences or wishes which Harris calls 'respect' for that person. The object of the respect, in this as in all cases, is the person as defined by Harris in the first chapter of his book. On his account, it is as persons in this sense – mere subjects of desires – *and not as people* that we can be shown, and are entitled to be shown, respect.

When Harris introduces his concept of a person he concedes that he is not using this term in the way in which it is ordinarily used; as 'just another . . . term for "human being" ', for an individual man, woman or child.[3] His definition of 'person' is *stipulative*. It is clear that Harris could have used some other term to designate the possessor of a valuable life, and clear too, I suggest, that he should have done so; his use of 'person' is nothing if not tendentious. It is not surprising, however, that Harris himself should be unconcerned by this; because for him what matters about persons in the ordinary sense – people – is that they are persons in his stipulative sense. Harris never returns to people; from his standpoint he does not need to do so, because he has abstracted everything which he regards as morally important about people and subsumed it under his stipulative concept of a person. When we describe the moral life of persons, therefore, we are describing the form that the moral life of *people* should take in Harris's view; and that form, as we have seen, is a utilitarian form.

If we reflect on the form that the moral life of people actually *does* take, however, what strikes us is how much an account like that of Harris leaves out; what strikes us is how *unlike* the moral life of persons the moral life of people is. When we transform persons into human beings leading human lives, we transform also the picture of morality which utilitarians like Harris paint. In this chapter I shall begin to effect the transformation by looking at the various moral relationships in which people, as opposed to persons, can stand to one other.[4]

What moral relationships can exist between persons? The answer is that there can be only one such relationship, that of mutual respect in the sense defined above. Each person is required to respect the autonomy of other persons and to concern himself with their welfare; and he can have no basis for regarding the welfare of some persons as more properly his concern than the welfare of others. Harris, like all utilitarians, is committed to a *generalist* account of obligation.[5]

Consider a given person, whom I shall call person A (letters of the alphabet are singularly appropriate designators for persons in Harris's sense). A can have no obligations to another person B that he does not have also to person C and to person D, and so on for all of the other persons on whom his life could conceivably impinge. In relation to A, all of these persons are on the same moral footing as one another. In other words, A can have no *special* obligations to other persons, for there is nothing upon which such obligations could be founded.[5] Looked at in this way, there can be only the *general* obligation to respect wishes and satisfy desires, an obligation which is binding in equal measure upon everyone. It can never matter, from the moral point of view, *whose* wishes and desires are in question, or *whose* respect and help happen to be forthcoming.

So on Harris's account, the identity of a person, who he is, can be of no relevance at all to the character of his moral relationships with other persons, and no more can their identities, who they are; for it is as *people*, human beings in a social setting, and not as persons in Harris's sense – bare subjects of desire – that he and they have identities at all. According to Harris, *who one is* can be in no way relevant to the form that one's moral relationship with another individual must take. Yet if we look at how things are for people, this is not so. A person's identity relative to another can determine what he may and may not do with regard to that other; it can determine what actions are and are not available to him as moral possibilities. It can determine, too, what, from the moral point of view, it is necessary for him to do with regard to that other – what he *must* do.

It is important to guard against a particular misinterpretation of this point. It might be thought that I am simply drawing attention to the obvious fact that, for various reasons, some people have more *power* to do good – to help the needy, for example – than others. A millionaire, for instance, has it within his power to give more support to worthy causes than could be given by the vast majority of ordinary people; his wealth opens up for him possibilities which are closed to them. Similarly, someone with medical training may be able to save the lives of people injured in an accident outside his house, whilst his next door neighbour, knowing nothing of medicine, can do little more than telephone for an ambulance and bring out blankets. Some individuals, then, are enabled by (for example) wealth or education to do things which are outside the power of those who lack such advantages; and we may express this by saying that what is possible for the former differs from what is possible for the latter.

The above, however, is not what I have in mind when I speak of someone's identity as determining what it is and is not morally possible for him to do in relation to another person. My point is this: that in order to transform persons in Harris's sense – mere subjects of desires – into people, we must do more than clothe them with human flesh and blood and endow them with some desires that are characteristically human. We must also give them *roots* in a human way of life. Man, as Aristotle observed, is a *social* animal, and it is from his social background that a particular man or woman derives his or her identity. I am not referring merely to *names*. The question 'who is that?' is not answered informatively by giving the name of the person in question, unless that name is already known to the questioner. If I am asked 'who was the man you were speaking to just now?' and I reply 'John Smith' the response may be 'so *that's* John Smith' (the famous actor); but it is more likely to be 'and who is John Smith?' This question will usually be answered in terms of John Smith's social role or roles; and it is in this way that an account of who someone is can carry implications for how he may act towards or be treated by certain people in certain circumstances.

Let us suppose, by way of simple illustration, that John Smith is my doctor and that he has a brother, Paul, who is my bank manager. John's role in relation to me is such that he may act towards me in ways that Paul may not, and vice versa; much of what is open to the one is closed to the other. As my bank manager, Paul's proper concern in relation to me is the state of my finances; as my doctor, John's proper concern in relation to me is the state of my health. Were Paul to suggest, on the basis of my overdraft, that I am living beyond my means, I could not with justification tell him to mind his own business; for that is precisely what he is doing. I made my financial circumstances his business when I opened an account at his bank. Similarly, I made my health John's business when I registered with his practice, and I cannot tell him to mind his own business if he advises me to give up cigarettes or to drink less alcohol. I may not take his advice, but I cannot justifiably object to his giving it; he is *entitled* to give it. Furthermore, were I actually to object, John could rightly reply that he has an *obligation* to warn me about the damage I may be doing to my health by indulging in such activities. It is not just that he *may* do it; it is also that he *must* do it, if he is to do his duty as my doctor. Paul has no such obligation; though, unlike John, he does have an obligation to warn me of certain other dangers – for example, the danger of getting myself into serious financial difficulties.

It is not the case, therefore, that all obligations are general obligations. That is not to deny that *some* obligations are general obligations. Consider John and Paul again. There are doubtless some obligations towards me which they share, along with everyone else – the obligation not to deceive me without good cause, perhaps – but there remain other obligations which they do not share. These are *special* obligations, in that they are specific to certain relationships which derive their character and moral significance from the social arrangements, institutions or practices which create and sustain them. Thus an exclusively generalist account of obligations is not appropriate to the lives of people (as opposed to persons). My moral relationship to John is not that of one mere subject of desires to another, but that of a *patient* to her *doctor*; my moral relationship to Paul is that of a *client* to her *bank manager*.

I have been attempting to illustrate and clarify my claim that a person's identity can determine what it is and is not possible for that person to do in certain circumstances. It is, of course, *physically* possible for my bank manager to comment on my unhealthy habits and for my doctor to give me unsolicited advice about my financial affairs; I am not denying this obvious truth. My point is that neither can do these things without overstepping the moral limits defined by the nature of my relationship with him. It is not *morally* possible for them to do these things (within the boundaries of their professional roles).

There is an important point to be made here about *action*. Unlike an event, an action is *something someone does*; it is the work of an agent, and the identity of that agent frequently has implication for how his action should be described. Consider the question 'how many sexual partners have you had in the last twelve months?' Were my

41

bank manager to ask me this question, he would commit a gross impertinence; yet I can conceive of circumstances in which my doctor's *not* asking it would constitute gross negligence on his part. Suppose that my bank manager and my doctor both ask me this question. The question they ask is the same, but what is not the same, despite that, is the act which asking the question constitutes. My doctor is discharging his responsibilities towards me, whereas my bank manager is prying into matters which are not his concern. They may be asking the same question; but they are *doing* different things.[6]

So far, the only social roles I have mentioned are ones which are occupational or professional in character. Normally the people who fill such roles have chosen to fill them, and it follows that normally the obligations internal to the roles are ones which their occupants have deliberately undertaken. However, not all social roles are chosen and not all obligations deliberately undertaken. I chose to become a university lecturer, and I shed the obligations this role involves when I resigned my post. I did not choose to be a daughter and a sister, and although *I* chose to be a mother, some mothers are not mothers by choice.

There may be some resistance to the idea that words standing for biological relationships also designate social roles; surely, it might be said, the relationship between a man or woman and his or her child, for example, is natural not social, a matter of biology not society; how can it be placed in the same category as the relationship of a doctor to his patient, or a bank manager to his client?

I do not dispute, of course, that there is a biological relationship in the former case (though it is significant that in particular instances it may be absent); what I am doing is drawing attention to the moral significance with which the relationship is endowed. Moral ideas are written into our conception of what it is to be a parent – we think of parents as having *obligations* to their children and *rights* against or in respect of them. Once again, these are *special* obligations; I do not have to the children of others the obligations I have to my own, nor can I claim the same rights against or in respect of them. It does not follow that I need never concern myself with their well-being, or that they need never concern themselves with mine. If I know that my neighbour's children are being seriously neglected or abused by their mother, then I should do something about it – alert social workers or the police, for example. It is not my business to bring those children up, but their neglect or abuse by the person whose business it is *is* my business, whether I like it or not. To say that some obligations are special is to say that *not all* obligations are general, not that *none* are.

The examples given above show how it is possible for the identities of people relative to one another to determine, at least in part, the character of the moral relationships which obtain between them. It is not the case that there is only one such relationship, that of mutual respect defined in utilitarian terms. What we must do now is consider the bearing of this point upon the account of moral action which utilitarians like Harris give.

Let us look again at the situation described in the first chapter, that of the unenviable individual who can rescue one but not both of two people trapped in a burning house, and who has to decide which of them it should be. On the utilitarian account, the 'persons' account, both of these individuals are entitled to the rescuer's respect. It does not follow, however, that it is a matter of moral indifference which of the two he saves; for he must consider the respect he owes to all of the other persons whose interests stand to be affected by his choice. He must fulfil his obligations to these persons too; which means that he must give priority to whichever of the trapped people makes the greater contribution to the general welfare or happiness.[7] If, then, one of the people inside the burning building is a well known cancer researcher and the other is that person's charlady, the rescuer must save the former at the expense of the latter.

Suppose, though, that the charlady, as previously stated, is the mother of the man who must choose whom to save. On the 'persons' account, it is clear that this can make no moral difference to the situation. The reason is that on this account, as we have seen, the identity of persons relative to one another can have no bearing upon the moral relationship that obtains between them. The rescuer can have no obligation to the charlady that he does not have in equal measure to everyone else; he can have no obligations which are not general in that sense. The transformation of persons into people, however, changes this; it makes special obligations possible. The fact that the charlady is the rescuer's *mother* is one that in the lives of people (but not of persons) can be invested with moral significance or importance.

It is possible, therefore, for the rescuer to take a view about whom he should save which is the opposite of the utilitarian view stated above.[8] He may say that he should save his mother; indeed, that he *must* save his mother, because she *is* his mother and for no other reason. This is not, it must be emphasised, his excuse for omitting to do what is morally required of him; it is his reason for thinking that saving the charlady *is* what is morally required of him. It is not open to him, he may say, to do otherwise. He need not deny that the considerations to which the utilitarian appeals are important ones; he may even say – though he may not – that were both the trapped people strangers to him, he *would* feel morally required to save the cancer researcher. As things are however, he maintains, it is morally impossible for him to do that – to repeat, he *must* save his mother, he *cannot* leave her to die.

Consider a different situation: a child is killed in a traffic accident, and a team of doctors asks his parents to permit the removal of his vital organs (his heart, lungs, liver and kidneys) for purposes of transplantation. If that were done, the doctors point out, the lives of several people presently facing death would be saved. However, the parents refuse their permission. Faced with this refusal, the doctors can deny that they should proceed with the removal of the child's organs anyway if they are to do what is morally required of them. They can say that it is morally impossible for them to proceed, despite the dire consequences for the people who would otherwise have received those organs. It is impossible because the child's parents have the right to decide what may and may not be done to their son's body; they have the right simply because they are his parents, and for no other reason.

For a utilitarian, as we have seen, moral action has an aim or end – in orthodox utilitarian terms, that of maximising happiness or satisfaction. Utility, in theory at least, is the only measure of what is morally necessary or impossible. What the above examples show is that this is not the case; there can be obstacles in the way of utility which are themselves moral in character. In a given situation, the action a utilitarian would regard as morally necessary – the so called 'optimific' action – may be closed to the agent or agents concerned on moral grounds.

Thus, in the first example discussed above, the rescuer sees himself as not *at liberty* to save the cancer researcher rather than the latter's insignificant charlady; for he cannot leave his own mother to die. Similarly, in the second, the doctors see themselves as not *at liberty* to use the dead child's vital organs in order to prolong the lives of other people; for they cannot override the wishes of the child's parents, who are entitled to have the last word on the matter. The 'cannot' here, as we saw, is a *moral* 'cannot' in both cases. The impossibilities in question are not physical ones; it is physically possible for the rescuer to save the cancer researcher at his own mother's expense, and for the doctors to disregard the parent's wishes; nor are they psychological – 'merely' psychological, as some people might be inclined to say. They are moral impossibilities, in that any account of them must refer to the moral significance of certain relationships.

In the preceding discussion I have sought to highlight one of the central dissimilarities between the moral life of persons and the moral life of people, human beings in a social setting; I have sought to show how *un*utilitarian the moral life of people is. Persons can have only general obligations; people, however, can have special obligations to one another, or special rights against or in respect of one another. These obligations and rights can set moral limits to the pursuit of utility, limits that cannot even be understood if we think of people as nothing more than the naked agents of utilitarian theory, mere subjects of desires the satisfaction of which is the be all and end all of moral action. Both of the examples just given involve family relationships; but there are, of course, innumerable special obligations which do not.

A contrast can be drawn, then, between the moral life of persons and the moral life of people. But, it might be objected, so what? What is the mere fact of this contrast supposed to show? If it is supposed to show that a utilitarian account of morality is inadequate then – utilitarians would insist – it simply fails in its object. If it shows anything at all, they would maintain, it shows not that the moral life of persons is inadequate *but that the moral life of people is*; it is inadequate from the standpoint of reason or rationality, precisely because it differs in the way described (and in other ways too) from the moral life of persons.

Thus utilitarians would urge in reply to the points made above that they are seeking not to *describe* our moral life, but to *change* it. They know very well that as things are we set *limits* to the pursuit of utility, and think of them as moral in character; but it is their characteristic claim that these limits cannot be justified from the standpoint of reason or rationality – that the moral conceptions which impose them have no rational foundation. As we saw in the previous chapter, that is exactly the line which bioethicists like Harris and Tooley take about the (so-called) belief that the lives of infants and foetuses have value. They maintain that this belief fails to withstand rational scrutiny, and that therefore it should not be allowed to impede utility any longer; we may kill foetuses and infants if it suits us to do so. Faced with the remarks I have made about special obligations, rights, claims and entitlements, utilitarians (including bioethicists) would reply to them in similar terms. The fact that such obligations are recognised, they would say, does not show that reason sanctions their recognition; and the utilitarian position is that it does not.

In presenting people as persons, then, utilitarians see themselves as stripping away from our moral lives all the irrational elements, leaving behind only what can be defended on rational grounds. As far as they are concerned, turning persons back into people, as I have sought to do, is simply attempting to keep back the moral clock – to reverse the progress towards a rational system of ethics which they are striving to effect.

Whatever we may think at the moment, we must think like utilitarians if we are to think *rationally*; that is what the utilitarian typically says (especially if he is a bioethicist). In chapter 2 we looked at this claim in relation to the argument just alluded to, the bioethical argument for the conclusion that the lives of foetuses and infants are valueless; and we rejected it. We must now look at the claim again in relation to the matters that concern us here; we must consider whether utilitarians really do show that it is *irrational* to recognise special obligations, rights, claims and entitlements. I shall argue that they do not. Once again, the expression of one moral view amongst others is masquerading as the standpoint of reason or rationality.

As we have seen, the question which Harris and other bioethicists regard as fundamental to the morality of killing is the general question 'what makes life valuable?' They insist, not only that we can answer this question, but that we must answer it if we are to make rational judgements about the value which attaches to particular lives, or particular sorts of lives. The point that the utilitarian must now establish about special obligations is similarly general in character: he must show, not that it is irrational to recognise a given special obligation or entitlement, in a given set of circumstances, but that it is irrational to recognise any special obligations at all, in any circumstances. Nothing less than this will serve his purpose, which is to establish utility as the only rational measure of moral action.

Thus the utilitarian believes, apparently, that the question 'is it rational or irrational to recognise special obligations' makes sense just as it stands; just as he believes that the question 'what makes life (or *a* life) valuable?' makes sense just as it stands.

I argued in chapter 1 that the second of these questions, the 'metaphysical' question about the value of life, does not make sense; it has no clear meaning. I did not argue that it never makes sense to speak of the value of (a) life; I pointed out that we do speak in this way on occasion, and that when we do it is the context in which we speak that gives what we say the meaning it has. We must attend to that context in each case if we are to understand what is being said.

It seems to me that we must respond to the first of the questions mentioned above in much the same way; we must dispute its very intelligibility. It is just too general to have any clear sense. Again, this does not imply that it never makes sense to question the rationality of recognising special obligations; it implies only that it needs to be stated precisely what obligations these are, and in what circumstances the rationality of recognising them has become an issue. It implies, in short, that a context is required for a question of this sort to count as a genuine question – one that can be understood and answered. Let us look at such a context and see what can be learned from it.

Consider the following story: a woman (Mary) is approached by a charity concerned with the homeless and told that her mother (Sarah) is living in one of the charity's hostels, having been discovered wandering about the streets of a distant city in a state of complete destitution. Mary herself has only dim recollections of Sarah, who deserted her when she was a child. Mary is married by now, however, and her husband is aghast when he discovers her reaction to the news; which is that she considers herself morally obliged to remove Sarah from the hostel and care for her in the home she shares with him. It is not only that he finds this prospect unwelcome, which he might have done had Sarah been the best of mothers; it is rather that he finds his wife's response to the situation *incomprehensible*, he can make no sense of it. To him, it is 'crazy' to suppose that Mary can have any particular obligation to Sarah, and if Mary herself believes otherwise then her belief is, to put it mildly, irrational.

I doubt if anyone would find it difficult to understand the view that Mary's husband takes in this case. What is crucial to it, however, is the history of a particular relationship, namely, Mary's relationship with her mother. It is in the light of that history that Mary's husband pronounces his wife's belief about her obligation to Sarah to be irrational, and it is to that history that he would refer in trying to get Mary herself to accept what he says. If we were to change the above story, then, it is probable that we would have to change Mary's husband's view along with it. He might still oppose his wife's proposal, but the grounds for his opposition would have to be different, and so – probably – would its character.

Suppose that Sarah had not deserted her daughter and that she were simply too old and too feeble to look after herself. It would be difficult in these circumstances for Mary's husband to argue for the *craziness* of a belief on Mary's part that she should take her mother in. He might still argue against her actually doing so; he might say, for example, that he and their children should come first, that a nursing home should be considered, that Sarah has another daughter who should play her part, and so on through a range of considerations that most of us would find familiar in this sort of context. My point is that whereas he might *disagree* with Mary's view about what her obligations were, he would be unlikely to find it *incomprehensible*; he would be unlikely to say that her view did not even *make sense*. I shall return to this point, however, in a moment.

'Why is my belief that I must take my mother in irrational? Why does it not make sense?' If, in the situation as originally described, Mary asks her husband this question, he can give her an answer: *she deserted you*. To repeat: the actual history of Mary's relationship with her mother is the key to understanding what her husband is saying. It is this which makes intelligible his judgement about the irrationality of what Mary believes.

There is a further point that needs to be made about this example, and it is an extremely important one. The judgement that Mary's husband makes about his wife's belief *is itself a moral judgement*. Mary knows the history to which her husband refers as well as he does; she is perfectly familiar with the facts that, for him, make it 'crazy' to suppose that she can have an obligation to care for her mother. In the husband's view, the rights correlative to such an obligation have to be *earned*; what he believes is that because Sarah has not *been* a mother to Mary, Mary is under no obligation to be a daughter to her. Yet this is not how *Mary* sees it. In reply to her husband's recitation of the facts about Sarah's past conduct, she might reply: 'when all is said and done, she's my *mother*'. If this is incomprehensible to Mary's husband, it is not incomprehensible to him in the way that sheer gibberish would be. When he says, in this situation, that Mary's belief 'makes no sense', he is delivering *a moral verdict*; one which Mary herself rejects when she gives 'she's my mother' as a moral justification for the action she is proposing to take.

We can see, then, that claims about the rationality or irrationality of beliefs and actions can be moral judgements. In the situation described above, neither Mary nor her husband is appealing to a standard of rationality which is value neutral or value free. Their dispute about what is 'rational' in this situation is a *moral* dispute – a dispute about what it makes *moral* sense for Mary to think and do about her mother. What makes moral sense to Mary herself does not make moral sense to her husband.

This point – that claims about rationality, or 'what makes sense', can be moral judgements – must be borne in mind in any attempt to move the discussion to a more general level from the one at which it has proceeded so far. I have emphasised the importance for an understanding of what Mary's husband says of the specific context in which he speaks. I have said that had Sarah not deserted her daughter, Mary's husband would be unlikely to say that he could see *no sense* in his wife's belief that she should provide a home for her mother. It is not impossible, however, that he might still be saying this, but for different reasons. For example, he might dismiss the whole idea of gratitude to one's parents as 'nonsense'. Where is the sense, he might say, in expecting people to be grateful to those who chose for their own pleasure to bring them into the world? Are people seriously expected to thank their parents for going to the trouble of bringing them up? Why should they? They did not ask to be born. This is a very different point from that made by Mary's husband in the situation as originally described, but it has one thing in common with it: it is just as clearly the expression of a moral attitude or point of view. Such attitudes need not be expressed in the language of right and wrong; they may be expressed equally well, and more forcefully, in the language of sense and nonsense.

Let us return in the light of this discussion to the claim whose intelligibility is in question: the utilitarian's claim that it is irrational to recognise special obligations.

I said above that the question 'is it rational or irrational to recognise special obligations' was too general to have any clear meaning; we need to know what obligations are being talked about, and in what circumstances, before we can make a judgement about the rationality of recognising them. A *context* is required for questions about the rationality of special obligations to make sense. The preceding discussion supports that point, though it shows also that we must not give too restrictive an account of what the need for a context involves.

In the example of the dispute between Mary and her husband, the latter's original claim (that his wife's recognition of an obligation to her mother is irrational) depends on the history of a certain relationship, Mary's relationship with her mother. He is saying that Sarah has forfeited by her behaviour the claims she would otherwise have had upon her daughter; he does not dispute that *generally speaking* people have obligations towards their parents of the sort Mary thinks she has towards Sarah.

Nevertheless, it is not impossible to do this. In the revised version of the example, Mary's husband maintains, not only that Mary owes Sarah nothing in these circumstances, but also that no-one owes their parents anything in any circumstances; he sees 'no sense' in special obligations of *this sort*. The reasons he gives however, do not apply to obligations other than ones of this sort; they are not applicable to special obligations *in general*. Thus we are still left, it would seem, with the necessity of asking anyone who speaks about the irrationality of special obligations to say what obligations he means, and how he would argue for their irrationality. An argument which applies to obligations of one sort may well apply *only* to obligations of that sort.

The onus is on the utilitarian, then, to give sense to what he is saying by producing an argument that is completely comprehensive, in that it applies *to all special obligations at once*, and is not confined to certain special obligations only. This condition of *comprehensiveness*, however, is not the only condition a satisfactory argument on his part must meet; it must also meet the condition of *impartiality*.

We saw above that the position adopted by Mary's husband (whether in the original or in the revised version of Mary's situation) is, like his wife's, a moral position; he does not appeal to a conception of 'what makes sense' which is value free or value neutral. To repeat: what is at issue between Mary and her husband is what makes *moral* sense in the circumstances. Mary's husband may speak of irrationality (indeed, of craziness), but he does not invoke a standard or criterion of rationality which is independent of his own moral perspective, and which those who do not share that perspective must accept. The same is true of Mary herself.

When the utilitarian produces his argument, he must do precisely this. He must show anyone who recognises special obligations – of any sort – that a point of view which denies all but general obligations is the more rational of the two, by some standard of rationality which is impartial between those points of view, and to which his opponents are already committed. It is not enough for him simply to express his own moral perspective in the forceful and rhetorically useful language of sense and nonsense.

The second condition just stated, that of impartiality in the sense described, immediately disqualifies the only argument that springs to mind as satisfying the first, that of comprehensiveness: namely, the argument from the *disutility* of special obligations. These obligations, as we have seen, can constitute barriers or impediments to utility; in the examples given earlier in this chapter, the recognition of special obligations and rights means that it is not open to the agents concerned to do what the utilitarian regards as right. The characteristic utilitarian response to such examples, as we saw, is to say that although special obligations and rights are *in fact* recognised, their recognition is *rationally indefensible*; and it is this point which the utilitarian must now establish. It is clear that if he were to do nothing more than appeal to *utility* as his criterion of rationality, he would not be invoking a criterion of rationality which was impartial between his own moral perspective and that to which he was opposed; *irrational* would mean *unutilitarian*; and no one disputes that it is *unutilitarian* to recognise special obligations.

It is not, let us recall, that the agents in the examples just referred to do not accept that the considerations the utilitarian urges upon them are important; they do accept this. What they do not accept is that *these are the only considerations which matter*. They maintain that in the circumstances described other moral considerations (the special claims of parents) carry more weight than the ones to which the utilitarian appeals. If the utilitarian is to establish his point, he must find a way of showing them that reason or rationality compels them to give up their view.

A bioethicist, Peter Singer, has argued that there is such a way. We can appeal to the very nature of reason, he has claimed, in order to establish the principle that we should in all our actions give equal weight to the interests of everyone they affect – his version of the Principle of Utility. It is to Singer's argument for this claim that we must now turn.

4

REASON AND REASONS

In his book *The Expanding Circle* Peter Singer argues that the principle of giving equal weight to the interests of all – which he calls the Equality Principle – is the only rational foundation for ethical judgements and decisions.[1] The standpoint the principle embodies, he says, is the standpoint of reason itself. The essence of his argument for this huge claim is that rationality requires impartiality (or disinterestedness) and impartiality requires the adoption of the Equality Principle. He writes as follows:

> We can progress towards rational settlements of disputes over ethics by taking the element of disinterestedness inherent in the idea of justifying one's conduct to society as a whole, and extending this into the principle that, to be ethical, a decision must give equal weight to the interests of all affected by it.[2]

We shall look at the details of this argument in a moment; before doing so, we should pay some attention to the context in which Singer presents it.

In the first two chapters of his book, Singer is concerned to assess the relevance for ethics of the discipline known as sociobiology, primarily as exemplified in the writings of Edward Wilson. We need not explore the content of these chapters in detail, but it is worth considering the general character of Singer's interest in, and response to, the claims that sociobiologists make.

Central to sociobiology is the idea of explaining the origin or genesis of ethics (morality) in evolutionary terms; that is to say, by the theory of natural selection. Some sociobiologists, however, including Wilson, think in addition that they can construct out of this explanation a system of ethics that will be justified on scientific grounds. According to these thinkers, sociobiology can provide not only an explanation of certain moral principles, but also a justification of them. Sociobiology, they believe, can tell us what moral principles we *should* adopt given the nature we have acquired as a result of evolutionary processes.

The above claim alarms Singer; and when we look at the ethical system which sociobiologists like Wilson describe it is not difficult to see why. The principles this system contains include ones which sanction exactly the kind of behaviour to which utilitarians are particularly hostile – the giving of 'preferential treatment' to people who stand to us in certain relationships, and especially to members of our own families. Furthermore, sociobiology purports to justify these principles in the name of something for which utilitarians themselves tend to have very considerable respect: science.

What the sociobiologist attempts to do is explain in evolutionary terms the origin and development of *altruism*, defined as action that is directed at the benefit of someone other than the person who acts. So far so good, one might think; utilitarians must surely approve of acting altruistically. The trouble is, however, that the altruism sociobiology explains is limited in scope; all that can safely be accounted for in evolutionary terms, sociobiologists say, is *kin* altruism – concern for one's genetic relatives – and *reciprocal* altruism – behaviour of the sort summed up in the dictum 'you scratch my back, I'll scratch yours'.[3] If this explanation were then made to serve as the basis for an ethical system, that system would be most unlikely to contain any version of the Equality Principle; rather, it would include moral rules which plainly violated that principle, in that they permitted us – indeed, required us – to give special consideration to the interests of those who happened to be our relatives or our benefactors.

It is in the face of this prospect that Singer makes the appeal that is central to his work: the appeal to reason or rationality. He does not contest the explanation sociobiologists give of the origin of ethics (indeed, as we shall see, he actually uses that explanation in an attempt to discredit the very principles sociobiologists think they have vindicated); what he does do is argue that when it comes to *justifying* moral principles, sociobiology can have nothing to say. It can have nothing to say because it is concerned with *facts*; and when we are talking about moral justification, Singer says, we are concerned not with facts but with *values*. Sociobiologists like Wilson, Singer contends, ignore the 'logical gap' between facts and values; between explaining and predicting on the one hand and prescribing and justifying on the other:

53

Science seeks to explain. If successful it enables us to predict how the world will be. Ethics consists, as Einstein puts it, of directives. Directives offer advice or guidance on what to do. In themselves, facts have no direction. They are neutral about what we ought to do.[4]

What is the source of a proper ethical directive, if it does not lie in the facts? How can we know what we ought to do, or what values we ought to adopt? In order to answer these questions, Singer says, we must bring in the rational component of ethics and see where it leads us. We can locate this rational component, he claims, by a careful examination of what he calls 'customary moralities'; for a customary morality is a halfway house between animal altruism and a fully rational system of ethics.

The example of a customary morality which Singer gives suggests the hunter-gatherer stage of human social development (see p.56); however, he thinks that customary moralities belong as much to the present as to the past. As long as we continue to acknowledge special rights and obligations, Singer says, we shall remain at the level of customary morality; we shall not advance beyond that level until we have accepted the principle which is incompatible with them, the Equality Principle. Thus most human communities have a long way to go, as Singer sees it, before they arrive at a system of ethics that is truly rational.

What exactly is a customary morality? It is, Singer says:

a system of rules and precepts guiding our conduct towards one another, supported by widely shared judgements of approval for those who do as the rules and precepts require, and disapproval for those who do not.[5]

Such a system, whatever its shortcomings, is properly called a system of *ethics* (or morality), on Singer's account, because it involves the making of ethical or moral judgements; and we must look at the notion of a moral judgement, he maintains, in order to locate the rational component of ethics. I shall set out as briefly as possible the bones of his argument; and in the course of putting some flesh on these bones, I shall advance an objection I consider to be fatal to it.

The first step in the argument has already been mentioned; it consists of the introduction, in connection with a customary morality, of the notion of a moral or ethical judgement. So:

1 A system of morality (or ethics) involves moral or ethical judgements, judgements about what ought or ought not to be done.

The second step connects the notion of a moral judgement with that of a standard to which the judgement must refer; it is this standard, Singer says, which furnishes the ground of, or the reason for, the judgement. 'The notion of a judgement', he writes, 'carries with it the notion of a standard or a basis of comparison, against which the judging is done'.[6] So:

2 A moral judgement requires a standard (or reason) by reference to which it can be supported.

The third step consists of a claim about the nature of the standard referred to in the second. This standard, we are told, must be 'disinterested' or 'impartial', in that it must be acceptable to the group (or society) as a whole, and not merely to whoever happens to be making the judgement which refers to it. It would not be sufficient, therefore, Singer says, for the latter to appeal either to his own self-interest or to some 'standard' which was purely subjective and which merely expressed his own feelings or opinions. In Singer's words,

'. . . the demand for a reason is a demand for a justification that can be accepted by the group as a whole. Thus the reason offered must be disinterested, at least to the extent of being equally acceptable to all.'[7]

So:

3 Moral standards (or principles of justification) must be 'disinterested' or 'impartial' in the sense described above. (Singer uses these two expressions interchangeably).

It is at this point that the move to the Equality Principle is made; for Singer thinks he can affirm that impartiality requires equality.
So:

4 Impartiality requires equality – it requires that equal weight be given to the interests of all those an action is likely to affect. As Singer puts it: 'Taking the impartial element in ethical reasoning to its logical conclusion means . . . accepting that we ought to have equal concern for all human beings'.[8]

This is Singer's argument for his central contention, the contention that reason or rationality requires the adoption of the Equality

Principle. I shall argue that the final move in the argument – the move to step (4) – is fallacious; Singer has failed to see that he has shifted from one sense of 'impartiality' in step (3) to another, different sense in step (4). At a crucial point he equivocates upon this expression. Once the equivocation is brought to light, the back of Singer's argument is broken; he can get no farther than step (3), which means that he cannot establish the Equality Principle. I shall now explain and defend this claim.

I have said that Singer uses the notion of impartiality in two different senses. What are they? Let us consider first the sense employed in step (3) of his argument.

What step (3) says is that the reasons offered in support of moral judgements must be 'impartial' or 'disinterested'; impartiality, Singer insists, is built into the very nature of moral reasoning. Given the importance of the move from this step to step (4), it is vital to understand exactly what step (3) means; and this is most easily done by looking at one of Singer's own examples.

We are asked to consider a situation in which one member of a group or primitive society lays claim to a greater share of the available food – nuts – than another. If this claim is to be a moral claim, we are told, it must be supported by a reason that is impartial or disinterested. What might such a reason be? The answer suggested by Singer is the claimant's prowess as a warrior. Putting himself in the position of the claimant, he says '. . . I may say . . . that my prowess as a warrior entitles me to a bigger share of the nuts. This justification is impartial *in the sense that it entails that anyone who equals my prowess as a warrior should get as many nuts*; . . .'[9]

Thus the impartiality (or disinterestedness) of the justification lies, apparently, in the implication that *anyone* who is like the claimant in the respect the latter cites as a reason for his having more nuts is similarly entitled to more nuts. Prowess as a warrior entitles *whoever possesses it* to a larger share of the nuts than someone who lacks such prowess.

Now it is quite plain, I suggest, that impartiality in the above sense can be present *even when the Equality Principle is breached*. That is to say, a judgement can be impartial or disinterested in the sense in which these expressions are employed in step (3), while at the same time being quite incompatible with the acceptance of the principle that one should give equal weight to the interests of all those affected by one's actions. In other words, impartiality in this sense does not imply the rejection of special rights and obligations, whereas the Equality Principle certainly does. The example of the warriors does not bring this out especially clearly, but it is not difficult to construct ones which do. The obvious sort of example on which to concentrate is one that involves kinship; but first we should return briefly to the case of the warrior and his claim for the lion's share of the nuts.

Singer himself, is suspicious of this claim; for instance, he speaks of the warrior who mentions his own prowess as giving his case 'an impartial *guise*,[10] and as clothing his justification for getting extra nuts with 'a *semblance* of disinterestedness'.[11] Might it not be the case, however, that warriors genuinely need more nourishment than people with less strenuous occupations? If they do, they have a perfectly proper case for extra food, and it follows that giving it to them does not constitute *preferential treatment*. It is not the case, in these circumstances, that *more* weight is being attached to their interests than to the interests of other members of the group; the weight being attached to their interests is no greater than the weight being attached to the interests of others. Indeed, if they are refused the food they need they can justifiably complain that *less* weight is being attached to their interests than to the interests of others. The needs of these others are being met; the warriors, however, are being refused the means of keeping up their strength, which has to be greater than that of (for example) the people in charge of gathering the nuts or weaving the baskets in which they are collected. Here, what seems at first sight to be preferential treatment turns out on examination to be no such thing. As yet, there is no breach of the Equality Principle whatsoever.

Let us now extend Singer's example in the following way: a particular warrior gives some of his nuts to two weak and elderly members of the group (to avoid complications, we shall suppose that he keeps enough of the nuts to maintain his prowess as a warrior; perhaps he has an especially strong constitution). When asked to justify giving his surplus nuts to these two people (rather than to others equally weak and elderly) he replies that they are his parents.

If the warrior's justification is to count as a *moral* one, then, according to Singer, it must be impartial or disinterested; it must be a justification 'that can be accepted by the group as a whole'.[12] Is there any reason at all why this justification could *not* be accepted by the group as a whole? I suggest that there is not. Even if they have not already accepted the standard implicit in the warrior's reply, the members of the group could now do so. They would be accepting, in that event, not that his parents *alone* were entitled to special consideration from their son, but that parents *in general* were entitled to special consideration from their offspring. That is what the warrior in question might be urging them to accept.

The justification the warrior gives for his action, then, is every bit as disinterested, in the sense proper to step (3) of Singer's argument, as that given by the original warrior for a larger share of the available nuts than people with other occupations. Just as it is *any* warrior who is entitled to extra nuts, so it is *any* parent who is entitled to special consideration from his or her offspring. However, whereas giving extra nuts to warriors does not breach the Equality Principle, the conduct of the second warrior towards his parents does; for it represents the acknowledgement on his part of a *special obligation* – one which he has to his parents but not to anyone else. Yet what is there to stop the warrior's group from acknowledging that obligation, from incorporating it into what Singer calls its 'system of ethics'? Were it to do so, it would be acknowledging, to repeat, that *any* parent was entitled to special consideration from his or her offspring.

Singer may reply that there is nothing to stop the group from acknowledging the obligation at issue; he has allowed, indeed he has insisted, that customary moralities are riddled with irrationality. But this brings us to the nub of the matter: what exactly is it that is supposed to make the acceptance by the group of this special obligation *irrational*? The only answer Singer seems to have available is that it is the Equality Principle, the principle that equal weight should be attached to the interests of all those affected by an action. The Equality Principle alone, he maintains, represents 'the standpoint of reason'. However, this answer will not do, because it has not yet been explained *why* the equality principle alone represents 'the standpoint of reason', *why* it is the uniquely rational basis for moral judgements and decisions. What has been said is that the principle results from 'taking the impartial element in ethical reasoning to its logical conclusion'.[13] But this is very odd. How does it so result? How *can* it so result, when *this* impartial element can be fully present in the justification of an action which is utterly incompatible with the principle of giving equal consideration to the interests of all? As I have shown, the appeal to kinship is just as impartial or disinterested in the sense appropriate to step (3) of Singer's argument as the appeal to prowess.

If we put steps (2) and (3) of Singer's argument together, we get the claim that moral judgements must refer to standards (or reasons) which are 'impartial' or 'disinterested' in the sense that they are 'equally acceptable to all' members of the group concerned. What Singer seems to mean by this is that a moral justification must appeal to something shared or shareable – some moral consideration or conception that is both available and applicable to others besides the person offering the justification; something that can be stated as a *principle*. However, this condition is satisfied by the first warrior's appeal to prowess *and* by the second warrior's appeal to kinship. Singer speaks of 'universal principles' in this connection,[14] but such talk can be misleading, and it appears to have misled Singer himself. A principle can be 'universal' even if it imposes an obligation which is *special* and not *general*. 'Warriors should receive extra nuts' is universal in that it is concerned with what *all* warriors should receive (namely, extra nuts); but similarly 'parents should be cared for by their offspring'; is universal in that it says something about what *all* parents should receive (namely, care from their offspring). Each of these propositions states a principle; but the first, as we have seen, is compatible with the Equality Principle, whereas the second is not.

Impartiality, then, in the sense in which Singer uses the expression in step (3) of his argument, is perfectly compatible with the recognition of special rights and obligations. Hence, contrary to what he says, there is nothing in the 'inherent logic'[15] of moral reasoning which must lead us to accept that equal weight be given to the interests of all those affected by an action.

It looks as though Singer himself was, at one point, on the verge of realising this. I am thinking of the following passage:

> That someone is related to *me* rather than to you, or lives in *my* village among the dozen villages that make up our community, is not an ethical justification for special favouritism; it does not allow me to do more for my kin or fellow villagers *any more than you may do for your kin or fellow villagers.*[16]

Here Singer seems to approach the recognition that impartiality of the sort alluded to in step (3) of his argument does *not* require the rejection of special rights and obligations. Yet on the very next page there appears the claim that 'Taking the impartial element in ethical reasoning to its logical conclusion means . . . accepting that we ought to have equal concern for all human beings'![17] Singer apparently thinks that there is a compulsory logical route from this statement:

Your kin are entitled to the same treatment from you as my kin are from me.

to this:

Neither your kin nor mine should be treated by you and by me respectively any differently from the way in which we treat other people.

But there is no such route. The first of these statements has no implications whatsoever for how one should treat one's kin, as compared with people who are not one's kin; the second insists that one should treat one's kin in exactly the same way as one treats everybody else. I am at a loss to understand how the second carries to its logical conclusion anything that is implicit in the first.

How on earth could Singer have made such a mistake? Because, it would seem, he is confused about the notion of *impartiality*. I said above that he equivocates upon this notion; the sense in which it is used in step (3) of his argument is different from the sense in which it is used in step (4). So far, we have looked at the first of these senses only; to say that a moral judgement must be impartial (or disinterested) in the first sense is to say that it must appeal to a general principle, in the sense of a shared or shareable standard. As we have seen, impartiality in this sense does *not* require that we attach equal weight to the interests of all; for a judgement which appeals to kinship, for example, remains disinterested in this sense. What, though, is the *other* sense of impartiality that is found in Singer's argument, the sense he employs in step (4) and that requires, he says, the adoption of the Equality Principle? When Singer says that impartiality requires equality, what sense of impartiality does he have in mind?

The answer to this question, I think, is that he has in mind impartiality in the sense in which this expression is most frequently used in ordinary conversation about moral, political and social matters. Impartiality, in this sense, is not a logical notion, as it is in the one discussed above, but a moral notion. Someone displays impartiality in this sense when he avoids *partiality* or *bias*; and it is not possible for him to do this, Singer seems to be saying, unless he acts in accordance with the Equality Principle. If one is to act in an unbiased manner, Singer believes, one must in all one's actions give equal weight to the interests of everyone they affect; one must give no-one preferential treatment by attaching more weight to his interests than to those of others. One must not show *favouritism*.

The Equality Principle, then, is required by impartiality in the sense just indicated; that is what Singer seems to be saying in step (4) of his argument. Since this sense of impartiality is not the one employed in step (3), the move from step (3) to step (4) rests upon an equivocation.

It is possible that someone might respond to this point by saying that even if Singer is equivocating in the way I have described, he has nevertheless succeeded in showing that the Equality Principle is one we must accept. This is because moral judgements must surely be impartial in the *second* sense as well as the first – they must, that is to say, be unbiased. Bias is a moral failing by definition, and it follows that it is necessarily something we must avoid. So if impartiality in the sense of lack of bias really does require the adoption of the Equality Principle, Singer has carried his point.

The reply to this is obvious. When Singer says that impartiality (in the second sense) requires us to give equal weight to the interests of all, he is making a *moral* claim; and people who recognise special obligations can and will reject it. As far as they are concerned, to recognise such obligations is not to show partiality or bias.

It does not follow from the above point, of course, that *nothing* Singer perceives as bias will be so perceived by people who reject the Equality Principle. To take a trivial example: if, acting as judge in a fancy dress competition, I award the prize to my own daughter because she is my daughter, and not because I consider her costume to be the best entered, I exhibit a bias in her favour. It would be hard to see how anyone could disagree with this; and we can all imagine cases of bias and consequent injustice which would be far more serious. To repeat: we can *all* imagine such cases, whether or not we would accept the Equality Principle. I may believe that I have special obligations to members of my own family, but I am not committed by that belief to a *cosa nostra* conception of the family. I do not believe that those obligations are the only ones I have, or that they can never be overridden, or that I can with justification do anything that will further my family's interests. I accept that many situations might arise in which some member of my family was involved but in which I should remain strictly impartial; that is to say, in a situation of that sort I would be obliged not to allow the existence of a family connection to have any bearing whatsoever upon the action I decided to take. It would be wrong – indeed, it would be foolish – to say that people who recognise special obligations have no room in their moral thinking for the idea of impartiality, in the sense under discussion; they might on some occasions lean over backwards to avoid even the appearance of partiality or bias, and in consequence act unjustly towards the very people to whom they consider themselves to have such obligations.

Utilitarians, therefore, have no monopoly on impartiality, in the sense appropriate to step (4) of Singer's argument. It is simply that what counts as partiality for them does not necessarily so count for other people, people who have values the utilitarian does not share. In the example of the fancy dress competition, one does not have to be a utilitarian to accept that proper impartiality was absent. Suppose, however, it were suggested that one should recognise no obligations to one's children that one did not also recognise to the children of others; that one's moral relationship to all children should be the same, whether they were one's own or not. That would be something which most people, myself included, would *not* be prepared to accept. I do not regard my *bringing up* of my children as showing a bias in their favour; yet in doing it I am not giving equal weight to the interests of all – I am giving more weight to the interest of my children than to the interests of other people's. I have, I consider, an *obligation* to bring up my children; I have no obligation to bring up the children of others.

But surely, the utilitarian will urge, the well-being of *your* children is no more important than that of anyone else's children; surely, the well-being of *all* children is of *equal* importance. Yes; but in rejecting the Equality Principle I am not saying otherwise. I am saying, not that the interests of my children are more important *absolutely speaking* than the interests of anyone else's children, but that they are (and should be) more important *to me*, more *my concern*. Nor am I saying that the interests of children other than mine are not my concern *at all*. There may be some people who would say this, but no commitment to it is implied by the recognition of special obligations to members of one's own family.

People who reject the Equality Principle, then, are not necessarily guilty of a reprehensibly narrow moral concern; though that is precisely the light in which they tend to be placed by philosophers like Singer. As I said before, people who recognise special obligations need not recognise *only* such obligations; nor need they consider that a special obligation must always take priority over a general obligation in cases of conflict between them. They are free to say that which of the two carries the greater weight in a given case will depend on the precise nature of the obligations that are in conflict, and of the circumstances in which the conflict has arisen. If (to take a different example) I could not go to the aid of an injured person without breaking a relatively unimportant promise, I would choose to break the promise, thus placing a general obligation before a special in that case. To say that an obligation is special, let us recall, is simply to say that it is *not general* – that is to say, that it is not owed to everyone. It is not to say that it is *especially important* as compared with general obligations. Some special obligations are also especially important ones; others are not.

I have argued that Singer fails in his attempt to show that reason or rationality requires the adoption of the Equality Principle, the principle that in all our actions we should give equal weight to the interests of everyone they affect. In the second part of this chapter I shall look more closely at the conception of reason or rationality to be found in Singer's work. This conception is not confined to Singer, nor to those philosophers who share a stable with him; it is, or has become, a *popular* conception, a legacy of the Enlightenment bequeathed even to what philosophers call the 'plain man', and not to intellectuals alone.[18] In what follows, I shall refer to this conception of reason as REASON; and I shall argue that despite its popularity, it is deeply defective. It will be convenient to begin the discussion by considering once again the way in which Singer reacts to the sociobiological enterprise of explaining morality in evolutionary terms.

We saw above that despite his advocacy of the Equality Principle Singer does not dispute the explanation of altruistic behaviour that sociobiologists give; nor does he dispute that the altruism thus explained is limited in scope. What he does dispute is the claim that explanations of how we *do* behave have implications for an account of how we *should* behave. As we have seen, he argues that we can establish the Equality Principle by taking to its logical conclusion the rational component in ethics; we are brought to this principle, he says, by the 'autonomy of reasoning'.[19]

Singer is led, therefore, to give an account of human nature and human life which consolidates the opposition between *reason* and *feeling* which is a recurring feature of philosophical writings on the subject. The picture which emerges from Singer's account is something like this:

The emotional constitution we possess as human beings has been formed by the evolutionary processes which sociobiologists describe. These processes have endowed us with *sympathy* – a feeling for or with other people that moves us to care about their sufferings and

63

take action to alleviate them, even at some cost to ourselves. There are limits, however, to how far sympathetic feelings generated by such processes can extend. In general, the further removed from us someone is the less his sufferings will move us; this being not a matter of physical distance, of course, but of the extent to which he *belongs* to us. This expression is normally used to speak of members of one's own family; and it is indeed our genetic relatives who have first claim on our sympathies. However, these sympathies can extend naturally beyond family connections to other people we regard as 'our own' – to, for example, members of our own tribe, or social group, or race. The sufferings of people who are not our own, though, may hardly move us at all. We are not *to blame* for this; it is a consequence of our nature as human beings, a nature which has been moulded by the evolutionary processes already mentioned.

Our emotions, then, cannot but move us to treat people differently from one another. If we act as our natural sympathies incline us, we will attach a great deal more weight to the interests of some people – those who are 'our own' – than to the interests of others – those who are not. An ethical system founded upon these sympathies, as customary moralities are, will have rules that reflect them by imposing special obligations and conferring special rights; and in this way it will sanction the preferential treatment of those we *feel* for. For sound moral guidance, Singer supposes, we should turn from feeling to reason, which shows us that we should in all our actions give equal weight to the interests of everyone affected by them, whoever they are and whatever their relationship to ourselves.

I have already exposed the fallacy in Singer's attempt to move from the 'impartiality' of moral judgements to the Equality Principle. It is important to do so, because the claim that this principle embodies the only standpoint from which rational moral judgements can be made is supported in Singer's work, so far as I can see, only by the argument which involves this move. If we fail to see that the argument is unsound we may allow it to conceal from us the artificial nature of Singer's account of reason; we may think that he is describing *human* reason, when the truth is that he is not.

We can begin to see that this is so if we reflect on the *schizophrenic* character human nature has, on the account which Singer gives of it. According to his account, there is a split (or gap) between reason on the one hand and feeling on the other; the former moves logically in a direction the latter must resist. Our feelings pull us towards our own, but reason – REASON – pulls us away from our own towards what

Singer calls a 'universal' point of view – a point of view from which the interests of all are to be assigned equal weight in our actions.[20] In other words, on Singer's account REASON requires us to go *against the grain* of our emotional make-up or constitution; we must transcend our own natures, apparently, if we are to succeed in meeting the exacting requirements of a fully rational system of ethics.

There are two points which Singer might make in reply to this. The first is that on his account our emotional constitution is not the *whole* of our nature; we are rational as well as emotional beings, and REASON, therefore, is as much a part of us as the feelings it must hold in check. We must simply give this part its head. The second is that he does not, in fact, expect us to act with no guide except a single injunction to promote the interests of all, impartially considered. This, he concedes, would be too much to ask of normal human beings. Instead of resisting our natural inclinations and sympathies, he says, we must give them expression in a system of rules that will work as a whole for the good of all.[21] Such a system will not deny satisfaction to our self-centred desires for the well-being of ourselves and our own; but if it is well designed it will transform those desires into an instrument by means of which the general good can be achieved. It will not do, Singer adds, for *everyone* to know that the rules of the system – which rules correspond to Mill's 'intermediate generalisations' (see pp.10–12) – are without 'ultimate authority of their own';[22] this knowledge will be appropriate only for those individuals who are clever enough to put the Equality Principle into practice directly.

Let us consider what can be said in reply to these two points.

It is clear, I suggest, that there is considerable tension between the first and the second. The first maintains that REASON is as much a part of us as feeling; the second reveals the dominance of what Singer presents as our emotional constitution, that part of our nature which, he says, inclines us towards our own and away from the universal standpoint of REASON. On Singer's own account, our natural inclinations are so powerful that we must be *manipulated* if we are to act as REASON requires.

Consider, once again, family obligations and rights. On the account Singer gives, these would be certain to have a place in any system of morality which a sensible utilitarian would design. For example, there might be a rule in that system that people should care for their parents in the latters' old age. Someone who obeyed the rule – Mary, for instance, whose situation was described in the last chapter – would see herself as having an obligation to her mother which she did not have to anyone else (except her father). The question is: would she really have that obligation? It seems to me that Singer must say that she would not; for her having that obligation, *really* having it, would be incompatible with the Equality Principle. She would *think* that she had such an obligation, of course, and that is what the utilitarian would want her to think; but she would not know that her thinking it was all part of a plan to channel people's natural sympathies in the right direction. She would be ignorant of the *derivative* status which attached to the rule she obeyed, and she would need to be kept in ignorance of it unless she possessed those exceptional qualities that would enable her to operate with the Equality Principle alone.

For Singer, then, there is *in reality* only one obligation which can be rationally justified: the general obligation to promote the interests of all, impartially considered. This is what REASON dictates. People may be allowed to *believe* that there are others; but this is no more than a concession to human nature, one that must be made if the good of all is to be secured.

I suggest that reflection on this point should help us to see that we must not identify human reason with REASON. Human reason is *human* reason; and any account which sets it at odds with the nature of human beings should be rejected. Although Singer recognises that his account threatens to divorce ethics from human nature,[23] he is not prepared to re-think it; all he is prepared to do is make the concessions to human nature described above. What he should have realised is that human reason cannot be alien to human nature – to the way people naturally feel, think and act – in the way that it is on the account he gives of it. Human reason, in short, is not REASON.

Earlier, I referred to Singer's conception of reason as a legacy of the Enlightenment; and Part IV of Jonathan Swift's *Gulliver's Travels*[24] gives us an idea of what the life of creatures with REASON would be like. The Houyhnhnms encountered by Lemuel Gulliver in this part of the book personify the ideal of reason characteristic of Enlightenment thinking; they are almost walking REASONS. Let us take a look at them.

According to Gulliver, who becomes their ardent admirer, the Houyhnhnms have one 'grand maxim', which is 'to cultivate reason and be wholly governed by it'.[25] In their moral life they display without the slightest effort the impartiality of Singer's Equality Principle; Gulliver tells us that their 'principal Virtues' of 'Friendship and Benevolence' are 'not confined to particular Objects, but universal to the whole Race'.[26] The Houyhnhnms, then, act in accordance with the single injunction to promote the interests of all, impartially considered, recognising no *special* obligations of any sort. They do not make, as Gulliver puts it, 'a Distinction of Persons'; except – and the parallel with utilitarian thought is striking – 'where there is a superior degree of Virtue'.[27]

Let us recall a situation described earlier, that of the two people who are trapped in a burning house (Singer himself discusses the original of this situation from the standpoint of the Equality Principle[28]). One of the trapped people is a cancer researcher whose work promises to confer great benefits upon the sick, and the other is this man's charlady. There is someone who can save one but not both of these people, and the question arises, therefore, of whom it should be.

As we have seen, the utilitarian insists that even if the rescuer is the charlady's son, he should rescue the cancer researcher, because it is the cancer researcher who makes the greater contribution to the general welfare or happiness. Of the two endangered people he is the more important. There is nothing here which offends against the Equality Principle; for the greater importance of the cancer researcher is entirely a function of the benefits he confers upon society at large. The rescuer, by saving this man, will do more to promote the interests of all the people affected by his action than he would by saving his own mother; for we must include among those people all the ones who stand to benefit from the researcher's work. It is on account of his social worth in this sense, according to utilitarians, that the cancer researcher and not his charlady should be saved. They may insist that all people are equal; but their position implies that some people are more equal than others.

Ideally, then, for philosophers of Singer's persuasion, human life should be like Houyhnhnm life. Yet Singer himself, as we saw above, sees little chance of this actually coming to pass. We must do the best we can, he thinks, by designing a system of rules that will both reflect our natural partialities and advance the interests of all. We must strike a *compromise* between REASON and feeling; and this means that we must adopt a system which is bound to sanction the wrong action on occasion.

If, therefore, the charlady's son were to save his own mother rather than her employer, Singer would say that we should not *blame* him for doing so, nor even for thinking that it was *right* to do so. Any rules we might realistically formulate for human conduct would have to permit that way of thinking; what we must ensure is that their general tendency would be sufficiently utilitarian to facilitate the doing of what was right most of the time. It would be better to have a system of this sort, Singer thinks, than to trust our fallible selves to the guidance of the equality principle alone; and *much* better to have it than to allow our conduct to be governed by a customary morality which merely codified our natural partialities.

So, in effect, human beings must take Houyhnhnm life as the ideal in shaping their moral code; although the code they shape will have to make major concessions to human nature. That is what Singer's view amounts to. I said above that *human* reason (unlike *Houyhnhnm* reason) should not be identified with REASON, and I must now say something further in defence of this claim.

Consider once again the Houyhnhnms. How does Houyhnhnm behaviour differ from the behaviour of people? Well, Singer would say, it is more rational; Houyhnhnms are more rational than people. (Gulliver's master would have agreed with him; he will concede to Gulliver himself only 'some tincture of Reason'.[29]) However, it is not that Houyhnhnms are better than people at transcending or controlling their passions – their 'irrational' desires and inclinations; it is rather that Houyhnhnms, unlike humans, have scarcely any passions at all. In them, as Gulliver puts it, reason 'is not mingled, obscured or discoloured by Passion and Interest'.[30] Thus the 'love' Gulliver refers to in describing their views and conduct is very different from the human love of individuals which advocates of the Equality Principle see as a threat to moral behaviour; it is, rather, precisely the kind of disinterested benevolence which lies at the heart of utilitarian thought. The Houyhnhnms recognise no special obligations; but, as Gulliver's account makes clear, they have no special *affections* either.

The Houyhnhnms, then, are doing what comes *naturally* to them when they occupy 'the impartial standpoint' of the Equality Principle. Houyhnhnm family life, for example, is as it is because the Houyhnhnms are as they are. Gulliver tells us that Houyhnhnms marry out of (once more) friendship and benevolence, and that 'they have no Fondness for their Colts and Foals . . . the Care they take in educating them proceedeth entirely from the Dictates of *Reason*'. He adds that he observed his master 'to shew the same Affection to his Neighbour's issue that he had for his own.'[31] Houyhnhnm existence as a whole is one of passionless calm, undisturbed even by the prospect of death or the fact of bereavement:

If they can avoid Casualties, they die only of old Age, and are buried in the obscurest Places that can be found, their Friends and Relations expressing neither Joy nor Grief at their departure; nor does the dying Person discover the least Regret that he is leaving the World, any more than if he were upon returning home from a Visit to one of his Neighbours.[32]

On the same page, the lateness of a female Houyhnhnm for an important engagement is explained as follows:

Her Excuse for not coming sooner was that her Husband dying late in the Morning, she was a good while consulting her Servants about a convenient Place where his Body should be laid; and I observed She behaved herself at our House, as chearfully as the rest . . .[33]

The Houyhnhnms are not, perhaps, incomprehensible to us, but they are certainly very different from us. Not that we ourselves are all alike. Different peoples (the members of different cultures) and different people (different members of the same culture) exhibit a variety of attitudes and responses to sex, procreation, death, bereavement, and so on; and some may even cultivate a 'stoical' attitude to life outwardly similar to that which is natural to the Houyhnhnms. Nevertheless, in so far as we can speak of a universal human nature at all, it is clear that it is quite unlike the nature with which Swift endows the Houyhnhnms; and this brings me to my main point.

Why should we think, as apparently Singer does, that there is a *single* ideal of rational conduct which can be applied to all rational beings, irrespective of the modes of thought and feeling natural to them? REASON is just such an ideal; but, as we have seen, if it is presented as *human* reason, a gap opens up between the emotional and the rational components of human nature and human life. There is no such gap as far as the Houyhnhnms are concerned; the form which their rationality takes is entirely appropriate to their nature, and the same should surely be true of human rationality. As I said above, Houyhnhnm reason – REASON – is *alien* to human beings; even Singer admits it to be antithetical to their natural constitution. If we are to give an account of human reason, however, we must describe something *integral* to human nature and human life, not something alien to it; and if our concern is with *moral* reasoning we should forget the irrelevant abstraction Singer describes and look instead at the perfectly ordinary business of *giving reasons for* (or *justifying*) moral judgements and decisions.

I suggest, therefore, that we should understand reason or rationality in the moral context in terms of the ability to give *appropriate reasons* or *grounds* for moral judgements and decisions – the sorts of reasons or grounds that people ordinarily give. This conception of reason in ethics, unlike that for which utilitarians (and many other philosophers) yearn, involves the recognition of *rational moral disagreement*. It acknowledges, not only that people can in fact disagree in the judgements and decisions they make, but that in many cases these disagreements cannot be resolved by finding out which of the competing judgements represents the standpoint of reason or rationality. All of the views in question may be rational, in that all of the parties to a disagreement may be able to give appropriate moral reasons for their judgements.

Let us go back to the incident of the burning house. On my account, people can make *different* judgements about whom the rescuer should save in this situation without it being the case that at least one of those judgements must be irrational. Suppose that the rescuer brings out the charlady, and that as the roof falls in upon the cancer researcher he is asked to justify his action. He replies 'she's my mother'. In saying this, he is giving an appropriate moral reason for his action; he is offering, not an excuse for it, but a moral justification or defence – one which the majority of people, I believe, would accept as entirely sufficient in the circumstances. (The appropriateness and sufficiency of 'she's my mother' as a moral reason or justification for certain actions depends *of course* upon what these actions are, and in what circumstances they are performed; this is a point I have already made).

Were the rescuer to save the charlady, then, he could provide a rational justification of his action; he could provide an appropriate moral reason for it. But the same would be true were he to save the cancer researcher instead – for he could point to the value of the latter's work as an appropriate moral reason for so doing. This, apparently, is the action Singer himself would take; or, at least, the action he would think it right to take.[34] Nothing I have said implies the 'irrationality' of Singer's position; it is not *irrational* to believe that (ideally) the rescuer should save the more useful life. But, to repeat, neither is it irrational to believe that he should save his mother. What we have here is a *moral* disagreement, a conflict between *moral* points of view, and not between rationality and irrationality.

Hence, in the situation described, there can be rational moral disagreement about what the rescuer should do. This is because there are several quite distinct moral considerations at stake; and even people who acknowledge the importance of them all might differ in their judgements about which should take priority in the circumstances in question.[35]

For creatures like the Houyhnhnms, on the other hand, a parallel situation could give rise to no moral dilemmas and no moral disagreements. If a Houyhnhnm were to encounter two of his fellows trapped in a burning house, he would save the Houyhnhnm of superior virtue as a matter of course, even if the other did happen to be his own mother. He would not be required to make a moral decision about the matter, for he would not be troubled by any suspicion that he should save his mother (nor, given the way Houyhnhnms are, would he be troubled by any temptation to save her). Furthermore, in saving the Houyhnhnm of superior virtue, he would be doing what any Houyhnhnm would do in the circumstances; no grounds would be available to a Houyhnhnm for making a different choice. 'She's my mother' could not count for a Houyhnhnm as a *moral thought*; however, it *can* count as a moral thought for a human being – a person not in the sense bioethicists stipulate, but in the ordinary sense, that in which it is interchangeable with individual man, woman or child.

I said above that people who acknowledged the importance of the same moral considerations could disagree in their judgements about which of those considerations should be given priority when they came into conflict. As we have seen, however, the disagreement between Singer and the man who rescues his mother is not a disagreement about moral *priorities*. People can differ, not only in the way they rank moral considerations relative to one another, but also in what they are prepared to count as a moral consideration at all; and Singer's view is that the charlady's relationship to the rescuer has, in reality, no moral significance whatsoever. Thus the reason the rescuer would give for saving the charlady rather than her employer ('she's my mother') does not count for Singer as a genuine moral reason or justification for acting. The only genuine moral consideration at stake, he would say, is that to which *he* refers.

We come, then, to the final point a utilitarian might make in the face of a decision by the rescuer to save the charlady. It is that the

rescuer must say *what makes* the reason he gives a morally appropriate reason, a moral reason *at all* from the standpoint of reason or
rationality. He cites the fact that the charlady is his mother; but he
must explain, in addition, what gives that fact moral significance. He
must say what makes 'she's my mother' a *moral* thought, rather than
a statement of fact charged with merely emotional significance.

Thus the rescuer has still something to do if he is to provide his
decision with a truly rational justification; he must say why the fact
that the charlady is his mother *matters* from a moral point of view. In
having *that* to do, however, he has everything to do; for what the
utilitarian wants from the rescuer now is nothing less than a
justification of the latter's values, the values which lead him to deny the
moral possibility of his doing what the utilitarian says he ought to do.

It is clear that there are ways of saying what gives moral
significance to the fact that the charlady is the rescuer's mother which
the utilitarian would dismiss as beside the point. It would not be
relevant, he would say, for the rescuer – or, more likely, a philosopher
talking about the rescuer's deed – to refer to the *social background*
against which he speaks and acts; it would be no answer to the
question the utilitarian asks to mention the moral import which
family relationships have in a certain culture, even if that culture were
typical in this respect of human cultures in general (as it seems to be).
The utilitarian knows all about the social practice of giving special
weight to the interests of one's relatives; what he wishes to know
about now, he says, is what *justifies* that practice from a rational point
of view. Why, from a rational point of view, should it matter morally
that someone is – for example – one's mother? Never mind, he would
say, that it may be universally held to matter; that is just what people
happen to think. Why does it matter *really*? This question requires an
answer, the utilitarian insists; if not from the rescuer himself, then
from any philosopher who defends the rationality of what the rescuer
says and does.

It is appropriate at this point to refer once again to Singer's attitude
to sociobiology. We saw above that he accepts the account
sociobiologists give of the origin or genesis of ethics; what he rejects
is the claim some sociobiologists make that in giving that account they
are providing at the same time a justification of certain moral
principles. As we have seen, he argues that this claim ignores the
'logical gap' between fact and value. Sociobiology in particular and
science in general, he says, can describe and explain, but not prescribe
and justify.

Singer is not content, however, to leave it at that; he goes on to argue that the explanation sociobiology provides of certain moral principles or beliefs (for example, the belief in special obligations to members of one's own family) actually 'debunks' those beliefs. Far from showing the principles to be justified, he claims, the explanation discredits them:

> Science provides leverage against some ethical principles when it helps us to understand why we hold our ethical principles. What we take as an untouchable moral intuition may be no more than a relic of our evolutionary history . . . Discovering biological origins for our intuitions should make us sceptical about thinking of them as self evident moral axioms.[36]

This, then, is what Singer would say about the charlady's son, were he to claim that he must save his mother – that he thinks he has a 'self-evident moral axiom', or 'untouchable intuition' when really he has nothing but a relic of his evolutionary history as a member of the species *homo sapiens*.

Utilitarians commonly represent moral views with which they disagree as resting upon 'intuition', thus contriving to associate anyone who defends the possibility of such views with a position for which few philosophers nowadays would wish to argue – intuitionism. Intuitionists did not all hold exactly the same philosophical opinions; perhaps the most obscurantist among them was H. A. Prichard, who argued that it is neither necessary nor possible to give reasons for moral judgements. On the account he gave, moral judgements are self-evident and one simply intuits their truth.[37]

It should be obvious that Prichard's is not the position which has been defended here. I have said neither that no reasons can be given for moral judgements nor that no reasons need be given for them. The charlady's son, for example, gives a reason for the judgement that he must save the charlady – the reason that *she is his mother*.

This, Singer might say, is mere quibbling; it is an attempt to evade the point he is making. The rescuer gives a reason of sorts, yes; but what is at stake is the *rationality* of that reason. What is required is not just his reason, but *the reason for his reason* – the justification for his values. If no such justification can be provided, then he *is* expressing a mere intuition; and one which sociobiology has exposed for what it is – a relic of our evolutionary past.

It should be clear by now what is wrong with this sort of response. Singer would maintain that the rescuer, *unlike the utilitarian himself*, has something – indeed, everything – to explain. He must show his values to be rationally justified; otherwise they should be dismissed (with the welcome but not strictly necessary assistance of sociobiological theory). Thus Singer would insist that it is not enough for the rescuer to say simply that these are the values he has, or that these are the reasons that carry weight with him and move him to act. The question is, however, *why* is it not enough for him to say this? Why is it not enough for the rescuer to point out that it is in terms of the reasons or values in question, among others, that he – and not only he – understands what it *is* to give a rational justification for a moral decision? Why does he have to provide something more?

It seems to me that all Singer could say in answer to this question is that *he* does not regard the justification which the rescuer has given as a rational one. A rational justification, for *him*, must refer – at least indirectly – to the interests of all, impartially considered. It must refer *always* to this and it must refer *only* to this (with the qualification made necessary by his acknowledgement of the need for rules). Given the preceding discussion, however, what could this be but the expression of Singer's own (somewhat eccentric) point of view – one point of view amongst others? What could he be saying here, if not that the reasons which move the rescuer to act are not reasons of the sort which move *him* to act? They do not refer to the only considerations *he* sees as morally important, or to the only values *he* holds dear.

Very well; but all that need be said in reply is that *the rescuer sees things differently*. He does not see *all* things differently; there are values which he shares with utilitarians like Singer – including the one to which the latter refers in the case in question, the well-being of the sick. The rescuer does not say, what do the sufferings of the sick *matter*? What he says is that other things matter too, and that one of them – namely, the claims upon him of his mother – must be given priority in the circumstances in question.

The point is this: Singer would claim the right to issue his challenge to the rescuer – the challenge to justify his values – because he thinks of himself as occupying a position which is *privileged*, a position which philosophical enquiry has shown to be the standpoint of reason itself. He maintains, as we saw above, that we are led to the Equality Principle by 'the autonomy of reasoning', and that this principle is therefore the only rational basis for moral judgements and decisions. As we have seen, however, this is not the case. Singer's argument for the privilege he seeks to confer upon his own position is fallacious, and it follows that he cannot maintain his position's title to that

74

privilege. It follows that he cannot maintain either his right to challenge the rescuer to justify his values. He can *disagree* with him, of course; he can say that he sees nothing in the rescuer's values. But that is all.

I do not dispute, then, that the rescuer is unable to justify the values in terms of which his decision must be understood. I do not dispute that he cannot give reasons for the reasons he gives. What I do dispute is that it follows from this that he can give no rational justification for his decision. He has already done *what is meant* by giving a rational justification for a moral decision. Singer, as I have said, is free to reject that justification; he is free to express disagreement with what the rescuer says and does. However, it is not from 'the standpoint of reason' that he does so, but from a moral standpoint which is on a level with that of the rescuer as far as justification is concerned. He is no more able than the rescuer to justify the values he has, or to give reasons for the reasons he gives.

What of the alleged 'debunking' power of sociobiology? I suggest that this is as illusory as the privilege with which Singer credits his own moral perspective. He claims, as we saw above, that the sociobiological explanation of how altruism developed provides 'leverage' against certain moral principles or beliefs (such as the belief that we have special obligations towards members of our own families). It exposes those beliefs as relics of our evolutionary history, and thus makes it easier for us to leave them behind as we advance towards a fully rational system of ethics.

The scientific credentials of sociobiology are open to question; but even if they were not sociobiological theory could provide no leverage at all against the principles of which Singer disapproves. Singer's claim to the contrary trades upon the schizophrenic picture of human beings already discussed, in which reason pulls in one direction and feeling, our emotional constitution, in another. His point is that those principles are 'relics of our evolutionary history' *as opposed to rationally justified beliefs* – beliefs, that is to say, which have the sanction of REASON. Once REASON is got out of the way, we are left with human reason or reasoning – the giving, I have argued, of appropriate reasons, reasons which people *find* appropriate, for moral judgements and decisions; and sociobiology cannot show us either that we *should* find certain reasons appropriate or that we should *not*. When Singer says that sociobiology 'debunks' reasons like 'she's my mother' he is making a claim which is quite incompatible with his own endorsement of the 'logical gap' between fact and value. As we have seen, he distinguishes between explaining and justifying; sociobiology in particular and science in general, he says, give explanations, not justifications. Thus Singer's view is that while sociobiology may explain how certain behaviour originated, it cannot *vindicate* that behaviour from a moral point of view. He should accept, then, it seems to me, that sociobiology cannot *discredit* that behaviour either; he should stop trying to have his cake and eat it.

In this chapter I have examined Peter Singer's attempt to establish the Equality Principle – his version of the Principle of Utility – as the uniquely rational foundation for moral judgements and decisions; and I have argued that this attempt does not succeed. I have also examined the conception of reason or rationality which emerges from Singer's discussion, and I have argued that this conception – which I called REASON – is defective as a conception of *human* reason in relation to moral matters. Singer, in true bioethical spirit, attempts to lay down the way in which moral thinking *should* proceed if it is to be rational; it is my view that we must attend to the way (or ways) in which moral thinking *does* proceed if we are to understand what rationality means in this context, or what counts as giving a rational justification for moral judgements and decisions.

There are certain stock objections against accounts of moral thinking of the sort I have given. For example, it is said that if we cannot justify, or give grounds for, our values, they must be the product of an arbitrary choice or decision on our part. To this, I would reply that we do not *choose* our values, or *decide* to find certain reasons compelling; they *are* our values, they *are* the reasons we find compelling. It is said further that the account implies the impossibility of criticising any of our values. To this, I would reply that the account implies nothing of the sort; what it does imply is that there is no *single* standpoint from which we must do the criticising, the supposed 'standpoint of reason' which philosophy identifies or brings to light. If we wish to understand how it is possible for us to criticise our values, we must attend, once again, to how we actually do it: piecemeal, and in terms of other values.[38] Finally, it is said that unless there *is* a single standpoint from which values can be criticised, and unless it is the sort of standpoint utilitarians like Singer describe, we shall have no ultimate philosophical weapon against values which are morally repugnant, or which have morally repugnant implications; values in the name of which some people – called *moral fanatics* – cause others to *suffer*. To this, I would reply that there *is* no ultimate philosophical weapon against such values; though there are, of course, a variety of *moral* weapons against them, of the sort with which we are all familiar.

I shall come back to the last of these objections at a later time, when I discuss an account of morality with which Singer's has much in common; the one given by R. M. Hare in his book *Moral Thinking.*[39] In the next three chapters, I shall be returning to the notion which occupied our attention in the first, and which is central to bioethics: the notion of *the value of life*. Those chapters, however, will not be irrelevant to the worry about morally repugnant values just mentioned; for they will provide ample confirmation of a point which should be clear already from chapter 1 – namely, that utilitarianism itself has its full share of morally repugnant implications. If the ethic which bioethicists urge upon us is supposed to be necessary for moral salvation, I, for one, would prefer to be damned than saved.

5

THE POLICY OF MAXIMISING LIVES

We saw in chapter 2 that bioethicists present a theory of the value of life as necessarily prior to a rational account of the morality of killing. We must know what makes for a valuable life in general, they say, if we are to know what lives or sorts of lives have value; and we must know what lives have value if we are to know what lives are ones that, other things being equal, it would be seriously wrong to end. We examined the version of the bioethical theory given by John Harris in his introduction to medical ethics, and we saw that he assumes in order to construct it that the lives of 'normal adult human beings' have value; he assumes that it is generally wrong to kill *people*.[1] Nevertheless, what the finished theory reveals, he thinks, is the reason why it is wrong. Let us recall the essential features of Harris's account.

A life has value, according to Harris, if and only if the possessor of that life has the capacity to value it. He must be capable of having the desire to go on living; and it follows, Harris says, that he must possess self-consciousness or self-awareness. Any being which is conscious of itself, therefore, possesses a valuable life and is, in Harris's sense, a person.

Harris's definition of the term 'person' is a stipulative one; and his choice of this term to stand for 'any being who has what it takes to be valuable'[2] is tendentious in the extreme. Nonetheless, most persons in the ordinary sense – people, what Harris calls 'normal adult human beings' – are also persons in his stipulative sense; for they do possess in fact the capacity to value their lives. Harris's account shows, he would say, that we are right to think it generally wrong to kill people, and it shows also why we are right to think so. It is generally wrong to kill a person because 'to do so robs that individual of something they value and of the very thing that

78

makes possible valuing anything at all'[3] – his life. Nothing that is not capable of valuing its life can be harmed by having it taken away from him.

So Harris thinks, as I said before, that his theory of the value of life explains why it is generally wrong to kill people. This is not the only virtue he supposes the theory to possess in relation to the killing of 'normal adult human beings'; for he maintains too that it enables us to make rational judgements about the circumstances under which it would *not* be wrong to kill people. If a person does not in fact value his life, the reason why it would normally be wrong to kill him no longer obtains; and if he positively wishes to die then we *ought* to kill him, or help him to kill himself. Given his desires, it is only by doing one of these things, Harris says, that we can discharge our obligation to show him respect, in the sense defined by Harris later on in his book.[4]

We can use his theory of the value of life, therefore, Harris would say, not only to establish what lives lack value, but also to establish under what conditions lives that have value may – or must – be ended. The life of someone who wishes to die has not lost the value that pertains to it as the life of a person – it has not lost the value I described in chapter 2 as 'absolute' or 'metaphysical'; but it has lost its value to or for the person whose life it is. In these circumstances, Harris believes, there is no moral reason not to kill this person, and every moral reason actually to do so.

When a life becomes valueless to its possessor, then, it may be ended, on Harris's account, despite the fact that it retains its value in the metaphysical sense. The account implies, moreover, that there can be circumstances in which valuable lives may be ended despite the fact that the possessors of those lives have *not* ceased to value them; and it is with circumstances of this sort that I shall be concerned in the present chapter and the two chapters which follow. As far as the lives of persons are concerned there is, as Harris puts it, 'value in numbers'; and for this reason, he says, a policy of maximising these numbers is the only rational policy to adopt, even in cases where some lives have to be ended in order to implement it. Let us examine the policy of maximising lives.

The basis of the policy is declared to be that 'precisely because each person's life is individually valuable, two lives are more valuable than one'.[5] It is for this reason, Harris maintains, that 'in cases where we have to choose between lives when we cannot save all at risk, we should choose to save as many lives as we can'.[6]

At first sight, perhaps, this remark might seem to be thoroughly unobjectionable. Harris's words call to mind situations of the kind commonly presented for our entertainment in 'disaster movies'; and surely, it might be said, the people who have to cope with real disasters of this kind do right in seeking to save as many lives as possible – to maximise the numbers of lives saved, as bioethicists would say. The concern of rescuers in these situations, quite properly, is to save alive as many people as they can. But how does the *ending* of lives come into this? How is it that the policy of maximising lives can be used to justify killing people, rather than saving them?

The short answer to this question is that sometimes situations arise in which some people can be saved only if others are killed. There are so many examples in the relevant literature that one is spoilt for choice in selecting a small number to make the point; I shall take those of the fat potholer and the runaway trolley. Here is one version of the example involving the fat potholer:

A party of potholers is trapped in an underground cave which is rapidly being flooded. There is a way out of the cave, but it is blocked by an especially fat member of the party, who is stuck so tightly that he cannot be freed either by his companions or by the members of the rescue party which has just arrived. Were this not so, all of the potholers could be saved alive. What stands between the occupants of the cave and safety, then, is the life of a single individual; for the exit from the cave can be cleared if and only if the fat potholer is blown up with the dynamite the rescue party has brought. According to the policy of maximising lives, that is the action which must be carried out; it would be irrational, on Harris's account, to refuse to carry it out, despite the fact that it would mean, of course, killing the fat potholer.

In this particular example, if the fat potholer is not blown up he may well die anyway, along with his companions in the cave. In many other examples, the individual or individuals whose killing is prescribed by the maximising policy would not die anyway; and this is the case with the second example I shall take, a version of the example of the runaway trolley. The gist of it is as follows:

A trolley – or tram car – is running out of control along a track at the end of which several people are trapped. These people will almost certainly be killed if the trolley hits them. While the trolley cannot be stopped, it can be diverted into a siding at the end of which only one person is trapped; and, once again, that is the action required by the policy of maximising lives.

The policy dictates, then, that in all situations involving a choice between lives, the course of action that must be taken is the one which will result in the smallest number of deaths; even if this means that the particular deaths which occur would not have occurred at all if the policy had not been followed.

Let us glance for a moment at something Harris says about *moral beliefs* in his introduction to *The Value of Life*. If someone believes an action to be right, he says, this person must think that 'the world will be a better place'[7] in consequence of the action; and he must be able to say, therefore, in what way the word will be a better place. It is this, he says, which 'makes rational debate about ethics possible'.[8]

Harris is committing himself here to a *consequentialist* account of the moral justification of actions – the sort of account Mill gives, as we saw, in his essay on utilitarianism. The moral justification of an action, on this account, resides solely in the value of its *outcome* – the state of affairs the action effects or brings about.

It is this conception of moral justification which is embodied in the policy of maximising lives. If, for example, the runaway trolley were diverted, the world would be 'a better place' in consequence (Harris would say); it would be a better place because fewer valuable lives would be lost than by allowing the trolley to remain on its present course. There could be no rational justification, on this view, for a refusal to divert the trolley; and generally speaking, in any situation of this sort, the rational action will be the one that would maximise the number of lives saved. We shall see how far Harris is willing to press the point in the chapter which follows, 'Plain Murder'.

Thus the policy of maximising lives incorporates the utilitarian assumptions which Harris writes into his very conception of what it is to hold a moral belief. The right action, the rational action, is in every case the action that will have the best outcome, or that will 'make the world a better place'.

However, as we have seen in previous chapters, this sort of account is open to a fundamental objection: that there are moral conceptions which can place an action *out of bounds*, despite the fact that it is the action which would have the best outcome in utilitarian terms. In chapter 3 I discussed moral conceptions internal to social roles in a broad sense, and I showed how those conceptions could rule out certain actions despite the benefits they would bring. For example, the team of doctors discussed on p.44 regard the act of removing the dead child's vital organs as not available to them; it is the parents of the child, the doctors believe, who have the right to say what may be done with his body, and they have refused to permit the act. I shall now describe a situation in which it is clear what course of action is required by the policy of maximising lives, but in which the taking of that course of action is likewise ruled out for the agents concerned by a moral conception or belief. This conception, then, will be like the conceptions discussed in chapter 3 in its power to set limits to what may be done; but it will be unlike them in that it will have no connection with any particular social role or with any particular special obligation.

Suppose that a group of terrorists invade and seize a foreign embassy with the intention of killing one of its occupants (the ambassador), who manages to hide himself so successfully that he cannot be found. The only person the terrorists are able to capture is a visitor to the embassy, a tradesman who is wholly unconnected with the regime the terrorists are fighting but who happens to know the ambassador's whereabouts. The terrorists take this man hostage and threaten to kill him unless he tells them where the ambassador is. He replies that he cannot tell them, because it would be shameful for him to buy his life with the life of another human being.

In the situation as described above, the policy of maximising lives is inapplicable; for one life will be lost and one saved whatever the hostage's decision – though it is possible that the terrorists will find the ambassador after they have killed the hostage or that they will decide to blow up the whole building. Ignoring these complications, the description of the situation can be altered so that the maximising policy clearly applies to it; the number of the hostages can be increased. There are, let us suppose, three of them, and they all know the whereabouts of the terrorists' target. If they tell what they know, one life will be lost and three saved; if they do not, three lives will be lost and one (probably) saved.

It is obvious in these circumstances what course of action is required of the hostages by the policy of maximising lives; they should surrender the target – indeed, it is the obligation of each hostage to do this, whatever the views of the others may be. Suppose, however, that all three of these people hold the same belief as the single hostage mentioned previously, the belief that it is shameful to buy one's life with the life of someone else. On this ground, they each decide to keep silent, knowing that their silence will mean the death of them all. An advocate of the maximising policy would have to say that theirs is the wrong decision, the morally wrong decision, because three lives are three times as valuable as one. There is, however, a different way of playing the numbers game here. If three people buy their lives with the life of another there are – the hostages might say – three shameful acts; it makes no difference that the other person is the same other person in all three cases.[9]

The situation could be altered again, of course, in order to complicate the issue still further. It might be the case, for example, that only one of the three hostages knows where the target is, and that the two who do not are begging him to save their lives and his by giving the terrorists the information they demand. However, we need not enter into these further complications; enough has been said already to make the point, which is this: the maximising policy, like any outcome centred policy, can fall foul of moral conceptions which have to do with the *character* of actions rather than their *consequences*. The hostages know what the outcome of their decision will be; they know that in terms of the number of lives lost it will be worse than the outcome of a decision to speak. They believe, nonetheless, that this would not make speaking any the less shameful.

It will not be difficult by this time to anticipate exactly how Harris and other bioethicists would respond to this point. They would say that the hostages are acting *irrationally*; they are acting irrationally in that they are choosing to save only *one* life when it is possible for them to save *three*. If we call to mind previous discussions, however, we can see what the objection to saying this is. It is that as far as the hostages are concerned, it is *not* possible for them to save three lives in this situation; the course of action which would save those lives, they would say, is simply not open to them.

Let us look back at the example discussed on several previous occasions; that of the man who has to choose whom to save from the burning house, the cancer researcher or the latter's charlady. I said when discussing this example in chapter 3 that although it is *physically* possible for the rescuer to save the cancer researcher, he regards that course of action as closed to him on moral grounds; the reason is that the charlady is his mother, and he cannot, morally cannot, leave her to die.

What is physically possible, the example shows, may be morally out of the question; and that is precisely what the hostages would say about the act of telling the terrorists where the ambassador is hiding. They regard it as not available to them. Furthermore, just as the charlady's son can give a reason for what he says ('she's my mother'), so too can the hostages; they cannot betray the ambassador's whereabouts for the reason cited above – that it would be *shameful* to do so; it would be shameful because they would be buying their lives at the price of his.

There is no doubt that a supporter of the maximising policy would continue to urge against this that the hostage's decision is an irrational one. It is clear, however, that if he does he must meet a similar challenge to that which was put to him at the end of the third chapter: the challenge of *demonstrating* the irrationality of which he speaks. Once again, there is nothing to prevent a maximiser from expressing his own moral opinions in a forceful way; he is perfectly at liberty to say that the hostages' view 'makes no sense' to him. But so far this *is* nothing but the forceful expression of his own point of view. If he is to make it something more, he must appeal to a conception of 'what makes sense' which is *impartial* in the sense described in chapter 3; he must show that the hostages's stance is irrational by some standard they themselves accept, or to which they are committed. The question is, can he succeed in doing so?

Eventually, the pursuit of this question will take us back to the notion of the value of life. In the present chapter, however, I want to consider a possible attempt to convict the hostages of irrationality which will highlight a fundamental feature of utilitarian (and therefore bioethical) thought: namely, the conception of *action*, or of what it is *to act*, which it embodies. The attempt I have in mind would proceed by way of the following argument:

The hostages say that surrendering the target would be a shameful thing to do; but what about the conduct of the target himself? It is possible that the ambassador does not know what is happening; if he does know it, however, or even if he merely suspects it, is it not the case that on the hostages' own account of things he should give himself up to the terrorists? If he does not do this, then surely *he* will be acting shamefully, according to them; for he will be buying *his* life at the price of *theirs*. But in that case it follows that the hostages must say of *the same action* both that it is morally prohibited and that it is morally required; and this is, quite simply, incoherent.

Thus the argument is that the hostages position makes no sense because it commits them to incompatible judgements about the same action. The act of surrendering the ambassador cannot be right if the ambassador does it an l wrong if the hostages do it; for it is the same action in both cases. Either way, the ambassador's life will be lost and the hostages' lives saved. *What is done* will be the same; what will not be the same is *who does it*. But if what is done is the same, the moral

84

value of what is done must be the same too; what can it matter who does it?

We need to make explicit the conception of action which is presupposed by this argument; and we can do that by asking the question: what is it, according to the argument, that would make the surrender of the ambassador by the hostages *the same act* as the act the ambassador himself would perform were he to give himself up?

It is clear that the main focus of the argument is on the sameness of *the outcome*.[10] Were the hostages to surrender the ambassador, the terrorists would kill him and free them; one life – his – would be lost and three lives – theirs – would be saved. This is the state of affairs that their surrendering the ambassador would accomplish or bring about. Exactly the same state of affairs, however, would be accomplished or brought about were the ambassador to surrender himself; three lives – the same three – would be saved, and one life – the same one – would be lost. Hence the argument concludes, *the same deed* would be done in each case, the same action committed or carried out; what would differ would be the identity of the person who committed it. The *agents* would differ, but the *actions* would be the same.

I suggest, then, that the conception of action with which we are concerned can be defined as follows: to act is *to cause something to happen* or *to effect a change in the world*; actions, on this account, are primarily instruments for bringing such changes about. It follows that if two people cause the same thing to happen, or effect the same change in the world, they do the same thing, they carry out or perform the same action. I shall refer to this as the *instrumental* conception of action, and I shall argue that it is a *mis*conception: actions cannot be reduced to instruments for effecting changes in the world.

Let us return to the situation of the hostages in the embassy. As we have seen, a maximiser would say that the hostages are not morally required to lay down their lives for the ambassador. But it is important to realise that one does not have to be a maximiser in order to say this. Maximisers are utilitarians; they have a theory which they apply to all cases. We saw in chapter 1 that bioethicists follow Mill in their conception of the relationship between particular truths and general theory; the former, they insist, must be established by means of the latter. We must determine what makes for a valuable life in general before we can determine whether or not this or that life is valuable; similarly, we must choose between lives, when we have to do so, in accordance with a general policy which recognises that where lives are concerned, there's value in numbers.

It is clear, however, that one could disagree with the decision the hostages make without thinking that all one must do ever in situations like this one is 'maximise lives'. It is possible to think that *in this case* the hostages are not required to sacrifice their lives without thinking that no one is *ever* required to sacrifice his life except when more lives are to be saved than lost by so doing. Other things being equal, we might say, it is right to save as many lives as possible; but other things may not be equal, and whether or not they are can be determined only by looking at the details of the particular case.

One need not have a general theory, then, utilitarian or otherwise, in order to think that the action which would save the hostages' lives is not closed to them on moral grounds. In chapter 6 I mention some of the considerations which might be urged in support of such a response, and I shall not anticipate that discussion here. But there is one question which I do want to raise at this point; it is the question of what attitude might be taken towards *the hostages themselves* by someone who does think that they are mistaken in their judgement about what they must do. The relevance of this question to the topic of the instrumental conception of action will soon become clear.

We are considering the attitude to the hostages that might be taken by someone who is not a utilitarian but who agrees with what a utilitarian would say about this case; he agrees that the hostages are not morally required to lay down their lives for the terrorists' target. The course of action which would save their lives – telling the terrorists where the ambassador is hiding – is not, in this person's view, one that is closed to the hostages on moral grounds.

So this person dissents from the hostages view that it would be shameful for them to surrender the ambassador. Nevertheless, he might well say that the hostages themselves are thoroughly admirable people. Each of them is prepared to sacrifice his life for another person, a man he does not know and whom he might despise if he did; they are all willing to lay down their lives for someone who is a stranger to them. The personal qualities that show themselves here, this person might say, are virtues, and virtues which few possess to the extent that the hostages do. However, he might continue, people can be led astray by their virtues as well as by their vices, and that is what has happened here. Since the hostages are *not* morally required to lay down their lives in this situation, they are in error in supposing otherwise; thus they are heroes, certainly, but (as far as the present situation is concerned) misguided heroes.

I have put this point of view into the mouth of someone who has no moral theory at all, but who agrees with the maximiser – the utilitarian – that the hostages are mistaken in this instance. Not only is a utilitarian able to take this view himself, however, it is probable that he will be anxious to put it forward; for he will be likely to regard it as expressive of a *general* distinction which has played a crucial role in utilitarian theory from its inception, and which is bound up with the instrumental conception of action described above. This is the distinction between judging *people* on the one hand and judging *actions* on the other. A utilitarian might well wish to invoke his characteristic account of the significance of this distinction in responding to examples such as that of the hostages in the embassy.

Let us recall the reason for introducing that example in the first place. I wanted to show that the outcome-centred policy of maximising lives can fall foul of certain moral conceptions, ideas or beliefs. The hostages hold just such a belief, the belief that it is shameful to buy one's life with that of another; and it rules out, for them, the action dictated by the maximising policy, that of telling the terrorists where the ambassador is. I went on to describe a view of the hostages which one could take without being committed to the policy of maximising lives; the view that they are misguided heroes. They are heroes because of their willingness to sacrifice their own lives; they are misguided because they are not in these circumstances morally required to do so. They have been led into moral error, therefore, by their virtues.

What the utilitarian would say now is this: implicit in the response sketched above is a *general* distinction which most opponents of utilitarianism fail to mark. Once this distinction is made clear, the sort of example under discussion can be seen in the correct light – one in which it loses the anti-utilitarian force it might seem at first sight to possess.

The utilitarian's argument would be as follows: utilitarianism is a theory about the morality of actions, or about what makes actions right or wrong. The theory says that what makes actions right or wrong are their outcomes, and the policy of maximising lives reflects this. But there is more to a situation than the morality of the actions to which it gives rise; there is also, for example, the worth of the agents, or the people who perform those actions. The hostages do what is wrong, in that they allow three lives to be lost rather than one; but it by no means follows that they are bad men, or even that in this instance they have let their characters down. Far from it; they are exceptionally brave men and they act with exceptional bravery on this occasion. Nevertheless, they do *not* do *the right thing*.

The hostages then, as the utilitarian would see it, do the wrong thing, but for reasons that must be admired. They shrink from delivering a man to his death, and they would be worse men, he would say, if they did not, if they were able to hand the ambassador over to his executioners without a qualm. On this view, the sort of person who can be relied upon to do what is right in a situation like the one described is – paradoxically – the coward, the man who thinks of nothing but saving his own skin. If one of the hostages were a character of this sort, 'the right thing' would stand a much better chance of being done. Thus it is not difficult, the utilitarian would say, to understand why the action that is in fact *right* should seem to the hostages to be a shameful thing to do; it is the sort of thing one might do for reasons of which one *should* be ashamed – reasons of cowardice and selfishness. So it is easy to explain, he would conclude, why people are impressed by examples like that of the hostages in the embassy; such examples depict fine people acting out of fine motives. However, they do not constitute examples of *right action*. People are tempted to think otherwise because they have run together two distinct things: the assessment of agents on the one hand and the assessment of actions on the other.

The point is that according to utilitarian theory, the motives from which people act are relevant *only* to the assessment of their *characters*; all that is relevant to the assessment of their *actions* are the outcomes those actions have. The hostages do the right thing, on this view, only if they do what will save most lives; if they do not they do the wrong thing, and we should not allow our admiration for their courage to blind us to the fact. Opponents of utilitarianism, it is claimed, trade on our tendency to do just that when they put forward examples of the sort under discussion. They are failing to attend to the distinction between judging *people* on the one hand and judging what people *do* on the other.

We must not confuse our admiration for the hostages's characters with approval or endorsement of what they do; that is what the utilitarian would say. The hostages' motives are indeed admirable; but motives, as Mill put it in a well known passage, have 'nothing to do with the morality of the action'; their sole relevance is to 'the worth of the agent'.[11]

It will be clear, I think, that this account of the irrelevance of motives to the moral judgement of acts is an essential constituent of the instrumental conception of action, the conception presupposed by the argument outlined on p.84. If to act, to do something, is to cause something to happen, then we know what someone has done when we know what he has caused to happen; we do not need to know why he has caused that thing to happen, though we may, of course, have an additional interest in this matter. So whatever we discover about a person's motives, or his reasons for acting, our description of his action – of *what* he has done – must remain dependent upon the change in the world he has effected or caused to happen; for to act *is* to cause something to happen. If, therefore, two people cause the same thing to happen, it follows that they do the same thing; they perform an action of the same sort, even if their motives or reasons for acting are quite different. In these circumstances what they do is the same, it is *why they do it* that differs. It follows that we may judge *them* differently, but we cannot without inconsistency judge their *actions* differently. The worth of the agents may be different, but that of their actions must be the same.

It is essential to the instrumental conception of action that the question of what someone does is *in all cases* entirely separate from the question of why he does it. If we treat these questions as connected, then, even in some cases, we show that we do not think of actions as the utilitarian does – as nothing but instruments for effecting changes in the world. I want to suggest that we do indeed treat these questions as connected. Our ordinary talk about conduct, I maintain, does not sustain the distinction between what people do and why they do it which is necessary to the instrumental conception of action. I shall take as the basis for my discussion a re-statement of this distinction by a bioethicist, James Rachels. Let us begin by looking at the context in which Rachels makes use of the distinction.

In his book *The End of Life* Rachels sets out to 'examine the ideas and assumptions that lie behind . . . the rule against killing';[12] and he gives an account of this 'rule' which is similar in certain fundamental respects to the one given by Harris. I shall attend to the details of his account in a later chapter; suffice it to say here that its object is to show, among other things, that *euthanasia* can be defended on moral grounds. Rachels takes issue, accordingly, with various traditional aspects of anti-euthanasia thinking; and among these is a doctrine or principle that assigns an essential role to the 'intention' with which an act of killing is performed: the doctrine or principle of 'double effect'.

Rachels explains what this involves in the first chapter of his book, going on to argue in the sixth that it relies upon an 'irrelevant distinction' which requires to be 'debunked' – namely, the distinction between 'intentional and non-intentional termination of life'.[13]

If we look at how Rachels explains this distinction, we will see that he uses 'intention' in a broad sense; he stretches the term far enough to include 'motive' also, for intention has to do, he says, with 'what one is trying to accomplish by an action'.[14] One kills intentionally, on this account, when one aims at the death which results from one's action; one kills non-intentionally when one foresees the death but aims at something else. In the latter case, the death is merely, as Rachels puts it, a 'foreseen but unintended by-product of an action which is aimed at some other goal.'[15] According to the doctrine or principle of double effect, non-intentional killing (in the sense described) is morally permissible in certain circumstances; but intentional killing (of innocent people, at least) is not. Since euthanasia involves intentional killing, euthanasia is not permissible.

Rachels argues in reply that different intentions assume relevance only when we are concerned to judge *people* (or *agents*); as far as judging *actions* goes, intentions are beside the point. He attempts to convince us of this by taking an example that has nothing to do with killing, but that shows, he says, the proper role of intentions in moral judgement. The example he takes is as follows:

> Jack visits his sick and lonely grandmother, and entertains her for the afternoon. He loves her and his only intention is to cheer her up. Jill also visits the grandmother, and provides an afternoon's cheer. But Jill's only concern is that the old lady will soon be making her will; Jill wants to be included among the heirs. Jack also knows that his visit might influence the making of the will, in his favour, but that is no part of his plan.[16]

The conclusion Rachels invites us to draw from this story is that Jack and Jill 'do the very same thing,'[17] the right thing; they do it with different intentions, to be sure, but that is relevant only to what we should say about Jack and Jill themselves, as people. Jack, we should say, is an admirable person, but Jill is not. The story shows, Rachels says, that the intention with which an act is done 'is not relevant to deciding whether the act is right or wrong, but instead is relevant to assessing the character of the person who does it, which is *another thing entirely.*'[18]

According to Rachels, then, we must say about Jill's action what we say about Jack's; if we judge his action to be right, we must judge hers to be right too. This is because 'Jack and Jill *did the very same thing*' and 'consistency requires that *we assess similar actions similarly*'.[19]

I said above that Rachels stretches 'intention' to cover 'motive'; and it might be argued that if we take the distinction between intentions and motives into account, Rachels' claim that Jack and Jill 'did the very same thing' is on even stronger ground than his own discussion suggests. He speaks of Jack and Jill as having done the same thing ('cheering up their sick grandmother'[20]) with different intentions; but the intention of *cheering her up* was common to them both. Jack intended to cheer up the old lady, but so, we may be sure, did Jill. Her visit might have done that had she not intended it; but, as it happens, she certainly did intend to leave her grandmother more cheerful than she found her. Her aim was to secure a legacy, and she would have been less likely to succeed in that aim if her visit had made no difference whatsoever to her grandmother's spirits. For this reason she may well have put her heart and soul into entertaining her grandmother, and she may have met with more success than Jack, who, with the best will in the world, might have bored his grandmother for much of the afternoon by talking about subjects in which she had no interest.

So not only is it the case that Jack and Jill both brought about the same state of affairs (or effected a similar change in the world), it is also the case that they both did so intentionally and in the same way. They *both* visited their grandmother, they *both* cheered the old lady up, and they had *both* intended to cheer her up. Must it not follow that they did the same thing as each other?

We must allow, it seems to me, that *some* of the descriptions that are applicable to Jack's action are also applicable to Jill's (and vice versa). There are descriptions of what people do which depend for the most part on what they intentionally effect; and arguably, at any rate, the descriptions Rachels himself selects in his discussion of the example are of this kind. He says that both Jack and Jill spent an afternoon 'cheering up their sick grandmother', or 'comforting an elderly relative',[21] and since, as we have seen, both visits did cheer or comfort the old lady, and were intended to do so, we might be prepared to allow these descriptions in both cases (though we might not; see below).

It does not follow from this, however, that *all* of the descriptions applicable to the one action are also applicable to the other. This is because there are *other* descriptions of what people do which do *not* depend solely on what they intentionally effect; descriptions to which the motives or aims of the agents in question are crucial. A little reflection reveals that many of these descriptions apply to Jack's actions but not Jill's, and vice versa.

Consider what Rachels has told us about the visits Jack and Jill paid to their grandmother. Jack, he has said, paid the visit because he loved his grandmother and was concerned about her well-being. Jill, on the other hand, paid the visit because she wished to secure a legacy for herself; she did not care about her grandmother's well-being at all. Now in telling us this Rachels has given us information, not only about the *characters* of Jack and Jill, but also about their *behaviour* or *conduct*. Jack and Jill *behave* or *conduct themselves* differently from one another – that is to say, the actions they perform are actions of *different kinds*. In short: they do different things.

What are the different things they do? What descriptions can we apply to Jack's actions that we cannot apply to Jill's, and vice versa? Well, we can say, for example, that Jack showed his grandmother the respect that was due to her and Jill did not do that. Or we can say, for example, that Jill manipulated the old lady for her own purposes, and Jack did not do that. In saying these things, we are talking about what Jack and Jill *did* (or *did not do*); we are describing their *actions*.

A little reflection will bring to light some more ways in which we can speak of the one act but not the other. We can say of Jack's actions, but not of Jill's, that they were acts of love, compassion and concern; it is not simply that *Jack* is loving, compassionate and concerned but Jill is not. Similarly, we can say of Jill's actions, but not of Jack's, that they were acts of hypocrisy and greed; it is not simply that *Jill* is hypocritical and greedy but Jack is not. These concepts or categories apply as much to actions as to people, because when we talk about actions we are talking about *what people do*. To insist, as Rachels does, upon describing what is *done* solely in terms of what is *effected* is to cut an action loose from the agent whose action it is, and treat it as if it were an *event* rather than a *deed*, a piece of human conduct.

There are descriptions of what people do, then, which depend, at least in part, upon why they do it, and not only upon what they intentionally effect or cause to happen. Indeed, it might be argued that even the descriptions Rachels himself selects fall into this category. Jack spent an afternoon comforting (or cheering up) his sick grandmother. Is it so certain that that is what *Jill* did? It might well be argued that given her ulterior motive she should more properly be described as having spent an afternoon *pretending* to comfort her grandmother.

However, even if we do not insist on the above point, it remains true that Jill's actions can be described in ways in which Jack's cannot, and vice versa. Hence, contrary to what Rachels says, they did *not* do the very same thing. We can, therefore, without the slightest inconsistency, assign to what Jill did a very different moral value from the one we assign to what Jack did. Jack acted well; Jill acted extremely badly – despite the fact that what they both *effected* was exactly the same.

'But isn't it a *good thing* that Jill visited her grandmother?' Perhaps. If Jill's grandmother is *very* lonely, we might be glad that Jill paid the visit, whatever her reasons for doing so; the old lady enjoyed the visit and felt more cheerful because of it. From her point of view, and ours, if we care about her, better a visit such as Jill's, we might say, than no visit at all. But even if we are prepared to say this – and we might *not* be; after all, the old lady has been *manipulated* by her granddaughter – it has no bearing on the moral character of Jill's actions; for the focus and the kind of concern in question has been shifted. A concern with the sort of day Jill's grandmother had is quite different from a moral concern either with Jill or with what she did, and the same holds true with respect to Jack. If he did bore his grandmother to the extent that she wished she had spent the day alone, we might be glad if pressure of work were to reduce the number of his visits; but now our sole concern is with the old lady's enjoyment.

Consider, by way of comparison, door to door collections in aid of worthy causes. The collectors' concern is with how much money they can collect for their chosen charities; they are interested in neither the moral character of the people who give that money nor the moral value of their actions. The collectors may know perfectly well that most donors contribute grudgingly, in order to get the collectors off their doorsteps, and that for this reason their acts are not truly acts of charity; the money will do the collectors' causes good all the same.

It is not the case, then, that questions of motive (aim, goal, purpose), let alone questions of intention proper, are of no relevance to the moral assessment of what people do. This is because questions of motive can be relevant to the *description* of what people do; it is not enough, in many cases, to know only what has been effected or caused to happen.

Rachels' central concern in The *End of Life*, as we have seen, is with *euthanasia*; and even the briefest of reflections upon what this notion means will suffice to confirm that his account of action must be inadequate. Suppose Jack and Jill to be not two cousins visiting their grandmother, but two doctors deliberately hastening the death of a terminally ill patient by means of a lethal injection. Jill, who retains her mercenary character, is doing this in order to secure sooner rather than later the legacy she knows the patient to have bequeathed to her; Jack is doing it in order to release the patient from the suffering and indignity he knows her to dread more than death. The consequences of their actions, let us suppose, will be exactly the same (we can even make the patient the same patient, injected by Jill at 2 a.m. and by Jack, who does not know about this, a few minutes later). What Jack is doing (or setting out to do) can be described as an act of *euthanasia* (whether or not we approve of it). What Jill is doing cannot be so described, and what explains this difference in description is the difference in motive. It is a *necessary* condition of describing a killing as an act of euthanasia that the agent in question should have a certain motive for what he does; what Jill is committing is not euthanasia, but murder.

We saw above that Rachels examines what he calls 'the relation between act and intention'[22] in the context of an attempt to discredit the doctrine of double effect. I will comment very briefly on this matter before returning to the bearing of the whole discussion upon the argument of the present chapter.

What the doctrine of double effect says, according to Rachels, is that the killing of an innocent person is not morally permissible unless the killing is unintentional or, better, unintended. What this means is not that the killing must be inadvertent, but that it must not be what is *aimed at*; it must be nothing more than a foreseen consequence (or 'by-product') of an action which has some other aim or object, such as that of reducing a patient's suffering.

Rachels thinks that there is nothing at all to be said for this doctrine. At one point he asks rhetorically: 'If [an] act is wrong with one intention, how can it be right with another?'.[23] But there is a perfectly proper answer to this question: because it is (or may be) *a different action* in each case (whether or not there is a difference in the outcome). In so far as the doctrine of double effect recognises this, there *is* something to be said for it, though not, in my view, for the application of it with which Rachels is particularly concerned. Indeed, thought of as a principle of justification, something which can be used to license some acts of killing as opposed to others, it is clearly open to serious abuse.[24] However, it does at least preserve the concept of a *deed*; Rachels' account does not.

This discussion of Rachels' work took its rise from a description of one possible way of reacting to the example of the hostages in the embassy. According to this reaction, the hostages are not morally required to sacrifice their lives for the ambassador who is the terrorists' target; it would not be shameful for them to reveal his whereabouts. They are in error, therefore, in thinking otherwise; but they have been led this error by their virtues – their courage and their integrity.

I have not sought to dispute that one might look at the matter in this way; what I have sought to dispute is that one *must* do so. That is the view to which utilitarians are committed, because their theory of morality separates the assessment of actions from the assessment of people and bases the former entirely upon outcomes. Implicit in this theory, as we have seen, is a conception of action according to which to do something is to cause something to happen. What one *does* is a matter of what one *effects*, and it follows that the moral value of what one does depends entirely upon the value of what one effects. So if two people effect the same thing, or cause the same thing to happen, they do the same thing, and the moral value of what they do must be the same.

Rachels uses the example of Jack and Jill visiting their grandmother to support the instrumental conception of action; but what the example really does, I have argued, is expose the inadequacy of that conception.

Rachels describes two people who cause the same thing to happen, but with different intentions (or motives). Contrary to what he says, however, they do *not* do the same thing. The example shows, therefore, that questions of motive – questions about *why* a person does something – can be relevant to the way in which the action in question should be described – to *what* that person does. Thus the response to the hostages' action which sees it as one of misguided heroism is *one possible response among others*; it is not the response one *must* make if one is not to run together two things which should be kept apart, the judgement of people and the judgement of actions.

We are now in a position to see exactly what is wrong with the attempt to convict the hostages of incoherence which was described earlier in this chapter. According to that argument, the hostages are committed to making incompatible judgements about the same action. Whether the ambassador surrenders himself or the hostages surrender him, his life will be lost and theirs saved. Hence what is done will be the same, and the doing of it cannot be both morally prohibited and morally required, as it must be on the hostages' account.

This argument depends entirely upon the misconception of action that the previous discussion has exposed. It is only if what is *done* is identified with what is *effected* (or *caused to happen*) that the hostages' surrender of the ambassador can be described as the same action as the ambassador's surrender of himself. What *is* the same in both cases is what is brought about, namely, the death of the ambassador as opposed to the three hostages; the identity of the agent makes no difference to that. However, it does not *have* to make a difference to that in order to make a difference to what is *done*. If the ambassador surrenders himself, he lays down his life for the hostages – this is what he does, this is how his action should be described. The hostages lay down their lives – that is to say, perform an action of the same sort – only if they *refuse* to surrender the ambassador. How a deed should be described depends not only upon what the agent has effected, but also upon who the agent is, in what circumstances he has acted, and for what reasons. The inadequacy of the instrumental conception of action is manifest in the way we ordinarily describe and classify what people do.

It is not the case, then, that the hostages are committed to making incompatible judgements about the same action. They may well be committed to the view that if the ambassador knows what is happening he should give himself up; but what *he* would be doing in giving himself up is not what *they* would be doing in giving him up, despite the fact that what he would *effect* would be the same.

I began this chapter by describing the policy of maximising lives which John Harris presents as the only rational policy to adopt. For Harris, and for bioethicists in general, it cannot be morally wrong to kill people or deliver them to their deaths if that is the only way of maximising the number of lives that are preserved in the end. I described the situation of the hostages in the embassy in order to show that the maximising policy can fall foul of moral conceptions, ideas or beliefs. The hostages are faced with a choice between lives – their own or that of the ambassador who is hiding from the terrorists. If they surrender him only one life will be lost, as opposed to the three that will be lost if they do not. They believe, however, that it would be shameful for them to surrender the ambassador, and for this reason they regard the action that would minimise the number of lives lost as closed to them on moral grounds. Were they to give the terrorists the information they seek they would be buying their lives with the life of someone else; and this is something they morally cannot do.

Bioethicists, as we know, are committed to the position that the hostages can give no rational justification for their refusal to hand over the ambassador. The claim that such an act would be *shameful* does not count for them as a rational justification, because it does not appeal to *outcomes*. The hostages' position, bioethicists wish to say, makes no sense; and they intend this to be more than a forceful expression of their own moral perspective. However, as we have seen, if they are to succeed in their intention, they must appeal to an impartial standard of rationality, one to which the hostages themselves are already committed. As yet, no such standard has come to light.

If we look back at what Harris says about the maximising policy, however, we find remarks that might be construed as an appeal of the sort I have said bioethicists must make. Consider the hostages once more. It is clear, the bioethicist might say, that they *value the lives* of individual people. They say, after all, that it would be shameful for them to buy their lives with the life of another person; and how could this be so unless the life of that other person were of value? Thus, that the life of an individual person (in the ordinary sense, at least) is a valuable life is implicit, on this account, in the moral conception which leads the hostages to act as they do. They *must* believe that the ambassador's life has value, and that the value it has does not depend on anything peculiar to its possessor, such as the sort of man he is; for they know little or nothing about him. The value of his life, then, must be the value of any human life, the life of any human being or individual person. To repeat: the hostages *must* believe this, the bioethicist might say, or their own behaviour would be incomprehensible.

But if they do believe it, the bioethicist might continue, *they are committed to accepting the policy of maximising lives*; for the policy is based on nothing more than that belief (that the life of an individual person has value), combined with the obvious and incontestable truth that if one life is valuable two lives are more valuable than one.

So the hostages' decision can be shown to be irrational by means of the consistent application of the very considerations which give it what sense it has; that is what Harris, or any other utilitarian, might say. Perhaps, he might add, it *would* be shameful, in the sort of situation the hostages are placed, to deliver someone else to his death rather than accept death oneself. That is to say, if *one* life must be lost in such a situation, strict integrity might demand that it should be one's own. The moment one hostage becomes two or more, however, everything changes. It would make no sense to allow three valuable lives to be lost when the loss of only one is necessary, and the hostages are already committed to acknowledging that this is so. If they regard the life of an individual person as having value, which they clearly do, they must regard three such lives as having three times the value of one; and they must concede, therefore, that it would be quite irrational to let three lives, rather than one, be lost. They must admit that the maximising policy is, as Harris puts it 'the only policy that can plausibly claim to value individuals'.[25]

I shall argue that we need not accept this conclusion; it is based on a profound misunderstanding of what it means, in the moral context, to see a human life, or a human being, as having value. Insofar as it makes sense to speak in the moral context of the value of a person, that value is not the value of an item. I shall attempt over the next two chapters to bring out the meaning of this statement; and in order to do so I shall move away from the situation that has occupied most of our attention in this chapter – that of the hostages in the embassy – to another, which is of Harris's devising. In his paper 'The Survival Lottery'[26] he attempts to take to its logical conclusion the policy of maximising lives which is rooted in the account he gives of the value of life; and we shall begin the next chapter by considering the argument of this paper.

6

PLAIN MURDER

In his paper 'The Survival Lottery'[1] John Harris makes a proposal intended to remedy the chronic shortfall in the number of vital organs that presently become available to physicians for use in transplant surgery. He writes as follows:

> . . .everyone [shall] be given a sort of lottery number. Whenever doctors have two or more dying patients who could be saved by transplants, and no suitable organs have come to hand through 'natural deaths', they can ask a central computer to supply a suitable donor. The computer will then pick the number of a suitable donor at random and he will be killed so that the lives of two or more others may be saved.[2]

What will be the moral justification for killing one person and giving his vital organs to two other people? It is clear from Harris's discussion that it will be nothing more than the policy of maximising lives explained in chapter 5. The idea of a lottery is beside his main point, which is simply that *there's value in numbers*; two lives are twice as valuable as one, and that is why one person may be killed so that two might live. It does not matter, on this account, that the one life lost in these circumstances will actually be taken; it is of no consequence that the donor of the organs which save two lives will have to be killed in order to make those organs available. However he comes to die, we shall be left with a better outcome in terms of the number of lives saved than if he had gone on living. Harris believes that we all have reason to support the setting up of the lottery he describes; each of us is more likely to gain from it than to lose. The lottery scheme, Harris says,

> . . . could offer the chance of saving large numbers of lives that

99

are now lost . . . the numbers of untimely deaths each year might be dramatically reduced, so much so that everyone's chance of living to a ripe old age might be increased.[3]

As I said above, however, the lottery proposal is beside the main point; for even without a lottery it would be right, on Harris's account, to kill one person so that two might be saved. It is because this would be the right course of action that the lottery is suggested; it is not that it would become the right course of action only when the lottery had been set up. The lottery, in true utilitarian spirit, would serve primarily to mitigate (to some extent) the 'terror and distress' that would be likely to result from a policy of '. . . snatching passers by off the streets and disorganising them . . .'.[4] Let us consider the situation that prompts the lottery proposal.

A team of doctors has two patients, Y and Z, both of whom need organ transplants if they are to go on living for any length of time. Y needs a new heart and Z new lungs. Unfortunately, no suitable organs are available for these individuals – none, that is to say, are presently 'in stock'. However, there is to hand a third person, A, whose own organs are suitable, as it happens, for both Y and Z, but who is alive and in good health. What the doctors should do, Y and Z maintain, is kill A and give his heart and lungs to them. They should do this because A's death constitutes the loss of one valuable life only, whereas the deaths of Y and Z would constitute the loss of two such lives; and it is obviously better that one life should be lost than that two should be.

I said when I introduced the policy of maximising lives in chapter 5 that at first sight it might seem to be thoroughly unobjectionable. This is because the way in which Harris describes it in *The Value of Life* calls to mind 'disaster situations', and when these arise we tend to take it for granted that rescuers should try to save as many lives as they can. I then described two situations in which saving as many lives as possible would necessitate killing people; specifically, the fat potholer stuck in the exit from the flooding cave and the single person at the end of the track down which the runaway trolley might be diverted (see p.80). I did not discuss those situations, but I did discuss a third, that of the hostages in the embassy who will be killed by terrorists unless they reveal the whereabouts of the fugitive ambassador.

The three situations just referred to are not similar in all respects; there are differences among them which would strike many people as morally significant. For example, it may be that the fat potholer who is blocking the means of escape for his companions is doomed (for it may be that he will die whether or not he is blown up to enable them to get out of the cave). But that is not the case with the individual who will be killed if the runaway trolley is diverted into the siding; if it continues on its present course his life is in no danger whatsoever. For this reason, it is likely that some of the people who would be prepared to blow up the fat potholer would not be prepared to divert the trolley. The position of the fugitive ambassador is like that of the single individual in the runaway trolley example in that he will be safe – probably – unless the hostages decide to tell the terrorists where he is. However, the situation involving the hostages differs from both of the others in respect of the place within it of *human iniquity*. There are certain to be people who would be willing to divert the trolley but not to co-operate in any way with terrorists, even at the cost of their own lives.

Nevertheless, there is one thing that all of the situations described have in common: they are *extraordinary* or *unusual* situations which require a decision or call for a choice. The rescuers who arrive at the cave in which the potholers are trapped must decide whether or not to blow up the fat potholer; the controller of the runaway trolley must decide whether or not to divert it into the siding; the hostages must decide whether or not to tell the terrorists where the ambassador is hiding. The situation described in 'The Survival Lottery', however, is not at all unusual, and it would not be perceived as one which requires a decision or a choice. Y and Z can be saved only if suitable organs are available for them, and none are; what the doctors would tell Y and Z's relatives, or Y and Z themselves, in these circumstances, is that *they cannot be saved*. This does not express a *decision* on the doctors' part; it is not that they have decided to go down one road rather than another. The only road they can see is the road they – and their patients – are on.

Harris must deny that there is only one road; and he does deny it. His claim is that whether or not they realise it, the doctors in charge of Y and Z *do* have a choice. Whatever the general attitude to this situation may presently be, any doctor involved must be brought to realise, Harris says, that '[he] must decide whether, in these circumstances, he ought to save two lives at the cost of one or one life at the cost of two'.[5]

The third life which suddenly appears here is the life of any healthy person who is to hand and whose heart and lungs would be suitable for Y and Z respectively. A happens to be such a person, but anyone with organs that suit would have done as well. Harris knows, of course, that it would not occur to the doctors to see A as a party to the situation; but this, for him, is neither here nor there. 'The fact' he says 'that so called "third parties" have never before been . . . thought of as involved . . . is not an argument against their now becoming so'.[6] He knows too that the doctors would respond to his proposal with incredulity and horror; but this, for him, is similarly neither here nor there. As far as he is concerned, it shows only that they (along with most other people) have not done their 'own moral thinking' about these matters, but have been content to appeal to what 'custom or authority' dictate.[7]

The doctors, Harris says, must be made to see that they have a choice; and once they do see it, he argues, it should be obvious to them what the right choice is. A should be killed in order to save the lives of Y and Z. If the doctors reject this course of action, they will be choosing to save one life at the cost of two rather than two lives at the cost of one; they will be acting, therefore, in a quite irrational manner.

Let us look at the argument Harris gives for his description of what the doctors would be doing if they refused to kill A; an argument which, like the lottery proposal itself, he puts into the mouths of Y and Z – two individuals so unpleasant, incidentally, that it would be difficult for anyone to lament their passing. I shall argue in reply that Harris has misidentified the point at issue between himself and the doctors; and that his claim for the irrationality of a refusal to kill A depends upon this misidentification.

The following is a summary of Harris's argument, divided into four steps or stages:

1 It is not strictly true that no suitable organs are available for Y and Z; there are any number of individuals walking around who have hearts and lungs suitable for them both. If one of these (A, for example) is killed the transplants can go ahead, with the probable consequence that the lives of Y and Z will be saved. So the doctors can save Y and Z.

2 Given that this is the case, if the doctors refuse to kill A they will be *letting Y and Z die.*

3 Since the distinction between letting die and killing is of no moral significance, if the doctors refuse to kill A they will be (as good as) *killing Y and Z.*

4 They will emerge, therefore, as people who, when faced with a

choice between killing one person to save two and killing two persons to save one, chose to do the latter when rationality plainly required them to do the former.

The way in which the conclusion of this argument is stated makes it look as if the step most vital to it is step (3), the equation between *killing* and *letting die* (or, as Harris puts it, 'positive and negative killing'[8]); and that is what Harris himself seems to think. He believes that those who reject his conclusion must do so because they do not accept this equation; it is only on that ground, he thinks, that the doctors could defend a refusal to kill A in order to save the lives of Y and Z. They could not, for example, defend it by protesting that killing A would be 'doing something [they] ought in no circumstances to do – kill the innocent'; for 'it is Y and Z's claim that failure to adopt their plan will also involve killing the innocent, rather more of the innocent than the proposed alternative'.[9]

The doctors, Harris thinks, must deny that letting die is tantamount to killing; otherwise, they would have to accept that it would be irrational not to kill A.

If we recall previous discussions, however, we can see that the equation between killing and letting die is not necessarily the issue between Harris and someone who refuses to countenance the killing of A. In saying this, I am neither accepting the equation nor denying that someone might choose to take issue with it; I am denying only that it *must* be the issue, certainly that it must be the main issue.

Suppose we accept, for the sake of argument, the piece of consequentionalist dogma which the equation constitutes; suppose we allow that there is no moral significance to the distinction between letting die on the one hand and killing on the other. Harris thinks that if we do this his case stands proven; but it does not, for steps (2) and (3) depend upon step (1), and step (1) may be rejected. If it is rejected, the truth of the equivalence thesis does not even arise; for the doctors can be said to be 'letting Y and Z die' *only if it is true that they can save them*. What the doctors say, however, is that they *cannot* save them. In saying this they are not denying that there are healthy people walking around with organs suitable for Y and Z; they know that perfectly well. They are not denying the *physical* possibility of getting organs for Y and Z by killing one of these people; they are denying the *moral* possibility of doing so. Killing A, they maintain, is morally out of the question.

So it is this, and not the equivalence thesis, which is the

fundamental point at issue between the doctors and Harris; for the moral impossibility of killing *A* means that his organs are not available, and therefore that *Y* and *Z* cannot be saved. Thus the doctors do not have to become involved in the debate about killing and letting die at all.

Let me restate the point in order to make it as clear as I can. Harris wishes to show that the doctors are acting irrationally in refusing to countenance the killing of *A*; and he seeks to do it by showing that they are choosing to kill two persons to save one, rather than one person to save two. This description certainly does depend on the equation between killing and letting die, the equation Harris uses to facilitate the move from step (2) to step (3); however, it does not depend *only* on that. It depends also on the acceptance of step (2), the proposition that the doctors are 'letting *Y* and *Z* die'. But that is just what the doctors do not accept. *Y* and *Z* accept it, because they regard the killing of *A* as something it is open to the doctors to do; the doctors themselves, however, deny that it is open to them to kill *A*. The killing of *A*, they say, is *physically* possible but *morally* out of the question; and it follows that *Y* and *Z* cannot be saved. But if *Y* and *Z* cannot be saved they are not being 'let' or 'allowed' to die; and the question of whether letting them die is tantamount to killing them does not even arise.

Hence, even if the equivalence of letting die and killing is conceded for the sake of argument, the description Harris gives of the doctors' conduct – that unless they kill *A* they will be killing two persons to save one – can still be rejected; and with it his contention that they will be acting irrationally. His argument assumes that the act of killing *A* is morally open to the doctors; for that is implied by the statement that it is false, strictly speaking, to say no organs are available to them for *Y* and *Z*, false because the organs of *A* (for instance) are available. To this extent, the first premiss of Harris's argument is already an expression of the maximiser's perspective.

The killing of *A*, according to the doctors, is morally impossible or out of the question. Of course Harris (or any other bioethicist) would insist on asking *why* it is out of the question – for according to him, as we have seen, '. . . if something is . . . morally right or wrong, there must be some reason why this is so'.[10] On the assumption that the doctors could be persuaded to regard Harris's question as a serious one, what answer, if any, might they give to it?

A possible answer would be that killing *A* is out of the question because it would be the killing of an innocent person, and one ought never to kill the innocent. Harris himself attributes this belief to the doctors, though he also thinks, as we saw above, that it will not serve their purpose.

Now whereas it is possible for someone to believe that in no circumstances should an innocent person be killed, most people, I think, do not believe this. They would accept that killing the innocent must always be *justified*; but in doing so they would be implying the possibility of a justification in certain circumstances. Killing the innocent, most people would say, is not always out of the question.

But the doctors need not give the answer just mentioned to the question the bioethicist insists upon asking (the question: 'why is it morally impossible to kill *A*?'). This is because there is a perfectly obvious alternative to it, namely, *because it would be murder*. The doctors need not deny that there are circumstances in which killing the innocent would be justified; they need deny only that such circumstances include the ones in which *Y* and *Z* are urging them to kill *A*. What they can say is that killing *A* would be an act of murder, and that therefore it is something there can be no question of doing. Thus they can give a *reason* for the moral impossibility of killing *A*; or rather they can *remind Y* and *Z* what killing *A* would be: murder.

Let us suppose that the doctors do remind *Y* and *Z* that killing *A* would be murder, and that therefore it is not open to them (or anyone else) to do it. Bearing this in mind, let us try to answer the following question: how should we describe the conflict between the doctors and Harris (whose spokesmen *Y* and *Z* appear to be)? What sort of conflict is it?

We have seen that there is, so far, no reason at all to accept the account of the conflict Harris himself tries to give – that it is a conflict between *rationality* and *irrationality* (he is thinking rationally, the doctors are not). If the doctors would only think about the situation in a rational way, he implies, they would be bound to conclude that they ought to kill *A*. As we have seen, the argument central to his paper is meant to show this by establishing that otherwise the doctors will be choosing to kill two persons to save one, rather than one person to save two. I have argued that it does not show this; or rather, that it shows it only if the perspective embodied in the maximising policy is presupposed from the beginning. It is only from within that perspective that *A*'s vital organs can be regarded as 'available' to the doctors (even 'strictly speaking'). As far as the doctors themselves are concerned, the moral impossibility of killing *A* means that his organs are not available, and thus the argument cannot get off the ground. There is in Harris's paper no argument for the irrationality of the doctors' behaviour which begins from a place outside the maximiser's own point of view.

The conflict between Harris and the doctors should not be described as a conflict between reasoned argument on the one hand and slavish obedience to custom and authority on the other. How should it be described? Were this discussion to follow the pattern of previous discussions, the answer would be that it should be described simply as a *moral* conflict or disagreement. Harris presents it as a conflict between reason (on his side) and unreason (on the doctors'); in reality, however, it is a dispute between people who hold opposing moral views about the same matter. Is that what we should say?

If we were to answer yes to this question, we would be presenting the conflict between Harris and the doctors as analogous to (for example) the conflict described in the previous chapter between the hostages and someone who believes that they may (or even that they must) tell the terrorists where the ambassador is hiding. I said when discussing the hostages' situation that it would be perfectly possible for someone to disagree with them; what the hostages say – that it would be *shameful* for them to reveal the ambassador's hiding place – is open to dispute (and not only by utilitarians). I shall argue, however, that what the doctors say now about the killing of A is *not* open to dispute. They say that the killing of A would be murder; but in saying this they are not making a *judgement* – they are not saying something with which others are able to disagree. Killing A in the circumstances under discussion, I maintain, is not only an act of murder, it is *incontestably* or *indisputably* an act of murder; a judgement that it would *not* be murder would be one to which no sense could be attached.

Consider once again the case of the hostages. Not one of them, as we saw, is willing to tell the terrorists where the fugitive ambassador has concealed himself, for they all believe that it would be shameful to do that. I have said that their judgement is open to dispute, and I have said also that someone who does dispute it need not do so because of some general theory to which he subscribes. Let us smuggle such a person into the embassy and consider what he might say to the hostages. His aim, remember, is to persuade them that it is morally permissible for them to tell the terrorists where the ambassador may be found; and if he is to succeed in that aim, he must convince the hostages that in giving their captors the information demanded, they would not, as they think, be acting shamefully. How might he do that?

It is clear that the newcomer must proceed by pointing to some morally relevant difference between what the ambassador himself is doing – if he knows what is happening – and what the hostages would be doing were they to tell the terrorists where he is. The newcomer might remind the hostages that they are innocent bystanders in this situation; unlike the fugitive ambassador, they have no connection whatsoever with the regime their captors are trying to bring down. He might add, if he believes this, that the regime in question is a brutal and tyrannical one, and that the ambassador must take the consequences of his support for it. He might point out instead, or in addition, that the man is a stranger to the hostages, whereas the people who will suffer as a result of their self-sacrifice are their own dependents. He might even suggest that although the hostages are evidently far from cowards in the usual sense of the word, there is a certain kind of courage in which they may be wanting; they are afraid, perhaps, of being *thought* cowards, something that would be a mark of *moral* cowardice. What does it matter, he might say, if other people misconstrue their actions? And so on.

Whether or not we agree with the view the newcomer puts forward – the view that the hostages should tell the terrorists where the ambassador is – it is surely the case that he can produce some moral support for it. He can argue, as I have said, that there are morally significant differences between what the ambassador is (or might be) doing and what the hostages are being asked to do. There is no guarantee, of course, that the hostages will be prepared to accept this; they may continue to think that surrendering the ambassador would be a shameful thing to do whatever the newcomer says. The hostages and the newcomer may remain on different sides of the argument. My point is only that there *are* different sides to the argument in this case; there can be dispute over the judgement the hostages make because there is *room* for dispute about it – there are moral considerations which count both for and against the judgement. It is, precisely, a *judgement*.

We cannot question, then, the moral intelligibility of the view the newcomer to the embassy takes; we cannot question the intelligibility of his denial that it would be shameful for the hostages to reveal the fugitive ambassador's whereabouts. We may not *agree* with it; but we must allow it to count as a possible moral response to the situation the hostages are in.

What I am suggesting is that this would not be true of an attempt to deny what the doctors say about the act of killing *A*. We could question the very intelligibility of a claim that it would not be murder to commit that act; and it follows that the conflict between Harris and the doctors is not analogous to the conflict between the hostages and the newcomer to the embassy. The latter is a moral disagreement, but the former cannot be described in this way.

It is important to guard against possible misunderstandings of this point, especially in view of the tendency utilitarians have to foist generalisations upon their opponents. I have been talking about the act of killing *A* so that *Y* may receive his heart and *Z* his lungs; it is *this* act I have described as indisputably an act of murder (though there are, of course, other acts I would describe in the same way). I have not said that *every* killing is an act of murder, and I have not said that every act of murder is *indisputably* an act of murder. I recognise, that is to say, that there can be acts of killing about whose moral classification people might intelligibly and rationally disagree.

Suppose, for example, that a paediatrician deliberately kills a newborn baby in his care. The baby is grossly handicapped, and its parents have rejected it. He claims that he has committed, not an act of murder, but an act of mercy.

Many people would say that this man *has* committed murder; some, perhaps all, of the doctors looking after *Y* and *Z* might say so. Nevertheless, in these circumstances it would be possible to take a different view of the killing, the paediatrician's own. This is the sort of case in which a dispute is possible about whether or not an act of murder has been committed; there are moral arguments the paediatrician can use in defence of his action, moral considerations to which he can appeal – for example, the interests of the child he has killed. As far as the killing of *A* is concerned, however, there are – I maintain – no such considerations; there is nothing that could give sense to a denial that killing *A* would be murder.

The point is that some *reason* must be given for saying of a given act (or type) of killing that it does not count as murder; and not just *any* reason, but an appropriate reason. The concept of murder is *public property*; it is a part of our everyday moral vocabulary, and it is not up to philosophers to prescribe how it should and should not be used. We all know to what sorts of considerations people must appeal in defending themselves and others against the charge of murder; and it is from the standpoint of this knowledge that we must judge not only the truth, but also the intelligibility of a claim that a given act of killing is not an instance of the concept. My contention is that none of the relevant considerations are available in the case we are discussing, the case of the killing of A; thus no appropriate reason could be given for saying that the killing did not count as murder.

Harris himself neither uses nor mentions the concept of murder in 'The Survival Lottery'; nor, so far as I can tell, in *The Value of Life*. For the time being, however, let us suppose that he would be prepared to express his views about the killing of A in terms of this concept – that he would be prepared to deny that killing A would be murder. In order to meet the point I have just made, he would have to show that contrary to what I have said, there do exist in the present case considerations of the sort mentioned above – ones which could be invoked to give sense, at least, to this denial. If we look through the pages of 'The Survival Lottery', we find mention of two that might be suggested for the purpose – *absence of malice* and *self-defence*. Let us look at what Harris says about them, beginning with the less promising of the two: absence of malice.

Harris considers an attempt by someone he calls 'an absolutist' to make the following point:

> . . . while no one intends the deaths of Y and Z, no one necessarily wishes them dead, or aims at their demise for any reason, they do mean to kill A (or have him killed). But Y and Z can reply that the death of A is no part of their plan, they merely wish to use a couple of his organs, and if he cannot live without them . . . *tant pis*! None would be more delighted than Y and Z if artificial organs would do as well . . . .[11]

Y and Z certainly do not improve upon acquaintance. They are attempting here to appeal to a principle or doctrine which we have had occasion to mention once before – namely, the principle or doctrine of 'double effect'. This permits the killing of the innocent, let us recall, so long as their deaths are not what is *aimed at* by the acts which bring them about. The end or object of these acts must be something other than the deaths which result from them; the deaths, therefore, must be nothing more than a 'by-product' of what is done.

When this matter arose in chapter 5, I made the comment, in passing, that the doctrine of double effect is clearly open to serious abuse; and it would be difficult, I suggest, to envisage a more outrageous abuse of it than the one contained in the passage quoted above. A's vital organs can be given to Y and Z only if A himself is killed, and therefore his death is most certainly part of Y and Z's plan.

It is true that they do not seek A's death *for its own sake* (as one might seek the death of a person one hates); their sole concern is to secure his heart and lungs for themselves. The presence of malice in the sense just indicated, however, is not a necessary condition of murder. A jury would not be inclined to acquit of that charge a defendant who made a plea such as the following:

> Not guilty, my Lord. I was the principal beneficiary in my uncle's will, and it was for that reason alone I poisoned him. My only aim was to get rich quick; I bore my uncle no malice at all. No one would have been more delighted than I if something had occurred to render my killing him unnecessary to my prosperity.

If Y and Z were to kill A, their defence would be no better than this one. Their aim would have been to preserve their own lives; the aim of the man who killed his uncle was to become rich. The fulfilling of the first aim, like the fulfulling of the second, required that murder be done. This is so plainly true that it is hard to believe we are intended to take seriously the part of Y and Z's argument under discussion; it is probably nothing more than an attempt to satirise the doctrine of double effect. So let us leave it and turn to the second and more promising of the considerations which can be extracted from 'The Survival Lottery'; that of self-defence.

Harris begins by putting the appeal to self-defence in the mouth of A, the person Y and Z are urging their doctors to kill. Most people would allow, he says, that each of us has a right to defend himself against physical attacks by others; they would agree that if one's life is threatened by an assailant one may kill the assailant, if necessary, in order to save it. Might not A invoke this right to self-defence, Harris asks, in order to protect himself from Y and Z? He goes on:

> . . . Y and Z would reply that the right of self defence must extend to them as much as to anyone else, and while it is true that they can only live [i.e. live only] if another man is killed, they would claim that it is also true that if they are left to die, then someone who lives on does so over their dead bodies.[12]

I would not dispute that Y and Z, like other people, have a right to self-defence; I certainly would dispute that their killing A – or their having him killed – could be seen as an exercise of that right. Such a claim is simply perverse. Stretching concepts beyond their legitimate bounds almost counts as an occupational hazard in philosophy; but in some cases, at least, there is an element of justification for the extended use to which a concept is put. In this case, however, there is no justification at all. It is worth pursuing the point, because it provides an excellent illustration of a persistent bioethical tendency – that of seizing upon familiar moral concepts and proceeding to apply them with little or no attention to the proper contexts of their use. Here, I shall argue, the kind of setting that gives talk of self-defence its sense is wholly absent.

In what sort of circumstance would it be proper to say that one person has killed another in self-defence? There follows a straightforward case (courtesy of Alfred Hitchcock's *Dial M for Murder*):

A woman gets out of bed late one night in order to answer the telephone. As she picks up the receiver she is set upon by an intruder, who attempts to strangle her. She struggles with him and her hand touches the pair of scissors in her sewing basket, which happens to be lying on top of the telephone table. She picks them up and stabs her attacker to death.

No one, I think, would find it difficult either to understand or to accept the judgement that this woman did not murder her assailant, but killed him in self-defence. She had a right to defend herself and she exercised that right. But what on earth could be meant by the suggestion that *Y* and *Z* would be acting *in the same way as this woman* in carrying out their plan; that, were they to kill *A*, they would not be murdering him, but exercising their right of self-defence?

There is, it must be admitted, one point of comparison between the two actions: just as the woman in the film kills the intruder in order to save her own life, so *Y* and *Z* kill *A* (if they do) in order to save theirs. Both acts are acts of self-*preservation*. However, not every such act is also an act of self-*defence*. That of the woman is, because the intruder is trying to kill her; but *A*, as Harris admits, is *not* trying to kill *Y* and *Z*; their lives are in danger, not from him, but from natural causes. *A* is not *attacking* *Y* and *Z*; so how could they be *defending themselves* by killing him?

It might be suggested that the notion of an 'innocent threat' could be applied to *A*, and that it would then be possible to present killing him as an act of self-defence on the part of *Y* and *Z*. *A* is not an assailant, he is not trying to kill or otherwise harm *Y* and *Z*; but all that follows from this, it might be said, is that he could not be described as a *guilty* threat to their lives, in the way that the intruder is a guilty threat to the life of the woman who answers the telephone. People can threaten the lives of others without either wanting or intending to do so, and when they do the individuals whose lives are threatened have a right to defend themselves. At the very least, talk of self-defence will *make sense* in such cases. Let us look at this notion of an innocent threat and consider whether or not it could really be applied to *A*.

When might a person be described as an innocent threat to the life of someone else? Consider the following situation: someone has planted a bomb with the intention of killing at their house two people whose movements, together with those of their neighbours, he has watched closely for several months. The bomber has so arranged matters that his bomb will be detonated at a time when his targets are within feet of it by the action of an innocent person – the postman – opening their front gate. At the very last minute, one of the targets discovers the bomb and works out the precise method of its detonation. The postman (who is deaf) has just reached the gate, and must be prevented from opening it if the bomb is not to go off; and he is prevented by the action of one of the targets, who shoots him dead with a legally held gun.

It is possible to understand how the notion of an innocent threat might be applied in this situation, and with it the notion of self-defence. The postman might be spoken of as an innocent threat to the occupants of the house; though devoid himself of the slightest intention to harm them, he plays, quite unknowingly, a crucial part in the scheme of someone who acts with just that intention. The postman is not an assailant, but there *is* an assailant and he is *using* the postman. Thus, when one of the occupants shoots the postman, he might be said to be defending himself and his companions against this assailant in doing so. He does not, therefore, (it might be said) *murder* the postman, who is, in a sense, the assailant's instrument. The occupant of the house acts in self-defence.

Not everyone would be prepared to take this line. It might be argued, for example, that although the postman's action *endangers* the lives of the occupants of the house, the postman himself should not be described as *threatening* those people or as being *a threat* to them; such expressions should be reserved for the man who planted the bomb. The point of saying that would be to reject the *moral implication* of calling the postman a threat to the people in the house. What matters above all, on this view, is the postman's own innocence of malign aims and intentions. The locution 'innocent threat' invites us to place the act of killing the postman in the same moral category as that of killing the assailant who is making use of him; and for this very reason, it might be said, the locution is best avoided.

There can be disagreement, then, about how the postman and the killing of the postman should be described; not everyone would be prepared to accept the descriptions which tend to exonerate the occupants of the house from moral blame. Nonetheless, they might be prepared to concede *sense* to those descriptions; they might be prepared to concede that even if talk of 'innocent threat' and 'self-defence' is morally tendentious in these circumstances, it is not unintelligible.

In the light of this discussion, let us move to some of the other situations described in this and the previous chapter. We must eventually come back to the killing of *A*, but let us consider first the case of the fat potholer. Might that individual – who is stuck, let us recall, in the only exit from a flooding cave – be described as an 'innocent threat' to the lives of his trapped companions? Would this description make sense here, and with it the claim that the potholers would be 'exercising their right of self-defence' were they to have him blown up in order to get out of the cave before they drown?

My own view is that the applicability of these expressions (except as *metaphors*) is doubtful in this case. The reason is that in the situation described, unlike the one involving the postman, there is no assailant *at all*. There is no *attack*, and where there is no attack there can be no *defence*. The potholers are in danger, certainly, from the water; and they kill the fat potholer, if they do, in order to escape this danger. Their lives are threatened, then, but in the way in which crops might be threatened by the weather. Since the fat potholer is blocking the exit from the cave, he is a threat to them; but in the way that a boulder stuck in the same place would be a threat to them, and not in the way that a murderous assailant would be a threat to them. If they kill him, they do so in order to save their own lives; but this, it seems to me, is (once again) self-*preservation*, not self-*defence*.[13]

If it is doubtful that the notions of 'innocent threat' and 'self-defence' are applicable in the case of the fat potholer, it is certain that they are *not* applicable in the case that primarily concerns us, the one in which the killing of *A* is proposed by *Y* and *Z*. This is like the case of the fat potholer, and unlike that of the postman, in that there is no assailant involved; there is no one who is trying to harm *Y* and *Z*, not *A* and not anyone who is making use of *A*. Furthermore, *A* would not be a threat to the lives of *Y* and *Z* even in the way that the fat potholer is a threat to the lives of the other potholers in the cave. The fat potholer is blocking the escape route; he and only he stands (quite literally) between the other potholers and safety. This, so to speak, is the *trouble* with him. The trouble with A, on the other hand, could be only that *he was alive and not newly dead*. It would have to be *that* fact which made him an 'innocent threat' to Y and Z – two people for whom his heart and lungs were eminently suitable. He would not be the only such 'threat'; *anyone* with organs suitable for transplanting into Y and Z would 'innocently threaten' their lives, on this account, simply by being in possession of his own. This would surely render ludicrous any attempt that might be made to use the notion in order to present the killing of A as an act of self-defence on the part of Y and Z. Thus my conclusion is that there is no foothold at all for such talk in the situation Harris describes.

There is yet a further difference between the killing of A and the killing of the postman; it is of crucial importance, yet no account can be given of it in terms of Harris's conception of the value of life.

For Harris, the killing of A would be entirely comparable with the killing of the postman, in that both would be killed, and killed rightly, in order to save the lives of two other people. The difference comes to light when we contrast the *way* in which A's death would save the lives of Y and Z with the way in which the postman's death saves the lives of the occupants of the house. The postman is killed, but he figures in the story of his death as a *person* (in the usual sense of the word); he is not robbed of his moral status as a *human being*. A, on the other hand, would be robbed of his status as a human being; he would figure in the story of his death as a walking organ bank, as nothing but the possessor of a heart suitable for Y and a pair of lungs suitable for Z. A's life is supposed to be a *valuable* life; yet in Harris's account the value he is said to possess as a person becomes entirely irrelevant as soon as he enters the vicinity of two people to whom his *instrumental* value could hardly be greater. Y and Z have a *use* for A; *he himself* would be the means of saving their lives. It would be rather as if he were butchered to provide a supply of food for two people who, by some quirk of nature, could be nourished only by human flesh of the rather rare sort that happened to clothe A's bones.

Y and Z, as we saw above, are made to express *regret* over the need for A's death; this is the sort of regret expressed by Lewis Carroll's walrus over the fate of the oysters:

'I weep for you' the Walrus said

'I deeply sympathise'
With sobs and tears he sorted out
Those of the largest size
Holding his pocket-handkerchief
Before his streaming eyes.

The point, I must emphasise, is not that *Y* and *Z* are such unpleasant individuals that they would be unlikely to *care* very much about *A*, or feel very sorry for him; *that* might be true of the man who kills the postman. It is rather that a certain kind of caring about *A* would be *inconceivable* on their part, given the way in which they are prepared to treat him. One cannot – *logically* cannot – value as a person someone whom one is prepared to treat as nothing but a bundle of vital organs.[14] People can certainly sink to such depths in their treatment of others; Harris, however, wishes to present *Y* and *Z* not as sinking to the depths, but as acting rationally and rightly. They are, apparently, people who can tell others what their *duty* is.

Let us pause for a moment to summarise the points which have been made in the latter part of this chapter.

I have presented the doctors as saying that killing *A* is out of the question because it would be an act of *murder*; and I have suggested that it would be an act of murder that was *undeniably* or *indisputably* such. It would be nonsense to deny that killing *A* would be murder, for there is nothing in our understanding of this concept which could render intelligible a refusal to count the killing of *A* as an instance of it. Harris, it would seem, must deny this; and it follows that he must produce considerations which show, at the very least, that 'killing *A* would be murder' is open to dispute. His reference in 'The Survival Lottery' to *absence of malice* and *self defence* could be construed as attempts to produce such considerations; but the conclusion I have reached is that they would not succeed.

It would appear, then, that Harris could not succeed in giving sense to a denial that killing *A* would be murder. It makes sense to say, for example, that the paediatrician described on p.108 did not commit murder in killing the handicapped infant; but it would not make sense to say that *Y* and *Z* (or their doctors) would not be committing murder were they to kill *A*. And if this point is correct, it would seem to follow that the position Harris adopts in 'The Survival Lottery' cannot count as a moral one; it is not coherent as a moral point of view.

If this conclusion were accepted, it would have devastating implications for Harris's position in general. As we have seen, the argument of 'The Survival Lottery' takes to its logical conclusion the policy of maximising lives described in chapter 5; and the maximising policy is a logical outcome of the account Harris gives of 'the value of life'. If this account has been shown to commit Harris to a position that makes no sense as a moral position, it has been reduced to absurdity.

Harris, it is certain, would not accept for one moment that his position has been shown to be absurd; indeed, he would doubtless continue to insist that far from being absurd, it is the only rational position to adopt. So he would have to launch a counter-attack upon the argument of this chapter; and it is time for us to consider the form such a counter-attack might take.

The argument Harris must meet can be briefly summarised in the following way:

1 Anyone who says that A should be killed must deny that killing A would be murder.
2 He can give sense to this denial only if he can appeal to some consideration which is recognised as being able to defeat the application of the concept of murder; or to an intelligible extension of one.
3 But no such consideration is available in the present case.

Therefore

4 'Killing A would be murder' is incontestable or indisputable – it makes no sense to deny it.

It is clear from this way of setting out the argument that there are at least two strategies that might be employed in order to meet it. Harris might reject the first premiss, maintaining that he does not need to deny that killing A would be murder; or he might accept that premiss and reject the second. However, I shall discuss a third strategy that combines aspects of both; one which accepts that killing A would be murder, but maintains that it would be murder *only as this concept is presently and defectively understood*. What must be rejected, according to the strategy, is the concept (or conception) of murder which the doctors employ; and it must be rejected precisely because it is incompatible with the policy of maximising lives. What that incompatibility is said to show is not that we must reject the maximising policy, but that we must reject the concept of murder which makes the policy seem absurd.

According to this strategy, then, killing A *would* be murder as we presently understand it; but it does not follow that we must not kill *A*. What follows is that *since we must kill A* we should expunge this concept of murder from our moral thinking. If we are to retain the concept of murder at all, we must reconstruct it along lines that would not permit its application to any act of killing required by the policy of maximising lives. We must change the way we think and behave, as utilitarians have always advocated.

The maximising policy can stand on its own two feet, without the aid of crutches borrowed from our present moral judgements about acts of murder; this is the position I am now putting into Harris's mouth. He repudiates as unnecessary any attempt he might have made to seek support for his view from such notions as *absence of malice* and *self-defence*, and he concedes that no amount of tinkering with familiar moral reasoning will suffice to defeat the application of the concept of murder to the killing of *A*. What he says instead is that we should *break* with what is familiar and fashion a new concept of murder.

But why should we do this? Why should we pay any attention at all to what a supporter of the maximising policy has to say? Why should we revise our thinking and our conduct in the way he wishes us to do? What is wrong with these things as they are?

The answer these questions would receive is the answer we have come to expect from the bioethicist; it is that the new way of thinking, the way he advocates, is *more rational* than the old. However, we must now allow him to press the point he made on a previous occasion – the point that the people to whom he is addressing himself are *already committed*, in logic, to the practices he is urging them to adopt.

We saw at the close of chapter 5 that this is what the bioethicist would say, in the end, about the hostages in the embassy. They believe that it would be shameful for them to buy their lives with the life of the ambassador who is the terrorists' target. This belief, the bioethicist would say, rests upon the assumption that the ambassador's life is a valuable life, not because it is the life of this person rather than that, but simply because it is the life of an individual person (or human being). If the hostages did not accept that assumption, their conduct would be incomprehensible. If one life is valuable, however, three lives must be three times as valuable as one, and the hostages are acting irrationally, therefore, when they propose to allow three lives, rather than one, to be lost. Their irrationality follows, the bioethicist would insist, not only from what *he* accepts but from what *they* accept, and *must* accept if their own behaviour is to make sense.

What the bioethicist would say now is that this goes for the doctors in charge of Y and Z too. They are, after all, *doctors*; and among the things that doctors do is *save lives*. If they do not think that the lives of their patients are valuable why do they bother trying to save them? Why did they bother looking for replacement organs for Y and Z, for example? Yet if the lives of Y and Z *are* valuable lives, as the doctors' own conduct implies, then it is irrational to baulk at taking only *one* valuable life in order to preserve them; simple arithmetic shows that the gain is greater than the loss.

So the bioethicists' point would be that the hostages, the doctors, all of us, already have conclusive reason to accept the policy of maximising lives. The break between this policy and our present thinking, he would say, is not total; if it were, we would indeed have no reason to make it. We have such a reason, however, namely, *the value we already place on individual lives*. We must bring our thinking about the taking of life into line with our recognition of this value; for it is not in line, the bioethicist would maintain, as it stands. We have not thought through the implications of what we already accept; instead, we conduct our moral thinking in terms of a concept of murder which does not adequately reflect the value we attach to the individual human life. The logic of the concept is incompatible with the only policy which does, the policy of maximising lives. This policy, and this policy alone, as Harris says, can plausibly claim to value individuals.

The bioethicist would insist, then, that the concept of murder he wishes to construct is the concept of murder we ourselves would employ were we to take to its logical conclusion the concern for valuable lives which we already have and in part express. The irrationality of the response the doctors make to the suggestion that A should be killed lies, he would say, in its incompatibility with this concern, its incompatibility with what they themselves believe – that each and every individual human life has value.

This point is a crucial one for the bioethicist; without it, as I have shown, he cannot defend his claim that reason or rationality requires us to abandon our present practices in favour of those he advocates. In the next chapter I shall argue that the bioethicist is fundamentally confused on this point. He thinks that there is a conception of the value of life which is common to himself and people like the doctors, and that he can appeal to it in order to show such people that they should relinquish their concept of murder (which fails to embody that conception) in favour of his (which succeeds). But this is not the case. Insofar as the doctors have a conception of the value of the individual life, it implies the rejection, and not the acceptance, of Harris's proposal. Even this remark is misleading, for it suggests that the doctors' conception can be elucidated apart from the judgements and actions which express it; but it cannot. What the doctors mean by 'the value of life' – what *we* mean – *shows itself* in those judgements and actions, and cannot be understood without reference to them.

7

THE VALUE OF LIFE

Seven sailors are cast away on a barren island with a plentiful supply of water – salvaged from their ship before it went down – but no food at all. The patrol boat which makes infrequent visits to the island is not due for a good while, and the sailors know that in all probability they will have starved to death by the time it arrives. The ship's captain, an old-fashioned sort of man entirely innocent of moral philosophy, says that all they can do in these circumstances is resign themselves to their fate; but the ship's doctor, who is fresh from a course in bioethics, is far from agreeing with him. Fortified by his newly acquired knowledge of the value of life, he proposes to the captain that one of the sailors – the fattest – should be killed and eaten by the remaining six. The captain is shocked by this proposal, and says that he has no intention of standing by while his crew commit murder and cannibalism, let alone of profiting from such acts.

The doctor (who was expecting this response) proceeds to argue that the captain is in a muddle. The captain, he says, has shown by his reaction to the proposal that he values the lives of individual people; for if he did not the killing of one sailor would not worry him in the least. He must see, then, that he is committed to the policy of maximising lives; and if he is committed to that policy he is committed to the implementation of it in the present instance. Why allow seven deaths when only one is necessary? If the captain does not accept the proposal, the doctor adds, he will be failing in his duty, which is to save as many valuable lives as possible.

The captain is caught at a disadvantage here; the doctor knew what to expect from him, but he did not know what to expect from the doctor. As I said before, the captain is innocent of moral philosophy and ignorant, therefore, of the ability of philosophers to justify anything. He is not naive; he knows what people are capable of doing

120

in order to save their own skins. He is fully prepared for weakness, villainy, evil and degradation. What takes him unawares is finding an act he regards as evil represented as a *duty*, especially by someone who claims to be qualified in a branch of philosophy, which the captain has always supposed to be a morally uplifting subject.

Consequently, the suspicion enters the captain's mind that courses in bioethics are not all they are cracked up to be. The doctor may have read a number of books, but he ignores distinctions that are evident to the captain himself. When, for example, the doctor describes the alternatives he says the sailors have, he tells them that they must choose between seven deaths and one death. If his proposal is accepted, he says, one death will occur; if it is not, seven deaths will occur, including the one that would have occurred had the proposal been accepted. The fattest sailor *will die anyway*.

The captain points out that the doctor is misrepresenting one of these (alleged) alternatives. It is certainly true that seven deaths will occur if the doctor's proposal is rejected; the captain does not dispute that. What he does dispute is the description of the alternative to those seven deaths as 'one death'. The fattest sailor will not simply lose his life if the doctor's proposal is carried out; he will not simply die, as he would were he to starve to death along with his companions. His life will be taken from him, he will be murdered. The doctor, the captain says, ignores this crucial point when he says that the sailor 'will die anyway', thus implying that his fate will be the same whether or not the captain accepts the doctor's proposal. His fate will not be the same. If the proposal is rejected, the sailor will die; but if it is accepted, he will be murdered. The captain concludes by reminding the doctor that whereas death is an evil, murder is *evil*; evils must be endured, he maintains, if the only alternative to them is evil. He cannot save the sailors or himself; what he can – and must – do is prevent a member of his crew from being murdered; and in so doing prevent other members of his crew from committing a murder, from becoming murderers. It is this which he sees as his duty in the present situation.

The distinction between a death and a murder is an instance of the general distinction between an event, something that happens or occurs, and an action, something a person does; where 'doing' here includes what is usually termed 'omitting' to do – forgetting, neglecting, or failing to do something. Moral judgements and concepts apply to people and to what people do, in this comprehensive sense; events are morally indifferent. This does not imply that what happens must be a matter of indifference to us, or that we cannot speak of some happenings as bad and others good; it implies only that when we do speak in this way about events we are not making moral judgements. There are *natural evils*; but natural evils are not *evil*, they are not *moral* evils.

I said above that the ship's captain regards the ship's doctor as ignoring the distinction between a death and a murder. It might be said in reply that of course the doctor does not ignore the distinction; at no point does he deny that were his proposal accepted the fattest sailor would have to be killed by his companions (though he does deny that this killing would be murder). A killing is the work of a human agent, someone who does the killing; the doctor knows that perfectly well, and is as able as the captain to distinguish between something which is brought about by human agency and something which is not. This is correct; but it does not follow that the doctor grasps the significance of the distinction, or that he understands what it is to act and what it is to commit moral evil. The doctor is a utilitarian; so let us go back to the utilitarian conception of action.

Utilitarians, as we saw in chapter 5, conceive of acting as *causing something to happen*, or *bringing about a certain state of affairs*. On their account, an action derives its identity or description from the nature of the change in the world it brings about (or effects), and it derives its moral character from the value of that change. In order to do evil, on this account, or to commit an evil act, one must effect, produce, or bring into being something which is *an* evil; and for a utilitarian, this must be something which is a natural evil. Moral evil, in short, is the bringing into being or causing to happen of some natural evil; this is what it must be for a utilitarian.

I want to take issue with this account of moral evil. I have already taken issue with the account of action it presupposes, the instrumental account. We saw in chapter 5 that two people may effect the same change or changes in the world, cause the same things to happen, and in the same way, without doing the same thing. In the example taken from Rachels, Jack and Jill both visit their grandmother, both leave her more cheerful than they found her, and both end up with a legacy. Nevertheless, despite what Rachels says, they do *not* do the same thing. There are some descriptions which apply to both actions, it is true, but there are others which do not. Jack's actions, for example, are ones of love and concern; Jill's are ones of hypocrisy and greed. The changes effected are the same; the manner of effecting the changes is the same; but the actions are not the same. We cannot, therefore, reduce acting to causing to happen; and nor, I contend, can we reduce moral evil to the causing to happen of natural evil. This is implicit in the earlier discussion; I shall bring it out here in relation to acts of murder, and in so doing lend further support to my criticism of the attempt to reduce acting to the effecting of changes in the world.

The irreducibility of moral evil has a crucial bearing on the familiar bioethical claim that we must say why murder is wrong, or why it is normally wrong to kill people. This, as we know, is what Harris tries to do in *The Value of Life*. It is generally wrong to kill a person, on his account, because in so doing we frustrate his wish to live, and all of his other wishes at the same time. This is the natural evil that we produce when we kill a person, that is the harm we cause to happen.

It is clear that if we do deprive a person of his life we take from him something he was bound to lose some day, the day of his death. On Harris's account, had this person died of a heart attack before we were able to kill him (a few minutes before we arrived at his house, for example) he would have suffered through natural causes essentially the same evil or harm as the one we were intending to inflict upon him. It is the person's *death* that frustrates every wish he has, and the wrongness of what we do when we kill him resides, Harris would say, in the fact that it brings about his death. On the bioethical account the moral evil of murder derives from the natural evil of the death we bring about when we commit a murder; the first is a function of the second.

I shall now advance some objections to this sort of analysis, taking, not the version given by Harris, but the fuller version given by James Rachels in *The End of Life*.

Rachels' main purpose in this book, as we saw in chapter 5, is to provide a defence of euthanasia in certain circumstances. He maintains that what he calls 'the rule against killing' has a point, and that its point is lost in the circumstances with which he is concerned. In brief: death is frequently a harm to the person who dies, and the point of the rule against killing is to protect people from that harm. It follows that where death would not be a harm but a good to the person who dies, the rule against killing no longer applies. Rachels says explicitly that 'the explanation of the point of the rule against killing, and the explanation of why it is bad to die, should fit together',[1] and he thinks he can show that and how they do.

I shall argue that this sort of account is not consistent with the judgements we make about acts of murder; these judgements do not connect up with our judgements about deaths in the way they would and should if Rachels and other bioethicists were right. I say *our* judgements about deaths, but I am well aware that we do not all make the same judgements. In what follows, however, I shall assume a measure of agreement; I shall assume at least this, that many people would hold that death is sometimes an evil and sometimes not; or, that if it is always an evil, it is a greater evil in some cases than in others. I shall take Rachels' own account of death as an evil as a point of departure.

Rachels summarises his position as follows:

> Death is an evil for the person who dies because it forecloses possibilities for his or her life; because it eliminates the chance for developing abilities and talents; because it frustrates desires, hopes and aspirations; and because it leaves parts of lives pointless and whole lives incomplete.[2]

Let us allow that there is some truth in what Rachels says here. People do tend to regard the death of a young person, for example, with all her life before her, as more of an evil than the death of someone who has had a long and reasonably happy 'innings'. Rachels himself compares the death of Frank Ramsey with the death of Bertrand Russell; the former, unlike the latter, he says, was 'a tragedy', for three reasons: Ramsey's life was incomplete, his training proved futile and had he lived 'he could have done great things'.[3] Rachels does not say that Russell's death was not an evil at all (it was, he says, 'a bad thing in its own way'[4]); but people can and sometimes do think this about deaths, their own and other people's. It is possible to see a death as not an evil, but a good, for the person whose death it is. Many arguments for euthanasia (which is the subject of Rachels' book) are based upon the premiss that one can find oneself in a condition worse than death, a condition so dreadful that it is in one's best interests to die. Let us allow, then, that death is sometimes an evil for the person who dies, sometimes not; that it can be a good for the person who dies. The question is: what has this got to do with murder?

I suggest that it has little or nothing to do with murder; yet, if Rachels were right about the relationship between 'the rule against killing' and 'the badness of death', it should, it seems to me, have everything to do with it. The moral evil of an act of murder should be proportionate to the degree of natural evil that attaches to the death in question. It should be less evil, for example, to murder someone who has had a 'good innings' than to murder someone whose innings is in its early stages. Now it may be that we do regard some murders as more evil, as worse, than others; but not, I suggest, on the same grounds as we regard some deaths as worse than others. We might speak of a particular murder as, for example, especially brutal, or especially cold and calculating; and we do see some murders as particularly horrifying given the relationship of the murderers to their victims (matricide would be an instance). None of this goes any way to support the line that Rachels is taking, and I doubt if there is much in our thinking about murder that does support it.

There is, however, a good deal that counts against it. At one point, Rachels invites us to view the death of someone who is 'mentally defective' (or 'severely retarded') as 'less tragic' than the death of a young woman who is leading the sort of life liberal individualists admire – one crammed full of plans and projects of various sorts.[5] The latter's death means, he says, that 'she will not get to raise her children, finish her novel, learn French, improve her backhand, or do what she wanted for Oxfam'.[6] Well, we *might* consider the death of the 'mental defective' as 'less tragic' than the death of this energetic young woman. If the life of the former was nothing but a burden to her, we might regard her death as a blessing, as a good and not an evil to her. (This, as we shall see, is only *part* of what Rachels himself wants to say.) Suppose, however, that these two people do not die natural deaths, but are murdered. Is the murder of the 'defective' less evil than the murder of her 'normal' sister?

It seems to me that it is not. Indeed, in so far as we do make judgements of this sort, we might even be inclined to regard the murder of the 'defective' as the *more* evil of the two. I remember an incident in Belfast in which terrorists murdered a mentally handicapped man in the course of a robbery; this act was greeted with a greater sense of outrage than were many other such murders. And to go back to the earlier example, a similar response is often generated by the murder of an old person; it is surely true, at least, that the advanced age of the victim does not *diminish* the evil of the murder. An elderly night watchman, for instance, is murdered by thieves. Had he died of natural causes, we might have talked in a consolatory way about his 'long innings'; but the length of his innings has no bearing whatsoever upon the degree of evil attaching to his *murder*; no more does the character – the 'quality' – of his life. He may have been longing for death; indeed, he may have been contemplating suicide. His murder is evil just the same, no less evil than if he had been the happiest of men.

I am suggesting, then, that the good or evil, the natural good or evil, of a death, its being a benefit or a harm to the person who dies, is neither here nor there as far as the moral evil of a murder is concerned. I am not talking about *euthanasia*, but about acts that are unquestionably acts of murder. The terrorists just mentioned were not practising euthanasia when they killed the mentally handicapped man; they killed him because he got in their way, not because they believed it was in his best interests to die. My point is that even if it had been true that it was in his best interests to die, his murder was every bit as evil as the murder of someone of whom it would not have been true. If we are thinking about whether or not someone's death was an evil for her, then we should look, I suppose, at what her life was like for her. The 'quality of her life' may be relevant to a judgement about her death; it is not relevant to a judgement about her *murder*. Lives, let us allow, can lose their value for those who live them – that is to say, people's lives can be or become a burden to them. But *people* – it might be said – do not thereby lose their value, their worth as human beings; and *murderers kill people*.

It is possible to lose sight of the fact that murderers kill people when reading what bioethicists have to say, because for them the *quality* of a life, in a certain sense, is all that matters. Let us go back for a moment to Harris's account of the value of life. We saw in chapters 1 and 2 that in his attempt to say what makes life valuable, Harris rejects the moral relevance of being a person in the ordinary sense – an individual human being. One's life has value if and only if one is a person in his stipulative sense – if and only if one has a certain capacity (the capacity to value one's life). This capacity, he says, confers value upon the life of any being that possesses it, whether human or not.

People matter morally, then, on Harris's account, not because they are people – human beings – but because they are persons in his sense. The accounts given by other bioethicists of the value of life differ in this and that detail from Harris's, but never in essence. Nothing could be more characteristic of bioethics than its concern with identifying the features, characteristics or capacities which something must possess in order to have 'moral status'; or to have a 'valuable life'. As far as the morality of killing is concerned, the capacity to value one's life – that is to say, to wish or want to go on living – is crucial for all bioethicists, precisely because of the importance they attach as utilitarians to the satisfaction of desires or preferences.

On the utilitarian account, something can be wronged only if it can be harmed; and it can be harmed only if it has desires that can be satisfied or frustrated. Hence something can be wronged by being killed, on this account, only if it can have the appropriate desire, the desire to go on living. Of course, it may lack the capacity for *that* desire without lacking the capacity for any desire at all; it may have the capacity to feel pain, for example, and to desire not to feel it. If it does it can be harmed – and therefore wronged – by being caused unnecessary suffering. Michael Tooley puts the point in terms of *rights*. Something has 'a right to life', he says, if and only if it can have the desire to live – only, therefore, if it is a self-conscious being. It has a right not to be made to *suffer*, however, if it is merely *sentient*; as far as *this* right is concerned, self-consciousness is irrelevant.[7]

Thus the degree of moral status or standing which something merits depends, in the bioethicists' view, upon its *level of consciousness*; it is in this sense that the 'quality' of a life is all that matters for these philosophers. To repeat: as far as people – human beings – are concerned, their being people (persons in the ordinary sense) is, on the bioethical account, of no moral significance whatsoever. An individual human being has moral claims not possessed by a dog, for example, only because he or she has mental capacities the dog lacks – only because his or her level of consciousness comes higher up the scale than does that of the dog.

In *The End of Life*, Rachels states the point that moral status depends on level of consciousness in terms of a distinction between 'being alive' (in 'the biological sense') and 'having a life'.[8] Something may be alive in the biological sense, he says, without being 'complex' enough to have a life; in order to have a life it must have mental and emotional capacities that very 'simple' creatures (insects, for example) do not possess.[9] This is, of course, a matter of degree. The greater and higher these capacities – the more 'complex' the being that possesses them – the greater the value of the life involved; and the more objectionable, as Rachels puts it, the taking of that life without good reason. It is this, he says, which explains '. . . why we feel that killing a human is worse than killing a dog . . .'.[10]

The quality of an individual life, therefore, in the sense just explained, is all that matters for Rachels and for bioethicists in general; it does not signify to what sort of individual the life belongs. The value of any individual being derives entirely from the value of the life it has, or is capable of having. So from the standpoint of value or worth an individual being is treated in the bioethical account as a *reified life*; what he is (a man, a dog), as opposed to the kind of life he can lead, is irrelevant to his moral status or standing. As Rachels puts it, '. . . it is individual characteristics and not species membership, that makes beings morally special'.[11]

The sinister significance of this sort of account is evident when we consider its implications for individuals which lack the capacities normally possessed by creatures of the sort to which they belong. Let us go back, then, to Rachels' discussion of the 'severe defective'.

We saw above that Rachels invites us to regard the death of the 'defective' as 'less tragic' than the death of her normal sister. When we consider his reasons, we find that they do not concern only the value of the 'defective's' life *to her*. It is not only the fact that her life was, or might have been, a burden to her that Rachels has in mind when he makes the comparison; he is thinking also about her value in the absolute or metaphysical sense to which I referred in the first chapter of this book. Rachels wishes to place the 'defective' on a sliding scale of absolute value, a scale to which all living beings can be assigned, he thinks according to their level of consciousness. Since the defective's life was 'less complex' than her normal sister's, he says, less can be said about why her death was a bad thing; there are fewer reasons for regretting it, just as there are fewer reasons for regretting the death of a dog than the death of a (normal) human being.[12] The greater 'simplicity' of her life means, according to Rachels, that the 'defective' is *inferior* to her sister; not merely in intelligence, say, but in *value* or *worth*.

Rachels is of the opinion that most of us would agree with him about this, though we might not like to say so; he claims that 'Although we may be inclined to endorse "the equal worth of all human lives" almost by reflex – it sounds so noble, who could deny it? – Not many of us really believe this high sounding principle.'[13] We don't really believe it, according to Rachels, precisely because we would think, like him, that the two deaths (that of 'the defective' and that of her normal sister) are not 'equally tragic'.

I have conceded that we might think this; *but* if we do, we need *not* have in mind the position of these two women relative to each other on some scale of 'absolute value'. We may be thinking, as I said before, of the value of the two lives involved *to those who lived them* – we may be thinking, in other words, of whether the women found their lives a blessing or a burden to them. To say that the life of Rachels' 'defective' was of less value *in this sense* than the life of her sister is *not* to say that 'the defective' was inferior in worth to her sister. The 'defective' was a person, a human being; and, we might say, her worth as a human being was the same as that of any other human being, including her intelligent sister (see p.136).

The topic of Rachels' book, as we know, is euthanasia. His account of 'the rule against killing' is designed to show that the rule has a *point* – the protection of 'biographical lives' – and that its point is lost in certain circumstances. What people's lives are like for them is surely relevant, it might be said, to the subject of *euthanasia*. No doubt; but even here, the picture of people – human beings – as reified lives sends things disastrously wrong.

Consider, for example, Rachels' remarks about 'Baby Jane Doe' in chapter 4 of *The End of Life*. This baby, he tells us, is so grossly handicapped that she will never have a 'biographical life', though she is alive in what he calls 'the biological sense'. Rachels advocates euthanasia in this case, and I am sure that there are many people who would agree with him. That is to say: they would agree that the baby should be killed. I doubt, however, if they would agree with his account of *why* the baby should be killed. Rachels says that because she will never have 'a life' it follows that 'there is nothing to be concerned with from a moral point of view';[14] but there is *everything* to be concerned with from a moral point of view – *there is the baby*, who is as much an object of moral concern as any other baby.

Rachels' position is such that he cannot say this; he must move from saying that Baby Jane Doe's life can be of no value *to her* to saying that it can be of no value *simpliciter*; and from this to saying that *she* can be of no value. The quality of her life – her level of consciousness – implies, on his account, that she lacks the moral status or standing of a normal baby; that there is in her case, to repeat, nothing to be concerned with from a moral point of view. When people other than bioethicists argue for euthanasia in such a case, however, they generally do so on the grounds that *moral concern for the individual in question requires it*. As they see it, the act of killing that individual would be an act of *mercy* or *compassion*. It would be meaningless, of course to speak of showing mercy or compassion to something that lacked moral status.

Consider also the position to which Rachels is committed concerning people in a permanently comatose (or persistently vegetative) state – people such as Karen Quinlan (whose case he discusses in chapter 6 of his book). Here too he must say that given the quality of their lives, 'there is nothing to be concerned with from a moral point of view'. But once again, there is *everything* to be concerned with from a moral point of view; *there are the people themselves*.

The point might be put by saying that someone in a persistently vegetative or permanently comatose state is as much entitled to *basic moral respect* as someone who is not. To say this, it must be emphasised, is not to rule out euthanasia; it is, however, to clarify the form that a defence of euthanasia should take, and in particular to clarify the significance of considerations having to do with the condition the person is in (or the quality of his life). Such considerations do not determine *whether or not* a person is entitled to respect; they do determine, at least in part, what *counts* as respect in a given case.

Suppose we were to decide that the best and kindest thing we could do for a person in one of the conditions just mentioned was kill him. If we did make this decision, we would not be denying him respect in killing him, let alone denying that he still merited respect; we would be *showing* him respect – we would be doing what we thought respect for him *required* in the circumstances. We would certainly not be showing him respect, however, were we to treat him as though he were no longer a person, no longer a human being – by, for example, practising vivisection upon him (as some utilitarians are prepared to suggest).[15] On the bioethical account, there could be no objection to our doing so; for, as we have seen, on that account moral status depends entirely on quality of life. It follows that for bioethicists the prossessor of a life which has no quality at all has no moral status either; he may be treated in any way it suits us to treat him.

The focus of our attention is now squarely upon *people*, individual human beings: men, women and children. Should we say this: that value or worth attaches to these individuals (rather than to their lives, in the way it does for bioethicists)?

If we say that it does, we must explain what this means in such a way that the value of a human being does not emerge as *the value of an item*; which is precisely how it does emerge from bioethical writings. What I mean by the value of an item is something conferred upon a thing by its possession of a certain feature or set of features. That, as we have seen, is the sort of value Harris and other bioethicists attach to a person. If a particular human being does possess the appropriate features, does have 'what it takes' to be valuable, then he is of value, and we have good reason not to treat him in certain ways; not to kill him, for instance, without a sufficient moral justification for doing so. On this account, the value of a human being explains, or is the ground for, certain moral prohibitions and requirements; people must not – normally – be killed (for instance) because they are – normally – valuable.

If this is how the ship's captain, for example, understands the value of a human being, the ship's doctor would be right in asking him what he thinks he is about in refusing to accept the proposal that one of the sailors should be killed; for the captain would be committed to the policy of maximising lives, which is rooted in this sort of conception of the value of individuals. The maximiser would be correct in saying that a refusal on the captain's part to accept his proposal would be irrational.

Consider an analogy with the value of something that might appear as an item on an auctioneer's list: a vase. Not all vases are valuable, and not all vases that seem to be valuable are really such. Suppose that a collector acquires a vase about which he has doubts; perhaps, he thinks, it is not valuable after all. He will need to resolve these doubts if he is to know what to do with his newly acquired vase. If it is what it seems, if it is of value, then it must be treated in a way appropriate to its value; the collector must insure it and lock it up, or display it in a place where it cannot easily be stolen or knocked over. If it is not of value, there is no need for him to go to this trouble. So the collector must establish whether or not the vase is valuable before he can know how to treat it; he must take it to an expert, perhaps, someone well versed in the relevant list of features.

Suppose he does this and that the vase does turn out to be of value; and suppose further that six other vases, each of equal value with the first, find their way into the collector's possession. Fantastic circumstances arise in which he must break one of the vases in order to prevent the others from shattering spontaneously. When his friends protest that the vase is valuable, he reminds them that each of the other six is just as valuable and that he wishes to end up with as few valueless heaps of fragments as possible. He regrets having to smash the vase, of course; but it would be irrational of him to refuse to do so on the ground that it has value – for the other six have *in toto* more value.[16]

I hope that the aptness of this analogy (up to a point) will be clear. The points of comparison with bioethical accounts of the value of people can be summarised as follows:

First, the value of the collector's vase is something which can be explained in terms of the features or characteristics it possesses. Similarly, the value of a person derives from his possession of certain features (for example, his capacity to value his life, or to live a biographical life).

Secondly, the value of the vase is what determines the sort of treatment appropriate to it; *because* it is valuable it should be insured, and so on. Similarly, the value of a person is what determines the sort of treatment appropriate to him; *because* a person is valuable it would be wrong to kill him, for example (other things being equal). If he were to lose the features which make him valuable he would lose his value, and killing him would not be wrong.

Thirdly, there's value in numbers. It would be irrational for the collector to refuse to destroy one vase in order to preserve more than one. Similarly, it would be irrational for anyone to refuse to kill one person in order to save the lives of several.

So, for the ship's doctor and for Y and Z (that is to say, for the bioethicist), the value of a human being is the value of an item. It is this conception of the value of the individual person which underlies the policy of maximising lives, and this conception which Harris must attribute to, for example, the doctors in charge of Y and Z. He must attribute it to them, as we have seen, if he is to carry his crucial point about *rationality*.

What he must say, let us recall, is that these people are acting in a way which is inconsistent with their own beliefs. They believe that each individual human being has value; if they did not they would have no basis on which to object to the killing of A. But they must be made to take this belief to its logical conclusion; they must be made to see that far from prohibiting the killing, the belief necessitates it. The doctors must abandon their claim that killing A is out of the question, and this means that they must abandon the concept of murder which makes it seem so. They must employ instead a concept of murder which is consistent with the value they place on individual people, one which would not apply to any act of killing required by the policy of maximising lives.

Let us agree to speak of Y and Z's doctors as thinking that individual people have value. The point that needs to be made is that what it *means* to think this is not what bioethicists mean (or try to mean) when *they* speak of the value of a person. Bioethicists are speaking (or trying to speak) of something which *explains* how people should be treated; something which explains, for example, why it is generally wrong to kill people. The value people (generally) have is, as bioethicists see it, the *ground* of 'the rule against killing'. Thus there is a reason, they say, for this rule; one which can be fully explained without any reference at all to the concept of *murder*. On the bioethical account a given killing will be an act of murder only if it is wrong, and it will be wrong only if it is such that the rule against killing applies to it. Since the point of this rule is the protection of valuable lives, in giving an account of what makes lives valuable we are uncovering the foundation on which sound moral judgements about killing must be built.

When Y and Z's doctors speak of the value of individual people, however, they are not speaking about something which *explains* what may and may not be done to people. So what are they speaking about?

Let us go back for a moment to Harris's discussion of abortion and infanticide. We saw in chapter 1 that Harris wishes to present his views about these issues as grounded in a correct account of the value that attaches to the lives of foetuses and infants. Foetuses and infants, he says, do not possess the capacities which confer value upon lives, they do not have what it takes to make their lives valuable. So their lives are valueless, *they* are valueless, and it follows that we may kill them if it suits us to do so; their lives are at our disposal.

On Harris's account, then, people who oppose abortion and infanticide have made a mistake about the value which attaches to the lives of foetuses and infants. They are like a collector who erroneously believes that the vases in his collection are valuable, and who for this reason goes to all sorts of unnecessary trouble to protect them from damage. The collector can be shown (by experts) that he is mistaken about the value of his vases, and that in consequence he is treating them inappropriately; in the same way, people who believe that the lives of foetuses and infants are valuable can be shown (by philosophers) that they are mistaken about the matter, and that their treatment of foetuses and infants is therefore inappropriate. They can be shown, in other words, that their beliefs and their conduct have no *rational justification*.

As we have seen, the conception of the value of life which Harris employs – the *metaphysical* conception – is not confined to his work; it is central to bioethics as such. When I described this conception (as far as it can be described) in chapter 1, I pointed out that we cannot identify the value of a life in the metaphysical sense (non-sense) with its value *to* anyone. Bioethicists set out to discuss the value that living beings have *absolutely*, or in themselves, quite independently of anyone's attitude to them; this is eminently clear from the account given by Harris, which is why I have given his work so much prominence in my critique of bioethics. In Rachels' book, by contrast, the metaphysical conception is obscured to a greater extent by talk about the value of a life to its possessor; although it shows quite clearly in – for instance – the remarks about the 'mental defective' discussed above. (It is significant, in this connection, that Rachels at no point mentions 'the defective's' value *to others* – that is to say, the place she has, or might have, in the lives of people who *love* her.)

I said in the first chapter that the metaphysical (or absolute) conception of the value of life lacks sense; the question Harris and other bioethicists try to ask – what makes life valuable (in this sense) – has no clear meaning. When bioethicists say that the lives of foetuses and infants lack value, they are not, as they think, describing the position of foetuses and infants on a scale of absolute value which philosophical reflection brings to light; they are expressing their own moral attitudes, their own opinions about – for example – abortion and infanticide. 'The lives of infants are valueless' is nothing more than a way of saying, among other things, that we may kill foetuses and infants if it suits us to do so. It masquerades in bioethical writing as something else, namely, a *philosophical explanation* of *why* we may kill them if it suits us to do so. It is only in this guise that it can seem to provide the bioethicists views about abortion and infanticide with a grounding they say other views lack – a 'rational justification' of the sort they think it is the business of philosophy to produce.

So it does make a certain sense, therefore, to talk, in a moral context, about the 'valuelessness' of infants and foetuses, or of their lives. What someone who talks in this way is saying is that there are no moral objections to certain practices – abortion and infanticide, for instance; as I said before, that is all he *can* be saying. Anyone who thinks the opposite can be said to *value* the lives of infants and foetuses, or to regard them as having value; but his doing so, once again, is a matter of the judgements he makes about these (and other) practices. Such judgements are not *grounded in* (or *derived from*) more fundamental beliefs about the value of the lives in question; for we can explain the meaning of such beliefs *only* by speaking of the judgements that are supposed to rest upon them. To hold the beliefs *is* to make the judgements; it is not to have *reason* to make them.

It is in these terms that we must elucidate the conception Y and Z's doctors have of the value of individual people. If they speak of people as having value, they are not speaking about something which *explains* what may and may not be done to people; they are simply speaking *about* what may and may not be done to people. We cannot explain what it is to value people, in the moral context, except by referring to *the unthinkability of doing certain things to them* – for example, the things that Y and Z are proposing to do to A. Since our not doing such things is part of what it *means* to see (the lives of) people as having value, the suggestion that we should do them *in the name of* the value of people's lives is incoherent. Bioethicists think they can appeal to the value of the individual person (or of his life) as a justification for *getting rid* of certain moral limits to the way in which individual people may be treated; but insofar as it makes sense to speak of the value of the individual person (in the moral context), *it is a way of talking about these very limits.*

So the evil of murder, for example, is not something which can be explained by reference to something else – 'what makes (human) life valuable'; what Rachels calls 'the rule against killing' is not *derived from* a separate and logically prior conception of 'the value of life' (or people). We must refer to the evil of murder, to the 'rule against killing' (though not *only* to this, of course) in explaining what it is to value people, or to see their lives as having value. Bioethicists believe that 'the rule against killing' can and should be given a rational justification in terms of the value of life; their view seems to be that although we may reasonably believe, without knowing the justification, that it *is* generally wrong to kill people, we can come up with the justification for this belief if we try. We can then make use of the justification to resolve issues of life and death which are controversial, issues like euthanasia, abortion and infanticide. But we must say of the 'belief' just referred to what we said in chapter 2 of the 'belief' that it is generally wrong to kill infants: namely, that it is not a *belief* at all. Neither is it an *assumption*. It is not a moral *proposition* of any sort for us, it is not something we *think*, in the way that we might think, for example, that it is generally wrong to *execute* people. I do not mean that we think otherwise; I mean, as I said in the earlier discussion, that we are talking about something which is least misleadingly described as an attitude expressed in action. Our thinking that it is generally wrong to kill people, our 'valuing their lives', is not a matter of our assenting to the truth of a proposition; it is a matter of what we *do* (and do not do) *as of course* – for example, of our making people answer for it when they kill others, and counting only certain ways of answering for it as appropriate, or of our seeing certain situations – such as that described in 'The Survival Lottery' – as ones in which *there is nothing to be done.* We do not *contemplate* acting in certain ways; it does not *occur* to us to do certain things to people. And the question of whether or not we are *justified* in this does not even arise.

Thus the value of life (or people) is not something on which an

135

account of how people should be treated can be *based* (or *founded*). To value people is not to have *grounds* for treating them in certain ways and not in others; it just *is* to treat them in certain ways and not in others. Similarly, to regard all human lives, all human beings, as equal in worth is not to have *grounds* for saying that it is every bit as evil to murder Rachels' 'defective', for example, as to murder her normal sister; it just *is* to make no moral distinction between such murders, of the sort to which Rachels and other bioethicists are committed.

It is time to summarise the bearing of this whole discussion on the issue from which it arose in the first place – the disagreement described in chapter 6 between the team of doctors and *Y* and *Z* (Harris) about the killing of *A*.

Harris proposes, let us recall, that *A*, a healthy person, should be killed so that *Y* might receive his heart and *Z* his lungs. If this were done, he points out, one life would be lost rather than two. The doctors in charge of *Y* and *Z* reply, on my account, that it is morally impossible to kill *A*, because to do so would be to commit an act of *murder*; and I added to their reply the suggestion that 'killing *A* would be murder' is not open to dispute. Harris (as I represented him) concedes the latter point, but maintains that the concept of murder the doctors are using is incompatible with their own acknowledge-ment of the value of the individual person (or life). Thus the doctors' position is *irrational* and will remain so until they abandon the concept and substitute for it one that would not apply to any act of killing required by the maximising policy.

It is clear that this argument for the irrationality of the doctors' position makes a crucial assumption; the assumption, namely, that the doctors *share* with the bioethicists the conception of the value of the individual person (or life) that underlies the policy of maximising lives. What I have tried to show in this chapter is that the doctors do not share the bioethical conception of the value of the individual person. What *they* mean by the value of the individual person shows itself in their judgements and their deeds; it is not something that can be understood apart from these, let alone something that is incompat-ible with them. Thus the assumption on which the above argument depends is false; and without that assumption the argument cannot succeed.

Before bringing this chapter to a close, we need to be clear about the way in which the situation described in 'The Survival Lottery' differs from the one involving the shipwrecked sailors which was described earlier. When I brought Harris's paper into the discussion at the beginning of chapter 5, I pointed out that the situation depicted therein is unlike the various situations described in chapter 4 – those of the runaway trolley, the fat potholer and the hostages in the embassy – in an important respect. It is not at all an extraordinary or unusual situation, whereas the others are. This is not a minor point, because in extraordinary circumstances it may be morally permissible to do something it would be out of the question to do in circumstances that were not extraordinary. Now the situation of the shipwrecked sailors, like the situations described in chapter 4 and unlike the one that Harris describes, is extraordinary; and for this reason the proposal the ship's doctor makes – that one of the sailors should be killed – is not in the same category as the proposal that Y and Z make about A. That the killing of A would be murder is beyond dispute; that the killing of the fattest sailor would be murder, however, is not.

Let me try to make clear exactly what I am saying here. I am saying that the judgement that one of the sailors may be killed is not *senseless* as a moral judgement; whereas that A may be killed is. It must be emphasised, however, that the former judgement is not (or not necessarily) an application of the policy of maximising lives, or an expression of the conception of the value of life which underlies that policy. In the mouth of the ship's doctor, of course, it is – he is a bioethicist, and he argues accordingly. But it is possible to envisage a different individual, someone whose position is not that of the captain, but is not that of the ship's doctor either (it would be analogous, therefore, to that of the newcomer to the embassy described in chapter 6). This person says that one of the sailors may be killed; and he refers to the lives of the other sailors in giving his reasons. But what he does *not* do is argue that the captain is *confused* or *muddled* in regarding this action as out of the question. What leads him to part company with the captain is not a theory, but the sheer extremity of the circumstances in which the sailors find themselves. It is this extremity, he says, which permits the killing of one sailor, despite the fact that it will be a terrible thing to do; he is not *blind* to the terribleness of it, whereas the ship's doctor is.

The captain, of course, may not accept what this man says, any more than he accepts what the doctor says. His reply is likely to be that the deed would be *so* terrible that in no circumstances, however extreme, would it be permitted. He sees the extremity of the circumstances as something which has led this man into the temptation to commit *evil*. The conflict between these two people is a moral disagreement; but no such disagreement is possible, I have argued, about the deed advocated in 'The Survival Lottery' – the killing of A so that Y may have his heart and Z his lungs. This action, to repeat, would be indisputably or incontestably an act of murder, and it is therefore a deed there can be no question of doing. If, therefore, the doing of it is necessitated by the policy of maximising lives, that policy is reduced to absurdity, together with the conception of the value of life which underlies it. It is not the doctors who are confused about the value of life; it is Harris – that is to say, the bioethicist.

In this chapter I have tried to present an intelligible conception of the value of human life, or of people; a conception which – unlike the metaphysical conception central to bioethics – makes sense. As I said before, to speak (in the moral context) of the value of the individual person is to speak of the limits which certain moral conceptions impose upon the way in which a person may be treated.[17] It is *not* to speak of something which *justifies* those limits – some human essence, perhaps; still less is it to speak of something which justifies their removal. Bioethicists ask *what it is* which confers value on people. If we reply 'their *being* people', that is not to *answer* the bioethical question but to *reject* it.

It may be impossible to talk about 'the value of people' at all without misleading and without being misled; it may be impossible to avoid giving the expression a *metaphysical emphasis*. I suspect that it is impossible. Nevertheless, given the treatment it has received at their hands, some attempt must be made to rescue the notion of value at stake here from the bioethicists.

8

HOW TO IGNORE MORAL THINKING

When I described utilitarian theory in the first chapter of this book I made a distinction between two forms of utilitarianism. I contrasted *pure* utilitarianism on the one hand with *impure* utilitarianism on the other; and I said that impure utilitarianism recognises standards of conduct which are independent of (or separate from) utility, whereas pure utilitarianism does not. All of the philosophers whose work has been discussed up to this point are utilitarians; but their utilitarianism is of the impure sort. In this chapter and the chapter which follows, however, we shall be concerned with a pure utilitarian theory of morality, the one put forward by R. M. Hare in his book *Moral Thinking*.[1] I intend to argue that whatever Hare describes in that book, it is not moral thinking. Moral thinking, as I said before, must proceed in moral terms; but pure utilitarianism, I shall argue, eliminates moral terms – it contains nothing that can serve as a measure or standard of moral action. This is not true of impure utilitarianism; nevertheless, the arguments I shall advance over the next two chapters will draw upon certain aspects of preceding discussions.

It will be necessary at the outset to gain a fuller understanding of what pure utilitarianism is, and of how it differs from the impure sort of utilitarianism found in the writings of bioethicists. I shall begin, therefore, by looking once more at the bioethical position; and in particular at the implications of that position for the moral concept or category of *murder*.

What is the difference between the role the concept of murder plays in the moral thinking of (for example) the doctors in charge of Y and Z, and the role it plays in the thinking of a maximiser like Harris?

What the doctors say, let us recall, is that killing A is out of the question, because it would be an act of murder; its being such an act means that no moral justification of it is conceivable. The concept of murder is essential to the doctors' moral thinking about acts of killing; were they to abandon it, as the maximiser wishes them to do, they would have to change the entire character of their moral deliberations about acts of this sort.

The maximiser, on the other hand, does not need a concept of murder at all. He may, for reasons of convenience, use the *word* 'murder' as a label for acts of killing he judges to be wrong; but he can say everything he wishes to say about these acts in other terms. Unlike the doctors, he can say why a killing is wrong, or what is wrong about it, without reference to the concept of murder; for he can explain, as Rachels puts it, the *point* of 'the rule against killing'. As far as the maximiser is concerned, this rule is not, in Rachels' words, an 'end in itself'; it is derived from a more fundamental rule designed to protect those lives alone which have value.[2] In the case of the killing of *A*, for example, more valuable lives would be preserved by the act than lost; and for this reason – the maximiser says – killing *A* would not be wrong, even if it would be an instance of the concept of murder which the doctors employ.

For the doctors, we might say, murder is a *fundamental* moral concept or category. The question to be asked of any act of killing, for them, is the question: is it *murder*? If the answer to this question is yes, it follows that there can be no moral justification for the act. For the maximiser, however, murder, if a moral category at all, is not fundamental but *derivative*. The question to be asked of any act of killing, for him, is the question: is it *justified*? If the answer is that it is not, he may choose to *call* it murder – but the justification it lacks will be a utilitarian one. The act in question will not be wrong because it is murder; it will be murder because it is wrong.

The point might be put in the following way: for bioethicists, the concept of murder can have *moral import* only if it is the concept of murder a utilitarian would employ; only, that is to say, if it applies to those acts of killing which cannot be justified in utilitarian terms. The concept of murder, on this account, can function as a moral concept only if it can be prevented from playing the sort of role it plays in the moral thinking of people like the doctors – only if it can be prevented from setting limits to what may be done on utilitarian grounds.

It is important to realise that this point does not apply only to the concept of murder; it applies to all specific moral concepts, including those discussed in earlier chapters. As we saw in chapter 3, *social roles*, for example, can have moral significance; concepts which designate such roles can function as moral concepts, ones in terms of which moral thoughts can be expressed and moral judgements made. 'She's my mother', for instance, can be a moral thought; it can be offered as a moral reason for acting or not acting in a certain way. We saw also what attitude Singer takes to these concepts. On his account, they must be re-fashioned into utilitarian concepts if they are to retain a rightful place in moral thinking – they must be prevented (as far as possible) from impeding utility as he understands it. This sort of account is not peculiar to Singer; it is the one utilitarians in general must give of all so called 'secondary moral notions'.[3]

So according to utilitarians, if the power of a moral concept to set limits to the pursuit of utility cannot be (virtually) eliminated, the concept itself must be eliminated from moral thinking. It does not matter what concept it is; if it cannot be interpreted or reconstructed in a utilitarian way, it must not be allowed to function as a concept in terms of which moral judgements can be made. Bioethicists, as we have seen, are especially keen on making this point about the concept of a *human being*. That concept, they insist, must be drained of the moral import it presently has; it must be deprived of its power to limit what may be done to human beings in the name of utility. Singer, for example, like Rachels, has little time for talk of 'the intrinsic dignity of the human individual' or 'the intrinsic worth of all men'; these are, he says, nothing but 'fine phrases' which are the 'last resort' of those who – unlike him – have 'run out of arguments'.[4]

Concepts which cannot be rendered into utilitarian terms must go; as *moral* concepts, at any rate. That is the utilitarian's point at its simplest. My point, at its simplest, is that since utilitarian terms are not moral terms, what goes in these circumstances is morality itself. *Pure* utilitarian thinking does not count as moral thinking.

Let us remind ourselves once more of what pure utilitarian thinking is. I have described impure utilitarianism as admitting standards of conduct – values or ideals – which are independent of utility; a pure utilitarian theory, by contrast, admits nothing but utility as the measure of right and wrong; and it defines utility in terms of the satisfaction of preferences or desires. We act rightly, according to such a theory, when we maximise the satisfaction of desires or preferences; what is right is what is preferred.

As I said above, none of the philosophers whose work has been discussed so far adopts a pure utilitarian point of view. The notion of *equality*, for example, is prominent in the writings of most bioethicists; and, as I argued in chapter 1, equality, understood as a positive moral conception or ideal, goes beyond what is implicit in the Principle of Utility itself. Harris, for one, is emphatic in his commitment to equality; more so even than Singer. He insists upon the equal worth of all valuable lives;[5] and he insists too that the value of a valuable life cannot be outweighed by pure utilitarian considerations. In order to shed light on the nature of these considerations, let us look more closely at the way in which Harris departs from pure utilitarianism in the latter case.

We saw in chapters 1 and 3 that the principle which is fundamental to morality, according to Harris, is the principle of *Respect for Persons*; and we saw also that this principle is – in his hands – virtually indistinguishable from the Principle of Utility. Respecting a person, on his account, consists in allowing that person to do what he wants and in helping him to get what he wants.

There is a straightforward connection between this conception of what respect for persons requires and the explanation Harris gives of why it is generally wrong to kill people (persons). Persons are, by definition, capable of valuing their own lives, or of having the desire to go on living; and when a person does have this desire it would normally be wrong, Harris says, to frustrate it by killing him. The prohibition against killing, therefore, rests on the same basis, for Harris, as all other moral prohibitions; a person's desire for life, like his other desires, is one that – other things being equal – we must not frustrate.

Nevertheless, Harris is led to give the desire for life a special importance, an importance he gives to no other desire whatsoever. On his account, a desire for life can override other desires, *but cannot itself be overridden* (except by more than one desire of the same sort – as in the policy of maximising lives). Thus Harris attaches a crucial significance to the *content* of this desire; whereas *pure* utilitarianism disregards the content of a desire and attaches weight only to its *extent* (how many people have it) and its *intensity* (how strong it is). Quantitive considerations (as opposed to qualitative ones) are, on the pure utilitarian view, the only considerations that count.

I understand Harris's view to be as follows: a particular desire for life – that is to say, the desire for life of a particular person – can be overridden or outweighed by more than one desire *of the same sort*; but it cannot be overridden by any number of desires of a *different* sort. In other words, someone's life may be taken (despite the fact that he wishes to keep it) if this is the only way of saving several other persons from death; but not otherwise.

142

Consider again the situation involving Y, Z and A which was discussed in chapter 6. A's desire for life, Harris thinks, may be frustrated in order to satisfy the desires for life of Y and Z. Suppose, however, that Y and Z want A killed, not in order to save their lives, but for some quite different reason; suppose that A's death will satisfy some desires of theirs which are *not* desires for life. On the assumption that these desires are very intense – more intense than A's own desire for life – would it right, according to Harris, for A to be killed?

The answer, it would seem, is no. In *The Value of Life* Harris writes as follows:

> if there are any circumstances which justify the sacrifice of unwilling innocent people *and for which the justification does not at some point turn on the other lives that may now or later be thereby saved* I do not know what they are.[6]

In other words: however intense and however widespread a desire may be, it cannot, if it is not itself a desire for life, override or outweigh someone else's desire to go on living. To say this is to depart from pure utilitarianism; it is to assign a crucial place in moral judgement to something which cannot be reduced to utility, for utility takes no account of the content of desires or preferences – it takes no account of what a desire is a desire *for*.

One might point out, of course, that generally speaking desires for life are stronger than other desires; doing what is preferred, therefore, would rarely involve allowing a desire of this sort to be overridden by desires of other sorts. But it is clearly *possible* for a person's desire for life to be outweighed in intensity or strength by desires that his death would satisfy; and Harris seems to be saying that even when this is the case, it is the desire for life which must take priority. It must take priority simply because it is a desire *for life*; it is its content that makes it more important than any of the other desires involved, and not its strength.[7]

So Harris would appear to believe that the lives of individual persons may be sacrificed only if required by the policy of maximising *lives*; it would not be sufficient that the sacrifice maximise *satisfaction*. He would thus find unacceptable a pure utilitarian account of the morality of killing. His disagreement with pure utilitarianism is a *moral* disagreement; he cannot show, as doubtless he would like to do, that *his* view has a 'rational justification' while the view of the pure utilitarian does not. He can talk about 'the value of life'; but as we saw in chapters 2 and 6, this is a way of *expressing* his view and not a way of *justifying* it in more fundamental terms. Provided we bear that point in mind, we can say that the value of life emerges from Harris's work as a value or ideal which is independent of utility and which can set limits to what may be done in order to maximise the satisfaction of desires or preferences.

Harris's utilitarianism, therefore, is impure; and its impurity (in this instance) consists in his attaching moral significance to the content of a certain desire. If we wish to examine a pure utilitarian theory, we must leave the work of Harris and of bioethicists in general, and turn instead to that of Richard Hare.

Anyone whose acquaintance with Hare's work is confined to the early writings might well be surprised to find Hare rubbing shoulders with the bioethicists. To begin with, his first book, *The Language of Morals*, is a prime example – probably *the* prime example – of the 'linguistic' approach to ethics that bioethicists appear to regard as an evasion of the proper business of moral philosophy. Furthermore, the account of moral reasoning Hare gave in that book would be unlikely to recommend itself to people who take the attitude to moral disagreement that the bioethicists do; for it allowed the existence of disagreements on moral questions that were too fundamental to be settled by rational argument.[8]

The evolution of Hare's thought since he wrote *The Language of Morals* is beyond the scope of the present discussion, which will be concerned solely with the account Hare gives of *Moral Thinking* in his book of that title. However, this at least must be said: Hare's moral philosophy remains 'linguistic' in that it is rooted in what he calls 'the logical study of moral words';[9] and the logical properties he ascribes to moral words are none other than those he originally attributed to them in *The Language of Morals*. What has changed is Hare's account of the implications these properties have for the way moral reasoning must proceed; and it is in his account of moral reasoning that Hare's affinity with the bioethicists lies.

Hare's central claim in *Moral Thinking* is that the logical properties just referred to yield 'canons' or 'rules' of moral reasoning, a system or method which people must follow if they are to think rationally about moral questions; and he maintains in addition that *everyone who follows this method correctly will come to the same moral conclusions*.[10] These conclusions, moreover, will 'have a content identical with that of a certain kind of utilitarianism'.[11] To anticipate (and simplify): we follow a rational method when we ascertain the preferences of all the people involved in a situation and do that action, whatever it is, which will maximise the satisfaction (or minimise the frustration) of those preferences. The right action is whatever action is preferred. This is *pure* utilitarianism, as defined above and in chapter 1; and Hare is saying that moral philosophy as such reveals that we *must* think like pure utilitarians if we are to think about moral questions in a rational way. We must now look in more detail both at the content of the method Hare describes and – eventually – at his derivation of this method from the alleged logical properties of moral terms.

Hare's account is complex and minutely detailed; and it is not easy to summarise what he says in a way that is both accurate and succinct. In the following simplified description I am almost certain to have omitted something Hare himself would regard as crucial. What is more, I intend to ignore for some considerable time the distinction between two levels of moral thinking that he regards as the *pièce de résistance* of his account; In the first instance I shall look only at the level he calls the 'critical' level, that of the 'archangel'.[12] Hare says that we are rarely called upon to think at this level; most of our moral thinking is (and must be) 'intuitive' – it has to take place at the level of the 'prole'.[13] But as we shall see, it is critical and not intuitive thinking which is the more fundamental of the two; and it is the method of critical thinking that is imposed, Hare maintains, by the logical properties of moral words. 'Critical thinking', he writes, 'consists in making a choice under the constraints imposed by the logical properties of the moral concepts and by the non moral facts, and by nothing else'.[14]

The moral concepts Hare is speaking of here are those expressed by 'the more general words used in moral discourse',[15] such as 'ought' and 'must'; and the relevant logical properties he ascribes to these concepts are *prescriptivity* and *universalisability*.[16] Judgements about what *must* or *ought* to be done are, Hare says, both prescriptive and universalisable. Let us consider, very briefly, what he means by these terms.

Suppose I decide in a certain situation that I ought to act in a particular way – for example, tell the truth. My judgement, Hare says, is prescriptive (or action guiding), in that it entails an imperative ('let me tell the truth'); and it is universalisable, in that it commits me to extending that imperative to anyone who finds himself in a situation of the same sort. A moral judgement, whatever its content, is, or entails, a universal prescription; 'I ought to tell the truth in this situation' entails 'let anyone in a situation like this tell the truth'.

Hare claims that we can derive from this analysis the rules of procedure (or method) we must follow if we are to make moral judgements in a rational way. The derivation is in two stages or steps. The first step extracts from the analysis a statement concerning the *aim* or *object* of moral thinking; and the second moves from that statement to an account of what the moral thinker must do if the object is to be achieved. These steps, again in brief, are as follows:

A moral judgement is a *universal prescription*. Therefore, the object of critical thinking in any set of circumstances is to arrive at just such a prescription – one that the thinker can accept, not only for the actual situation which has made the thinking necessary, but also for any situation like it. So the place the thinker happens to occupy in the situation as it has arisen is irrelevant; in other such situations he might occupy a different place, or no place at all. In order to arrive at a universal prescription, Hare says, the thinker must pay attention to the preferences of everyone involved in the situation, including himself, and give equal weight to them all; he must in this sense make all the preferences in question his own. The only judgement (or prescription) which will be acceptable to him if he does so, Hare concludes, is the one that will maximise the satisfaction of these preferences; the one that 'does . . . the best, all in all, for all the parties concerned'.[17] In short, it is the *preferred* action which will be the rational and right action for him to take.

The procedure just described is best understood by looking at critical thinking in action; in order to do this I shall adapt one of the simple examples provided for illustrative purposes by Hare himself.[18]

I wish to leave my car in a particular parking space, but I discover that someone has left a bicycle there. It is possible, though, for me to move the bicycle out of this space; and that is just what I feel inclined to do. However, what *ought* I to do?

As we have seen, this amounts for Hare to the question: what universal prescription can I accept? What judgement can I accept, not only for this situation but for all situations like it, irrespective of my own place or position in them? I can answer this question, Hare says, only by identifying all of the preferences involved and giving them equal weight.

As it happens, there are only two preferences to be considered in the situation described – my own as the owner of the car, and that of the person who owns the bicycle. My inclination is to move the bicycle so that I can park my car in the place it presently occupies; but can I accept the prescription 'let the car owner move the bicycle' for *all* situations like this one, including those in which I *myself* am the owner of the bicycle?

Now it might be the case that were *I* the owner of the bicycle I would not object to its being moved, as long as it were moved carefully and repositioned only a short distance away. It might also be the case, however, that the bicycle owner himself has a disposition quite unlike mine, and that he would have a *strong* objection to the removal of his bicycle, even in the manner and to the place just described. Let us suppose that to be so. On Hare's account, I must represent to myself how I would feel in the bicyclist's place *were I him*, that is to say, were I possessed of *his* disposition and hence of *his* preferences. If I do this, I will acquire (Hare says) a *replica* of his desire that the bicycle should not be moved. The desire I thus acquire will be as strong as the desire it replicates, and it may, therefore, be stronger than my original (or 'antecedent') desire to move the bicycle to a different place. If it is, I will find myself unable to assent to the judgement that the bicycle be moved; for this is, or entails, a universal prescription which is incompatible with the desire I have acquired through putting myself in the bicyclist's shoes – the desire that the bicycle stay put. The reason is that this desire, as stated above, outweighs in intensity the only other desire involved, my own antecedent desire for the bicycle's removal.

Thus the judgement yielded by critical thinking in this case is that *the bicycle should not be moved*. This, Hare would say, is the only judgement I can accept whatever my position in the situation; and exactly the same would go for the owner of the bicycle himself, were he to embark upon critical thinking. Once each 'fully represents to himself the situation of the other' agreement is inevitable.[19]

I have tried by means of this example to explain as simply as possible the procedure Hare calls 'critical thinking'. His account of this procedure gives rise to a great many questions, not the least of which is the question of its coherence or intelligibility. It is my view that critical thinking is logically incapable of being carried out; but I shall argue for the rejection of Hare's account on a quite different ground – the ground that critical thinking, even if it made sense, would not count as *moral* thinking.[20] I shall now try to explain and defend this claim.

I said above that Hare' makes the *right* action in any situation the action which will maximise preference-satisfaction; what is right is what is preferred. Consider the bicycle example again. What is it that is supposed to make leaving the bicycle where it is the right thing to do? Essentially, it is this: *that the bicyclist's desire for the bicycle to stay put is stronger or more intense than the only other desire present.* Were the car owner's desire to move the bicycle the stronger of the two, it would be right to move the bicycle. Thus on the account Hare gives, nothing except the extent and intensity of the preferences involved has any relevance at all to the moral decision that must be made.

It must be emphasised that there is nothing peculiar about this example; whatever example were taken, critical thinking would proceed in exactly the same way. Hare does not *define* right action in utilitarian terms; but critical thinking will invariably pronounce as right the action a utilitarian would regard as right – the action that maximises satisfaction, and that (in this sense) does the best all in all for all of the people concerned. '. . . The logical apparatus of universal prescriptivism', Hare writes, '. . . will lead us in critical thinking . . . to make judgements which are the same as a careful act – utilitarian would make'.[21]

In a moment I shall look at some of the situations discussed in earlier chapters in the light of Hare's account; before doing so, however, I shall make some comments on the example just sketched and discuss some of the points to which these comments give rise.

The most striking thing about this example, as with so many of the examples Hare gives, is the *triviality* of the decision the agent has to make. Parking one's car may often make for a bad temper, but it is rarely a matter of tremendous moral significance. This is not an unimportant point, for where an issue is trivial we may be content to settle it in a way in which we would not dream of settling more important issues; for istance, by ignoring such moral considerations as are involved and letting an aggressive and irrational person have his way. In the circumstances described, the car owner may decide to take the line of least resistance with the owner of the bicycle, if the latter is making a great deal of fuss and there is another parking space not too far distant. The car owner may shrug his shoulders and drive on. Nevertheless, he may be *entitled* to the parking space the bicycle is occupying – for it is (let us suppose) the space immediately outside his own house. Being a good-humoured man, however, he goes to another parking space just the same. Were the car owner less good-humoured he might *insist* on moving the bicycle, however strong the bicyclist's feelings may be. The bicyclist, he might point out, is *in the wrong*;

and what puts him in the wrong is the car owner's entitlement to the space in question, and not the strength of anyone's *feelings*.

In the example described above, then, a procedure that takes no account of the question of *entitlement* simply ignores the moral issue – such as it is – which is at stake. So critical thinking ignores that issue, and must ignore it; all it takes account of, and all it can take account of, is the extent and intensity of preferences.

This point remains correct, it must be emphasised, even if the action that is right in these circumstances *happens to coincide* with the action that is preferred. An action can be *both* right *and* preferred without it being the case that the action is right *because* it is preferred. However, it is *possible* for an action to be right because it is preferred (or at least because it is the most *extensive* preference); and it seems to me that Hare's account trades on this possibility. Consider, for instance, the following situation:

There occurs at a non-conformist chapel a difference of opinion about the form that should be taken by the Sunday school treat. Of the two deacons in charge of this matter, one favours a seaside outing while the other favours a tea party. The dispute must be settled if the treat is to go ahead; how should it be settled?

Well, an obvious way of settling the dispute would be to find out which of the alternatives just mentioned is the more popular with the scholars – which of them is *preferred* by the intended recipients of the treat. As I said before, it seems to me that Hare's account of critical thinking trades on this sort of situation; it derives a measure of plausibility from the fact that we habitually settle many straightforward conflicts of preferences (or interests) in a way which seems to resemble the procedure Hare describes. If we cannot find some compromise that everyone will accept, we do what the majority would prefer, and by and large consider it right to do so. If most of the Sunday scholars would rather go to the seaside than have a tea party, we would be inclined to suppose that, other things being equal, to the seaside they should go. (We might even consider relevant the intensity of the preferences, involved, and not merely their extent, though this, I think, would be unlikely.)

It is extremely important, however, to consider *why* we would think it right to do what most of the scholars preferred. Why would we think it wrong to do something else – for example, what only the pastor's daughter wanted to do? The answer is, because it would not be *fair* to do so. The matter must be decided fairly, and this means (we would think) that it must be decided by finding out what the majority of the people affected want to do.

In the sort of situation described above, then, we would generally consider it right to do what most people preferred; but we could also say *why* it would be right to do that, and in saying why we would invoke a certain conception of fairness. This is of crucial importance in the present context, because fairness is a *moral* conception or value, and no such conception can figure in critical thinking. Critical thinking, to repeat, 'consists in making a choice under the constraints imposed by the logical properties of the moral concepts and by the non moral facts *and by nothing else*'.[22]

So we would be mistaken, I suggest, if we were to suppose that in situations like that of the Sunday school treat we actually resort to something that resembles critical thinking; we do not. What we do is attempt to settle the dispute in a way generally acknowledged to be *fair*, fairness being quite possibly the only moral consideration that bears upon the matter. In other situations there may be other moral considerations besides fairness to take into account; in yet others, fairness may not be a relevant consideration at all.

There are, therefore, situations in which we would consider it right, *because fair*, to do what is preferred (in the sense of what most people prefer). I have given as an illustration a situation in which there is a decision to be made about the form that a Sunday school treat should take. This is in all likelihood a straightforward conflict of preferences; hence all that matters from the moral standpoint is that the conflict should be settled fairly.

However, there are conflicts which are *not* straightforward conflicts of preferences; indeed, the dispute about the Sunday school treat may be one of them. Suppose that the deacon in favour of the tea party, Brother Jones, actually *disapproves* of outings to the seaside (which he supposes provide opportunities for lewdness); suppose that his objection to such outings is a *moral* objection, and not a mere aversion or disinclination. For this reason, he maintains that the matter is not one to be decided by finding out what the scholars would prefer: they might prefer something immoral (namely, the outing to the seaside). His fellow deacon, Brother Lewis, does not share Brother Jones's view at all; there can be nothing wrong with a little harmless sunbathing, he thinks, and the sea air will do everyone good. When he discovers what Brother Jones believes, Brother Lewis finds his own preference for the seaside outing hardening and beginning to change its character. They *ought* to go to the seaside, he now says; it is high time the chapel broke away from the kill-joy attitudes of people like Brother Jones.

The conflict as just described is not a conflict of preferences but of *moral beliefs*; it is a *moral* conflict or disagreement. Now the Sunday school treat must (let us suppose) go ahead, and it follows that a decision must be made as to the form it should take. How should that decision be arrived at?

Brother Jones maintains, as we have seen, that it would be inappropriate to consult the preferences of the scholars. He suggests instead that the matter be decided by the chapel deacons as a body at their next meeting, and Brother Lewis agrees. The meeting is held, and after a long and occasionally acrimonious discussion the deacons come out in favour of the seaside outing by a small majority.

What this part of the story illustrates is that even where a conflict is a *moral* conflict and not a conflict of preferences, we may frequently go about settling the matter of *what is to be done* in a way which resembles the way we settle conflicts of preferences. We find out what course of action is favoured or preferred by those whose business it is to make the decision; we put the matter to a vote. Again, this is not 'critical thinking' – for one thing, only the *extent* of a preference is taken into account – but it may seem to bear a resemblance to it. Of course, the differences are far more significant than the (apparent) similarities – for example, the deacons will doubtless vote according to their *moral convictions*, which will not have been arrived at by anything that resembles critical thinking.[23] Nevertheless, it is possible that once again Hare's account trades on the seeming resemblance between critical thinking and the sort of procedure described above, just as it trades on the seeming resemblance between critical thinking and the procedure we generally adopt when there is a conflict of the sort I have called a straightforward conflict of preferences.

In the names of *fairness* and *democracy*, then, we tend to adopt procedures for dealing with conflict, including, on occasion, moral conflict, which might seem to resemble critical thinking. However, the resemblance is only apparent; and moreover, fairness and democracy are *ideals* or *values* – the sorts of things that Hare explicitly excludes from critical thinking.

Let us go back for a moment to the moral dispute between Brother Jones and Brother Lewis. I said before that they agreed to let the matter be settled by a meeting of the deacons. But what matter? What was it that was settled by the deacons' vote? Was it the *moral issue* at stake between Brother Jones and Brother Lewis, the propriety of

Sunday school outings to the seaside? Surely not. The deacons would certainly have discussed this issue at their meeting, and voted, in the usual phrase, according to their consciences. Nevertheless, what was settled by the vote was that the Sunday school *would go* to the seaside, and not that it would be *morally right* for it to go. The show of hands may have been preceded by an engagement on the deacons' part with the moral issue at stake; it may have been preceded by some *moral thinking*. But it was not itself a piece of moral thinking, and the same would go, I suggest for the procedure described by Hare. If critical thinking were applied to this case, it would not engage at all with Brother Jones's *reason* for disapproving of seaside outings – that they provide opportunities for lewdness; thus it would ignore the moral issue involved.

Thus we are brought back to my fundamental objection to Hare's account of moral thinking: that it is not an account of moral thinking at all. Moral thinking must be *moral* thinking – if we are to think morally about some matter we must bring moral considerations to bear upon it, we must engage with the moral issues it raises. It may seem uninformative to say this, but there is some point in doing so when we find ourselves faced with an alleged description of moral thinking which makes no reference at all to the considerations that make it moral.

In the preceding chapters I have described several situations in which moral decisions have to be made or moral reasons offered for doing or not doing certain things. Let us look at one of them in the light of Hare's account.

Consider the stance of the hostages described in chapter 5. These hostages, let us recall, are threatened with death unless they tell their captors the whereabouts of the fugitive ambassador. Nevertheless, they refuse to do so – it would be shameful, in their view, for them to buy their lives with the life of another person. Thus it is a moral conception, idea or belief which accounts for the hostages' refusal to do the one thing that will save their lives; and as we saw, no one who wishes to take issue with them on moral grounds can ignore that conception. The newcomer to the embassy described in chapter 6, for example, cannot ignore it if he wishes to argue that the hostages may tell the terrorists where the ambassador is to be found. This is not a psychological point; it is a point about the form a *moral* argument with the hostages must take. The newcomer must present the act of surrendering the target in a different light from that in which it appears to the hostages themselves if he is to persuade them that the act is not closed to them on moral grounds. He must argue that it would *not* be a case of buying their lives with the life of another; or at least that it would differ significantly from other actions that could be described in this way. He may introduce other moral considerations, some of which were mentioned in the earlier discussion; but he must present them as either altering or overriding those to which the hostages refer in explaining their decision. What the newcomer cannot do, to repeat, is *pay no attention whatsoever* to what the hostages say about surrendering the terrorists' target; to do that would be to pay no attention whatsoever to the moral issue as they understand it.

The point I am urging can be expressed in general terms as follows: moral thinking must involve moral ideas, values or conceptions; it is with reference to such conceptions that we explain and support judgements about what *ought* or *ought not* to be done, and it is the possibility of that reference which makes those judgements moral ones. Critical thinking, however, is concerned only with identifying preferences and assessing their extent and intensity. The action it identifies as right will be in every case the action that is preferred, no matter what the action is and no matter how it is defended by those who prefer it. Indeed, it need not be defended *at all*: defence, justification, giving reasons, become simply irrelevant on Hare's account, as does anything that relates to the *content* of a preference. What a preference is a preference *for* is neither here nor there as far as critical thinking is concerned; all that matters is how many people have the preference and how strongly they have it. This has some interesting implications, to which I shall return in the next chapter.

I maintain, then, that critical thinking – the thinking of Hare's 'archangel' – is not moral thinking. It is not moral thinking because it does not involve moral conceptions, such as those discussed in earlier chapters. The hostages consider it *shameful* to buy their lives at the price of the ambassador's; Mary must look after Sarah because Sarah is *her mother*; the ship's captain condemns the killing of one sailor as *murder*; and so on.

It must be emphasised that I am not objecting to critical thinking on the ground that it might yield conclusions which most of us would consider to be wrong – conclusions which would run counter to our 'moral intuitions', as Hare puts it. I am making the *conceptual* point that critical thinking does not count as moral thinking, whatever its conclusions. It does not count as moral thinking because it is empty of moral categories or conceptions; it makes no reference at all to moral values or ideals.

It is time to consider what reply Hare would make to this point. Ultimately, as we have seen, he would say that the method of moral thinking he describes *must* be right, because it is the method imposed by the logical properties of moral words. We need not consider this reply yet, however, for Hare can appeal first to the fact that the description I have given of his account is only a partial description of it. Critical thinking, which is all I have expounded, is not the only form that moral thinking takes, according to Hare; indeed, it is his view this day to day moral thinking rarely takes that form. The kind of moral thinking in which we normally have occasion to engage, he says, is not *critical* but *intuitive*, it is the thinking not of the 'archangel' but of the 'prole'; and it is to the thinking of the prole, Hare would say, that the moral conceptions on which I have placed so much weight belong.

Thus Hare's reply to my objection (at this stage) would be that if his account of moral thinking is taken as a whole, it is by no means ignores the moral conceptions or categories to which I have referred. On the contrary, he would add, it assigns those conceptions to their proper place in moral thought and moral life, which is very different from the place to which I have assigned them. Let us look at what Hare supposes their proper place to be.

Consider once again the dispute between the owner of the car and the owner of the bicycle. We saw that each of the parties to this dispute must replicate, as Hare puts it, the preference of the other and compare its strength or intensity with that of his own antecedent preference. The situation under discussion is a relatively simple one involving only two people, and for that reason there is – Hare would say – no great difficulty in actually conducting the procedure he describes, the procedure of critical thinking. However, very few situations are as simple as this, and even when they are the time available to the agent or agents involved is usually limited. Hence it is impossible, Hare says, for us to make all (or even most) of our moral decisions by the method of critical thinking; and it follows that we need some general principles of conduct to which we can refer instead.

The point is a familiar one. In essence, Hare is insisting upon the need for what Mill called 'secondary principles' – moral rules which we must use to make particular decisions and judgements in the ordinary course of our lives.[24] We think 'intuitively', Hare says, when we apply such rules, which he calls 'prima facie principles'. These principles, he insists, are *necessary* for us, in that only a being possessed of 'superhuman powers of thought, superhuman knowledge and no human weaknesses'[25] – an archangel – could do without them.

Thus Hare says that we could not dispense with the level of moral thinking he calls the 'intuitive' level; we could not get along without the principles and concepts that belong to it. But how do we know what principles and concepts to use? The answer to this question reveals the relationship which is supposed to obtain between the two forms or levels of thinking Hare describes; for it is critical thinking and critical thinking alone, Hare says, that can establish the prima facie principles it is best for us to have:

> Critical thinking aims to select the best set of prima facie principles for use in intuitive thinking . . . The best set is that whose acceptance yields actions, dispositions etc. most nearly approximating to those which would be chosen if we were able to use critical thinking all the time.[26]

It is clear that the principles critical thinking selects must derive their authority *entirely* from the thinking that has selected them. A prima facie principle is a 'good' principle, on Hare's account, if and only if the outcome of inculcating it in people will be 'for the best'; if it is not, the principle should be modified or discarded. 'Intuitive thinking', Hare writes 'has the function of yielding a working approximation to [archangelic thinking] for those of us who cannot think like archangels on a particular occasion'.[27] The more specific our prima facie principles the better, for the less risk there will be of our encountering situations in which they might lead us astray. However, they cannot be completely specific if they are to play the role they are supposed to play; and it follows that we are bound to encounter some situations to which these principles are inadequate. In such highly unusual situations we must be prepared to engage directly in the kind of thinking on which prima facie principles depend, critical thinking.[28]

We have now identified and explained, albeit briefly, the distinction which is central to Hare's account – the distinction between 'critical thinking' on the one hand and 'intuitive thinking' on the other. Hare himself, as we have seen, refers to this as a distinction between two *levels* of moral thought; and he attributes almost all of the philosophical accounts of morality with which he disagrees to a failure to appreciate the distinction. We must consider, then, whether the objection I have made to Hare's account can be disposed of convincingly by means of it.

The objection was that moral thinking must involve moral conceptions (or categories), and that for this reason critical thinking, which is void of such conceptions, cannot count as moral thinking. It will now be clear how Hare would reply to this objection. I have accused him of giving an account of moral thinking which is fundamentally defective, in that it ignores the moral conceptions essential to it; but his reply would be that his account does not ignore those conceptions. They belong, not to critical thinking, but to intuitive thinking; they give content to the prima facie principles which we need to use in the normal course of our lives. Like many other philosophers, Hare would say, I have failed to see beyond such principles to the kind of thinking on which they are based; I have therefore mistaken their status and that of the moral conceptions which figure in them – conceptions such as *murder*. Since conceptions of this kind are *derived* from critical thinking, it can hardly be an objection to critical thinking that it does not proceed in terms of them, as intuitive thinking does. Once the distinction between the two levels of moral thought is made clear, Hare would say, nothing remains of the objection I have made to his account.

It is important to realise that according to Hare it is not only his philosophical opponents who are ignorant of the true status of 'secondary' moral notions (like the ones mentioned in this and previous chapters); the so-called 'plain man' is ignorant of them too. He makes his moral decisions, lives his moral life, in terms of those conceptions; but he knows nothing at all about the kind of thinking that has selected them and is the source of all the authority they possess. That is no bad thing, Hare would say; critical thinking, is (at best) very difficult, and not many people could be trusted to do it properly. It would be unwise, therefore, to weaken the hold which prima facie principles have upon the mind and heart of the ordinary person.

Hare's position with respect to ordinary moral thinking – the moral thinking of the 'plain man' – is thus very different from that of Harris, for example. Consider again the views of the ship's doctor described in chapter 7, the man who advocates the killing and eating of one shipwrecked sailor by all the rest. As a representative of Harris, the doctor regards the ship's captain (who opposes this proposal) as confused or muddled; there is a discrepancy, he says, between the captain's concept of murder and the value he himself places on the lives of individual people. Like the doctors in charge of *Y* and *Z*, the captain should drop this concept and substitute for it one that would not apply to any killings necessitated by the policy of maximising lives.

Were the ship's doctor a representative of Hare, however, he would be required to take a rather different tack. He would have to concede that the concept of murder the captain employs plays an invaluable and essential role in moral thinking. The trouble with the captain, in his eyes, is not that he is muddled, but that he is ignorant of the *limits* of this role. He is an excellent man who has received an excellent moral education; his intuitive thinking is impeccable. But he does not realise that his thinking *is* only intuitive, and that the situation in which he is now placed is one of those rare situations for which thinking of the intuitive sort will not suffice.

The captain, on this account, is trying to put the concept of murder to a use for which it was not designed. It was designed for use in ordinary circumstances, but the present circumstances are not ordinary, and for that reason the captain must set the concept aside and engage directly in the sort of thinking from which it was derived: critical thinking. What critical thinking will show, in all probability, is that killing one sailor would be the right thing to do; notwithstanding the applicability to this act of the *secondary* moral notion of murder.

However, there is a complication here which the original ship's doctor did not have to reckon with – that critical thinking may *not*, after all, license the killing of one sailor. The captain may be vehemently and passionately opposed to the killing, and the same might go for some at least of the other members of the crew. If the doctor (or anyone else) does his critical thinking conscientiously – if he fully represents to himself the intensity of these feelings – he may find that they are stronger than his own antecedent preference for killing one sailor, even when it is combined with the preferences of those members of the crew who support him. In that event it would be *wrong* to kill one sailor, for not doing so will be the preferred course of action. Hare begins to talk about the *alterability* of preferences when he is forced to contemplate the possibility of 'non utilitarian' preferences winning the day; I shall take up this point in the next chapter.

On Hare's account, then, the *significance that moral conceptions have for those who use them is not their true significance; their true significance is given by his theory.* We need to be clear about the difference between these two things, and we can best do so by recalling the intended point of examples like that of the shipwrecked sailors.

The example just mentioned was one of those given in earlier discussions in order to illustrate the *limiting* power of moral conceptions – the power of such conceptions to impose limits upon what it is permissible to do even to achieve an indisputably good end (such as the saving of lives). The ship's captain regards the course of action proposed by the ship's doctor as closed to the sailors, because it would involve an act of *murder*. Similarly, the hostages regard the action which would save their lives as morally forbidden them; it would be *shameful*, they think, to buy their lives with that of another. The captain and the hostages may be extraordinary in their moral strength, but there is nothing extraordinary about their understanding of moral conceptions as being able to set limits of the sort described.

Hare, unlike Harris, would not say that we must *get rid* of such conceptions if we are to think rationally about moral matters; what he would say instead is that we must gain an insight into their true character. His view seems to be that once that insight has been vouchsafed to us, we will see that the power of moral conceptions to set absolutely limits is an *illusion*. This illusion is generated, it would appear, by a combination of two things: moral education and philosophical ignorance. In a person who has been well brought up, Hare maintains, the prima facie principles which have been instilled into him are so deeply ingrained that the very thought of departing from them, even in highly unusual circumstances, will be grossly repugnant to him.[29] That is what has happened, he would be likely to say, in the case of the ship's captain. The captain's moral education has been so successful that he cannot help seeing the doctor's proposal as a proposal that evil should be committed; and since he is not a philosopher, he is unable to understand how an act could be an act of murder and yet be morally right. The captain's moral thinking, like the thinking of most ordinary people, is wholly confined to the intuitive level at which conceptions such as murder have their home.

To put Hare's point in general terms: people who are ignorant of the function of intuitive thinking, ignorant even that it *has* a function – as almost everyone is – will have nothing except such thinking to go on in making moral judgements and decisions. They will be aware of no grounds for saying of an action that it is right (or wrong) except the grounds which intuitive conceptions supply. They will believe, therefore, that if an act is an act of murder (for example) it *must* be wrong; it is incoherent, they will think, to suggest otherwise. A conception such as *murder* will seem to them to set an *absolute* limit to what is morally permissible. In reality, no such limit can be set; what is preferred is right, whatever it may be.

On Hare's account, then, the conceptions which belong to the intuitive level of moral thought do not determine the moral value that actions really have; at very best, those conceptions supply no more than a 'working approximation' to critical or archangelic thinking. Primary moral judgements, ones about what is *right* and *wrong*, or what *ought* and *ought not* to be done, are, Hare thinks, logically independent of judgements which involve 'secondary evaluative words' (like murder). 'If "F" is any secondarily evaluative condemnatory adjective', he writes, 'we can always ask "Granted that it would be F would it be *wrong*?" ';[30] and the archangelic reply in any given case might be that it would not.

So whereas Hare would concede that *in fact* most acts of murder (for instance) are likely to be wrong, he would insist that no act of murder can be wrong *simply because it is an act of murder*, simply because it is an instance of this concept. To say otherwise, he thinks, would be to elevate intuitive thinking to the status of critical or archangelic thinking; for '. . . the right and best way for us to live or act either in general or on a particular occasion is what the archangel would pronounce to be so if he addressed himself to the question'.[31]

Prima facie principles may be indispensable to us in practice, but they are not logically necessary constituents of moral thinking; they are not definitive of right action.[32] That seems to be Hare's view.

We saw in chapter 1 that bioethicists like Harris present their moral conclusions as *the rational answers* to moral questions. They are convinced that ordinary moral thinking is riddled with irrationality, and that this absolves them of the need to pay very much attention to how it actually proceeds. They are trying to *change* the way we think, they would say, and not *describe* it. As we have seen, that is not what Hare perceives himself as doing. True, his aim is to help us think *more rationally* about moral issues;[33] but this improvement in rationality is supposed to come about through a better understanding of the way we think already. Hare purports to give a *description* of moral thinking; and for this reason we might expect him to attach some importance to whether or not we can recognise the description. In fact, he attaches no importance to it whatsoever. On his account, we are ignorant of what our own moral thinking involves. If we say that we do *not* think as Hare says we do, we simply reveal our ignorance, in his opinion; we do not give him cause to revise the account he has given.

Hare's belief that our ignorance disqualifies us from taking issue with him is clearly a convenient one for him to hold; but Hare's convenience does not supply anyone else with a reason for going along with that belief; and what reason is there to go along with it? Why should we not say instead that the account Hare gives *falsifies* the way we think about moral issues? This, I suggest, is just what we should say.

Consider the example of the hostages. I said before that the newcomer to the embassy could not ignore their reason for refusing to surrender the ambassador if he wished to engage in a moral argument with them; he could not ignore the moral conception, idea, or belief which puts surrendering the target out of the question as far as they are concerned. Suppose, however, that the newcomer were a representative of Hare, not of Harris, and that he were to tell the hostages to *set the belief aside* and engage in critical thinking. Would he not be ignoring the belief I have said he could not ignore?

Hare would reply, as we have seen, that the newcomer would not be ignoring that belief but enlightening the hostages about its true status. They have taken at face value what they have been told by their parents and teachers, and they think in consequence that the moral conception to which they refer is a an autonomous measure or standard of right and wrong. They think it has its own authority; and they must be made to realise that it does not.

Hare, then, would see his representative as giving the hostages insight into something of which they are ignorant – the basis or ground of a moral conception they erroneously believe to be self-supporting. But why should we attribute ignorance to the hostages and insight to Hare? Why should we not attribute ignorance to Hare and insight to the hostages instead? Hare would insist that what the hostages are appealing to (without knowing it) is only a *prima facie* principle, one which has been inculcated into them and others because normally the consequences of abiding by it will be for the best. But again, why should we accept this? Why should we not say that the hostages are doing what they *think* they are doing – appealing to a standard of conduct which needs no foundation, which needs no authority beyond its own?

We have almost reached the point at which we must consider Hare's ultimate answer to this question: that the method of critical thinking he describes is the one imposed by the logical properties of moral words. However, there is something we should look at before we do that; namely, Hare's discussion of *moral dilemmas* – *intra*personal as opposed to *inter*personal moral conflicts. I shall begin the next chapter by considering his treatment of conflicts of this sort.

9

VALUES, PREFERENCES AND FANATICISM

In chapter 2 of *Moral Thinking* Hare writes as follows:

> The views held by moral philosophers about conflicts of duties are an extremely good diagnostic of the comprehensiveness and penetration of their thought about morality; superficiality is perhaps more quickly revealed by what is said about this problem than in any other way.[1]

Let us consider in connection with some examples what Hare himself has to say about 'conflicts of duties'.

A doctor believes both that he ought to be truthful with his patients when they wish him to be and that he ought to act in their best interests. A situation arises in which he cannot meet the first of these moral requirements without, he thinks, failing to meet the second. The doctor believes that telling a particular patient the truth about his condition would be contrary to that patient's best interests; yet the patient has made it clear that he wants to know what the truth is.

The dilemma the doctor faces is bad enough, but there can be worse. Consider, for example, the situation described in chapter 6, in which an innocent person is about to detonate a bomb intended to blow up the occupants of the house to which he is delivering mail. In the example as previously described, the postman is killed by one of the people in the house. Suppose instead that the person who works out the assailant's plan is a police marksman who has been detailed to provide the occupants of the house with protection. This man must either shoot the postman – whom he knows to be an innocent party – or allow him to set off the bomb that will kill or maim the very people it is the marksman's duty to protect. This sort of dilemma is frequently described as 'tragic', in that it is not possible for the agent involved to avoid doing something which is morally dreadful.

Hare, of course, will not hear of the tragic nature of moral dilemmas,[2] although he concedes that many people believe in the possibility of moral tragedy of this kind. On his account moral tragedy, along with the idea of absolute moral limits, is an illusion; one created by the psychological hold of intuitive thinking, together with ignorance of its proper role and status. In Hare's view, since prima facie principles – 'intuitions' – are all derived from critical thinking, we can use critical thinking – 'reason' – to settle any conflicts that may arise between them. Archangelic thinking, he says, has the role of resolving conflicts between the prima facie principles it has selected for our use. It can resolve such conflicts in various ways; I shall consider here only one of them. This particular method, Hare remarks, is 'dangerous' for human beings as opposed to archangels; nevertheless it is the method which reveals most clearly the entirely derivative status he accords to prima facie principles. The method consists in putting aside the principles which are in conflict and seeing what critical thinking itself has to say about the case in point.[3]

Suppose we were to offer the doctor whose predicament was described above this method of proceeding to a decision. We tell him, in other words, to proceed in the same way as the motorist described in chapter 8 proceeds when he is deciding whether or not to move the bicycle which has been left in his parking space. The doctor must pay attention to the various preferences involved and attach equal weight to them all, whether or not they happen to be his own. He himself, we must suppose, has two competing inclinations, an inclination to tell his patient the truth and an inclination to withhold it from him. He must replicate the patient's preference for knowing the truth and combine it with his own preference, in so far as he has one, for giving him that knowledge. He must then compare the intensity of the preference produced by the combination with that of the preference he also has for keeping the patient in ignorance. The stronger of the two preferences will win; that is to say, it will determine what the doctor ought to do. Thus the dilemma will be resolved, Hare would say.

I suggest that even if the procedure just described could be carried out, it could not be spoken of as resolving the doctor's dilemma. The reason is that critical thinking simply bypasses the moral issues at stake. In this respect it is analogous to a procedure which is certainly capable of being carried out, that of tossing a coin. The moral considerations which create and define the doctor's dilemma are completely ignored in Hare's account, in favour of a decision procedure which makes no reference at all to these considerations.

It is possible to overlook this point, because one of the factors which must enter into critical thinking in this instance is the patient's wish to know the truth about his condition – his 'preference' for the truth, as Hare would put it; and the fact that he does want to know the truth (and even, perhaps, *how much* he wants to know it) is certainly relevant to the doctor's decision about what he ought to do. Indeed, it is probable that the majority of people nowadays would consider this to be the crucial fact in the type of case under discussion. Doctors, they would say, should *respect their patients' autonomy*; if a patient wishes to know the truth about his condition, then the truth is what he should be told.

So in this case, as it happens, critical thinking must take account of a factor which is at least morally relevant, and is perhaps morally crucial, to a decision about what the doctor ought to do – but *only* as it happens. The situation in question happens to be one in which a certain preference – the patient's preference for the truth – assumes *moral* significance. But what gives it that significance is a moral conception, ideal or value – something which can have no place at all in critical thinking, as Hare himself insists. The moral conception I mean is that of respect for a person's autonomy (though see p.200), combined in this case with other moral conceptions, such as those of honesty and truthfulness.

The doctor believes, let us remember, that generally speaking he should be honest with his patients. He is in a dilemma because he also believes that generally speaking he should act in their best interests. There would be no dilemma for him if he did not hold these beliefs; it is the beliefs which create the dilemma. The dilemma cannot be resolved, therefore, by ignoring those beliefs, by putting aside the very considerations which give rise to it and make it the dilemma it is. The moral issue at stake cannot be resolved by a procedure that fails even to address it.

The point is that the moral values which define the doctor's dilemma play no role at all in the procedure for resolving it that Hare would offer him. The patient's wish for the truth plays a role in that procedure, certainly, but only as a preference, and as one preference among others; it cannot be given the kind of importance it has for those who speak of the moral obligation to respect a patient's autonomy. The doctor's moral concern for the best interests of his patient fares no better in Hare's account; it too plays a role only as a preference, a preference in this case for withholding the truth. If this were to emerge as the stronger or more intense of the preferences involved, it would win – *whether or not* it was an expression of the moral concern just mentioned. Thus once again critical thinking fails to engage with *the moral issue* the dilemma involves; it avoids the issue rather than resolves it.

How should the doctor proceed, then? If he is to deal with the moral issue he faces, he must decide which moral consideration outweighs the other in this case. Hare believes that it is pointless to say such a thing without saying also *how* the decision must be made – not only in this case, and not only in this type of case, but *in general*. But it is just not possible to do that; there is no *formula* for resolving moral dilemmas. People *do* resolve such dilemmas; that is to say, they do decide, in all sorts of situations, which of the competing moral considerations which confront them carries the most weight. Hare would not call this resolving the dilemma unless the decision arrived at were the one that all rational persons were required to accept; I have argued for the possibility of rational moral disagreement in such cases, and I shall not repeat those arguments here. What must be said, however, is this: whatever decision the agent makes, the moral consideration he regards as having been outweighed *will retain its own weight* – and this brings us back to the notion of moral tragedy.

Suppose the doctor decides that it would be best to withhold the truth from his patient. He may never change his mind about this decision; but he may still feel that he has been morally required to betray his patient's trust in him. We may not wish to describe his dilemma as 'tragic'; but the dilemma faced by the police marksman is surely a candidate for the description. If he shoots the postman, he will be killing a man who is innocent of any intention to harm the occupants of the house; if he does not, he will be failing to protect the very people he has been charged to protect.

Hare, for his part, claims to be well aware of the moral anguish that situations like these can produce for the people who are called upon to act in them – people like the doctor or the police marksman; and he would think badly, it seems, of people who felt no anguish at all in such situations. However, he looks at this anguish through the distorting medium of his own theory. People who have received a good moral education, he says, and who have acquired in consequence good dispositions and strong moral feelings, will breach their prima facie principles only with extreme reluctance. Thus they will find repugnant the very thought of killing an innocent person, for example, even when they know that it would be the right thing to do; and were they actually to perform such an act, they would look back at it afterwards with something rather like a feeling of remorse.[5]

The trouble is that what Hare is describing here is not what is meant by moral anguish. If the police marksman shoots the postman, he does something dreadful, and his anguish arises from his knowledge that this is so. It is not that his deed only *seems* dreadful to him because of his good moral education. The dreadfulness of killing an innocent person does not disappear when one is morally required to do it. Hare must say that it does; he must say that the marksman's remorse for his deed is, in the end, quite irrational. It is quite irrational because what he has breached, according to Hare, is only a *prima facie* principle; and prima facie principles have *no authority of their own* – they are not genuine moral gauges of action.

In short, moral tragedy is an illusion for Hare because moral conflict is an illusion for him. It can never be the case, on his account, *both* that a person should do one thing *and* that he should do another thing which is incompatible with it.[6] Since the moral considerations involved derive all of their authority from critical thinking, there is always, for Hare, only *one* thing a person should *really* do, namely, 'what the archangel would pronounce to be [right] if he addressed himself to the question.'[7] But we cannot give an account of moral anguish unless we preserve the mutual independence of the various considerations which create moral dilemmas by coming into conflict with one another. We must recognise that duties (to use the vocabulary favoured by Hare) really can conflict; it is not the case that they only seem to conflict, or that the conflict is between prima facie duties only. Moral conflict is a reality; and this means that moral tragedy is a reality too. Superficiality – see the passage from *Moral Thinking* quoted at the beginning of this chapter – lies in the denial of this truth, and not – as Hare thinks – in the acknowledgement of it.

I shall return in due course to some of the points touched upon in the early part of the preceding discussion. It is necessary now to consider Hare's ultimate answer to any objection that might be levelled against his account of moral thinking. The answer is, in brief, that since the account *must* be correct no objection to it can possibly succeed.

The account must be correct, Hare would say, because the method of moral thinking it describes is the method imposed by the logical properties of moral words. As we saw in chapter 8, his view is that a philosophical analysis of such works is sufficient to show that rational moral thought *must* take the form of critical thinking. I shall argue that this is not the case; although a full examination of all of the issues raised by Hare's analysis of moral terms must be regarded as beyond the scope of the present work.

As I said before, Hare maintains that the relevant logical properties of the more general moral words – words like 'must' and 'ought' – are those of *universalisability* and *prescriptivity*; a moral judgement is a universal or universalised prescription. The derivation of 'canons' of moral reasoning from this account proceeds in two steps or stages (see p.146). The first is to a statement of the aim of moral reasoning; the second is to a description of the method that must be followed if this aim is to be achieved. For any agent in any situation, the aim of moral reasoning is to arrive at a prescription which he can accept for that situation and for all situations like it, whatever his own position in them might be. In order to arrive at this prescription, Hare says, the agent must follow the method of critical thinking; he must pay attention to the preferences of everyone whose interests are affected, and give equal weight to them all. The prescription that expresses the strongest, most intense preference is the only prescription whose universal application in these circumstances he (or anyone else) can accept.

In sum, the method dictated by the logical properties of moral terms is one which requires us, in Hare's words, to

> pay attention to the satisfaction of the preferences of people (because moral judgements are prescriptive and to have a preference is to accept a prescription) and to pay attention equally to the equal preferences of all those affected (because moral principles have to be universal and cannot therefore pick out individuals).[8]

Hare is not saying that this is *one method among others* of arriving at a universal prescription; he is saying that it is the *only possible* method of doing so. In a moral situation we *must* 'pay attention to preferences' in the way he describes; there is, according to him, no other way of determining what prescription we can universalise in such a situation.

The example I used to illustrate Hare's method in chapter 8 involved a conflict over a parking space between a bicyclist on the one hand and a motorist on the other. If we reflect on this example, we shall see that the motorist can arrive at a universal prescription without doing critical thinking; he can identify a prescription he can accept for this case and for any case like it without paying attention to preferences in the way Hare says he must.

The disputed parking space, let us recall, is outside the motorist's own house. The motorist maintains that for this reason he is *entitled* to park his car in that space; and it is this entitlement, he says, which makes it the case that the bicyclist should move his bicycle.

The motorist, then, gives a reason for his prescription that the bicycle be moved; the reason being that the bicyclist is not *entitled* to the parking space, whereas the motorist is. If the motorist is right about his entitlement, it follows that – other things being equal – moving the bicycle is the right course of action. It is the right course of action, not only in this case, but also in all cases (actual or hypothetical) that are like this one in respect of the entitlement. So not only *may* the motorist universalise the prescription his judgement entails (let the bicycle be moved); he *must* universalise it if he is to be consistent. To repeat: he gives a *reason* for what he says (that he, and not the bicyclist, is entitled to the parking space in dispute), and he gives a reason, furthermore, for claiming this entitlement (that the space is outside his own house). Whenever the same reasons apply, the same judgement must be made – provided, of course, that there is no *further* reason involved to which they must give way (for example, that the bicyclist in *this* case is rushing to the aid of someone who has been injured).

I maintain, then, that the aim or object Hare says moral thinking has can be achieved without following the method he describes – without paying attention to preferences in the way he lays down. It is not necessary to follow this method in order to arrive at a universal or universalised prescription; it is sufficient that one gives *reasons* for the judgement one makes, in the way that the agents in all of the examples discussed in this book give reasons for their judgements. The reasons they give refer to, or invoke, moral conceptions or beliefs; and such conceptions cannot enter into critical thinking, which is concerned solely with the extent and intensity of preferences.[9]

It must be repeated that I am not denying the relevance of preferences to moral decisions in many cases; I made this point following my original discussion of the example involving the parking dispute, and again when I discussed the doctor's dilemma described above. The fact that an action is preferred can be a reason, I said, not only for doing it, but for thinking that it is *right* to do it. As we have seen, some moral conceptions are such that what people want is often relevant, and is sometimes crucial, to a decision about what ought to be done in a given case. What I am denying is that we can give an account of moral thinking that refers *only* to the satisfaction of preferences, and ignores altogether the moral conceptions which furnish us with *reasons* for moral judgements – including the judgement that in some circumstances it is right to do what is preferred.

Hare himself is aware that there are objections to his account of moral thinking which turn on a distinction between preferences and moral conceptions. In chapter 6 of *Moral Thinking* he envisages just such an objection:

> What is all this talk about preferences and desires . . .? What we are supposed to be talking about is *morality* . . . Moral duties are higher and more authoritative than mere preferences . . . and cannot be weighed in the same scales. In setting up your 'preference–utilitarianism' have you not in effect thrown morality out of the window, not given it a basis?[10]

In reply, Hare refers his readers to a later portion of his book, section 5 of chapter 10. In this section he discusses the example of a 'fanatical doctor' who believes that he should keep his patients alive for as long as possible, whatever the cost to them in suffering. That example will be discussed at length below; what concerns us at this point is the way in which Hare fulfils his promise to answer the objection which draws a distinction between *preferences* and *moral duties* (or, as the latter become in this part of Hare's discussion, *moral convictions*).

The reply which emerges is that a moral conviction *is* a preference. It is not a 'plain preference', Hare says; but his distinction between a 'plain preference' and a 'moral preference' amounts only to this, that the latter, unlike the former, is universal or universalisable. A moral conviction, according to Hare, is nothing but a universalised desire; and since it is the object of critical thinking in any given case to show what desire can be universalised, the need for such thinking, he maintains, cannot be obviated by referring to one's moral convictions.[11]

Hare is saying, then, not only that 'to have a preference is to accept a prescription', but also that 'all prescriptions, including moral ones, are expressions of preferences or of desires in a wide sense'.[12]

The inadequacy of this reply should be clear already. A moral judgement does not differ from an expression of preference only by being universal or universalisable. The motorist discussed above may say that the bicyclist should move his bicycle, but unless he can give a certain kind of reason for what he says (as he does, on my account) he is not making a *moral* judgement, even if he adds that he would say the same in all situations like this. He must be able to invoke some moral conception or other if what he says is to count as a moral judgement. Hare would reply that in invoking a conception of this sort he is merely expressing his 'intuitions', and that those intuitions require to be tested by critical thinking.[13] But this presupposes the correctness of his own theory, the very theory the objection under discussion is intended to call into question. The category of 'intuitive thinking' belongs to the theory, and it is not available, therefore, unless the objection can be answered in some other way. Hare is here assuming what is at issue: the acceptability of his account of moral thinking.

Let us pause at this point to take stock of the position for which I have been arguing in this and the preceding chapter. I have been concerned throughout with a pure utilitarian theory of morality, the one put forward by R. M. Hare in his book *Moral Thinking*. Most contemporary utilitarians, including the bioethicists, stop short of pure utilitarianism; they import into their theories moral values or ideals which restrict the application of considerations pertaining to utility alone. Harris, for example, as we saw in chapter 8, uses the notion of a valuable life (together with that of the equal worth of all such lives) to resist a pure utilitarian account of the morality of killing. For Hare, on the other hand, what is right is in every case what is preferred; for it is archangelic or critical thinking alone which determines what is right, and the aim or object of archangelic thinking is the discovery of what is preferred. 'The right or best way for us to live or act,' Hare writes, 'either in general or on a particular occasion is what the archangel would pronounce to be so if he addressed himself to the question'.[14] Once the archangel has made his pronouncement, the moral question which was put to him has been answered; there is no possibility of judging an action to be wrong despite the fact that the archangel has pronounced in its favour, for there are no standards of right and wrong which are independent of archangelic thinking. Such standards may seem to exist; but only to the philosophically unenlightened.

Critical thinking, then, is blind to the content of preferences; it can take account only of their extent (how many people have them) and their intensity (how strong they are). It is void, therefore, of moral conceptions, values or ideals. Since these are necessary to moral thinking, the procedure Hare describes does not count as moral thinking at all.

This claim may sound not merely false, but incredible. Hare is putting forward a *utilitarian* theory; and utilitarianism is associated with the championing of certain moral ideals or values. This is not to say that utilitarians never disagree amongst themselves about important matters; they do. However, we expect from all utilitarian thinkers arguments which reflect a characteristic pattern of moral priorities; and by and large that is what we get – *except*, as I shall now show, when the arguments are *pure* utilitarian ones.

Consider, for example, the case of the shipwrecked sailors discussed in chapter 7. These sailors have been cast away on a barren island with plenty to drink but nothing to eat. The ship's doctor proposes that one of the sailors should be killed and eaten by the remaining six, who will then be found alive by the patrol boat that will call at the island in a few months time.

The doctor's proposal, I suggest, is one we would expect any utilitarian to support. We would expect any utilitarian to say that however understandable the distaste of the ship's captain for the proposal might be, his opposition to it must be regarded as irrational; for what the doctor proposes is the only way of saving any of the sailors from death. This is what Harris, for one, would certainly say; and in saying it he would be expressing, to repeat, the point of view we would expect any utilitarian to take.

However, we saw in chapter 8 that critical thinking as described by Hare would *not* be sure to yield the conclusion that it would be right to do what the doctor proposes. This is because what the doctor proposes may not be what is preferred; and it is the discovery of what is preferred that is the object of critical thinking. The preferences of the doctor and his supporters may be outweighed in intensity or strength by those of the captain and his; and were that the case it would be wrong, the archangel would pronounce, to kill one of the sailors, despite the fact that not doing so will mean the death of them all in due course.

How would Harris, for instance, respond to this? I suggest that he would be committed to the view that, notwithstanding the intensity of the preferences which the captain and his supporters have, their preferences should be disregarded. On his account, it would be irrational not to kill one person so that six others might live; and for that reason the preferences just referred to should not be allowed to determine what is done. The sailors, Harris would say, should do what it would be *right* to do; and it would be right to do what it would be *rational* to do – kill one sailor.

Harris, then, would have to reject even an archangelic pronounce-

171

ment in favour of the captain's point of view. This is because Harris's theory, unlike Hare's, takes account of the *content* of preferences, and not only of their extent and intensity. The captain's preference is a preference for omitting to do what will *save lives*; and it follows, for Harris, that it should be disregarded in the name of *the value of life*. Thus, as previously stated, the value of life functions in Harris's thought as a moral conception or ideal, one in terms of which the content of a preference – what it is a preference *for* – can be measured or assessed.

Critical thinking, as we have seen, is empty of moral conceptions or ideals; it is empty of anything which could serve as a standard by which to judge the content of preferences. Such standards play a role in intuitive thinking, certainly; but nothing that belongs to the intuitive level of moral thought can have any application at all to the pronouncements of the archangel. To repeat: what is preferred is right, whatever it may be. Pure utilitarianism, therefore, eliminates moral values or ideals; *including those which are associated with utilitarianism itself*. In order to bring this out I shall examine Hare's discussion of a situation described by him in chapter 10 of *Moral Thinking*, the one referred to above as that of the 'fanatical doctor'.[15] But first I shall consider briefly 'the fanatic' in general as he is found in Hare's work, and the whole matter of 'fanaticism' as it relates to the account of morality which I give in this book.

Let us look back at Singer's Equality Principle. As we have seen, Singer maintains that we can appeal to the very nature of reason in order to establish that we must, in all our actions, give equal weight to the interests of everyone they affect. Singer's account of moral reasoning has clear affinities with Hare's; both the Equality Principle and the procedure Hare terms 'critical thinking' are variations upon the Principle of Utility.[16]

I argued in chapter 4 that Singer does not succeed in showing that the Equality Principle is the only basis on which rational moral judgements and decisions can be made; and I argued further that reason or rationality in ethics must be understood in terms of the ability to give *appropriate reasons* for moral judgements and decisions. Appropriate reasons are those which invoke moral conceptions or beliefs – ideals or values of the sort to which I have referred many times. Towards the end of the earlier discussion I mentioned some of the objections which are commonly levelled against accounts of morality of this kind; and in one of these there was a reference to *moral fanaticism*.

The objection in question can be stated in the following way:

according to utilitarianism, all legitimate moral ideals can be derived from a common source – a principle (or method of reasoning) which enjoins us to pay attention to people's preferences (or interests) and to pay *equal* attention to the preferences (or interests) of *all* people. If philosophy can show that this principle is the only rational one to adopt, it will give us a weapon against moral fanatics – people who trample on the interests of others in the name of certain ideals or values. If it cannot, we shall have no such weapon; and it follows that we shall have no ultimate defence against people whose ideals are morally repugnant in the way just described – people like the Nazis, for example, who set out to exterminate all manner of human beings (especially Jews) in the name of an ideal of racial purity.[17] According to the account I have given, philosophy cannot do it; the account, therefore, legitimises moral fanaticism – or, at any rate, fails to *illegitimise* it.

In response to this, I must repeat what I said in chapter 4: that in my view philosophy *cannot* provide an ultimate defence against moral fanaticism – it cannot show that fanaticism is ruled out by the sort of thing moral reasoning is. However, a further point must be made here. Hare himself has long been concerned with fanaticism. In his earlier work, he came to the conclusion that fanaticism could not be discounted as a logical possibility; it would be possible, he said, for someone to admit the facts utilitarians cite in support of their moral judgements, and follow the same method of moral reasoning – the method Hare described then – but nevertheless dissent, in virtue of his ideals, from the conclusions utilitarians would draw.[18] By the time he wrote *Moral Thinking*, however, Hare had changed his mind about this matter; fanaticism emerges from that work as not even a *logical* possibility. I shall argue in reply that the victory Hare appears to have won is hollow; and that it is his account, the pure utilitarian account, and not mine, which is properly regarded as the legitimiser of moral fanaticism. Hare's own example of the fanatical doctor brings this out very clearly; so let us turn to Hare's discussion of it.

The fanatical doctor, according to Hare, is fanatical in his attitude to a certain principle, the principle that doctors should save lives whenever they can. Hare sets out to describe a dialogue between this doctor and someone who 'can reason with perfect logic and knows all the facts'[19] – an archangel. The dialogue concerns a patient who, Hare says, '. . . will die at once if not put under intensive care; if he is put under intensive care, he will suffer a great deal and die in any case within a month or so'.[20] Hare's doctor brings to this situation 'a very strong moral aversion to omitting any step which could prolong life'.[21] Before we examine how the doctor's dialogue with the archangel actually proceeds, let us ask the question: how would we *expect* a utilitarian to respond to this case? What view would we expect him to take about the doctor's duty in these circumstances, and how would we expect him to argue for that view?

I suggest that we would expect a utilitarian – any utilitarian – to argue against the doctor's placing the patient under intensive care. The doctor, we would expect him to say, should withhold in this case any treatment that would prolong the life of the patient; and he should withhold it because the patient, as Hare says, *will suffer horribly* if such treatment is given. In the circumstances Hare describes it is this fact – together with the fact that the patient would *rather* die immediately than endure the suffering – which we would expect a utilitarian to regard as crucial. Utilitarians, after all, write books protesting about attitudes of the sort displayed by Hare's fanatical doctor – books that advocate not only 'passive euthanasia' – the withholding of life-prolonging treatment – but also 'active euthanasia' – killing – whenever a dying patient would prefer not to linger on in pain and distress.[22] This is the position adopted by Rachels, for example, in *The End of Life*;[22] and at the very least we would expect a utilitarian, as I have said, to support the withdrawal of treatment in such a case.

So in the circumstances described by Hare, we would expect a utilitarian to say that treatment should be witheld. And we would expect him to say, furthermore, that since this would be the *right* course of action, the doctor concerned should overcome any aversion he might have toward taking it. I said before that utilitarianism is associated with the championing of certain moral ideals; and the relief of suffering is surely paramount among them. No utilitarian worth his salt, we might think, would describe the fanatical doctor as anything but misguided. Let us consider, however, what Hare – a *pure* utilitarian – has to say about this case.

Here are Hare's initial observations concerning the position of the fanatical doctor:

> ... it is an excellent principle for doctors to save lives when they can; but if any doctor says 'my job is saving lives, therefore I must keep people alive to the last moment whatever the cost to them in suffering' he is showing himself a fanatic in elevating this good principle above another which would, after critical

thinking, override it in particular cases, namely the principle requiring him to prevent suffering.[23]

At first sight, this appears to be the response we said we would expect a utilitarian to make: what matters above all is that the patient should not be made to *suffer*. Thus it looks at first sight as though we could translate the passage into more familiar utilitarian terms, in the following way:

The doctor's fanatical attitude to the prima facie principle 'save lives whenever possible' is an instance of what is commonly called 'rule worship';[24] he has failed to realise that the rule he invariably follows in his treatment of dying patients is only a *secondary* principle, one which derives all its authority from the first or fundamental principle on which it depends – the Principle of Utility, which enjoins us to maximise happiness and minimise unhappiness, misery or suffering. If prolonging the life of a patient would serve only to increase that patient's suffering, he should be allowed to die. It is irrational to elevate a secondary principle above the first principle on which it depends; yet that is what the fanatical doctor is doing.

Is this a correct account of what the doctor is doing? Or rather, is it a correct account of what *Hare* says the doctor is doing? A closer look at the passage quoted above will reveal that it is not. Before we return to that passage, however, let us consider the dialogue Hare constructs between the fanatical doctor and the archangel.

The archangel is there, Hare says, to help the doctor rise above the intuitive level and do some critical thinking about the case before him. In virtue of his omniscience, the archangel can represent to the doctor the full extent of the patient's suffering, and with it the strength or intensity of the patient's desire for release. The doctor acquires in consequence a replica of the patient's preference; he acquires a preference that 'were he the patient he should not, *ceteris paribus*, suffer in that way.'[25] So the doctor now has two preferences, this one, and his own antecedent preference for placing the patient under intensive care. The stronger, more intense of these preferences will win; it will determine not only what the doctor does do, but what he *should* do – what it would be *right* for him to do.

It is clear that critical thinking can yield one of only two outcomes in this case. The doctor's antecedent preference for treating the patient may be less strong than the patient's preference – and therefore its replica – that treatment should be withheld. If it is, then the latter preference is the one that should be implemented; the right course of action will be the one we said we would expect a utilitarian to favour. On the other hand, the opposite outcome is possible. The doctor may be so averse to withholding treatment, Hare says, that 'his own suffering if he does it will exceed that of the patient if he is kept alive'.[26] In this event, Hare continues, '. . . even critical thinking will say that the suffering of the two taken together will be minimised by putting the patient under intensive care'.[27] The right course of action will be the one we said we would expect a utilitarian to argue *against*.

Let us return in the light of this discussion to the passage quoted above, the passage in which Hare explains what it is about the doctor's position that makes it 'fanatical'. The passage presupposes Hare's distinction between intuitive thinking and critical thinking, for it locates the doctor's fanaticism in his attitude to the 'good principle' that doctors should save lives whenever they can. This is, Hare says, a prima facie principle, one that belongs to the intuitive level of moral thought; and like all such principles it derives the authority it has from the critical thinking which has selected it. It can be disregarded, therefore, in those cases when following it would not be for the best.

In my earlier remarks about this passage, I suggested that it might be read as finding the doctor guilty of 'rule worship'; he has failed to realise that the rule or principle he is following (save lives whenever possible) is only a secondary or, in Hare's terminology, prima facie principle. When the doctor insists upon obeying the principle even when suffering is actually increased thereby, he is elevating it above the first principle on which it depends (in orthodox utilitarian terms, the Principle of Utility). On this interpretation of what Hare says, it is *the first principle itself*, according to him, which overrides the doctor's prima facie principle in this case.

What will now be clear, I think, is that this is *not* the account Hare gives. What overrides – or *may* override – the doctor's 'good principle', on his account, is certainly a principle 'requiring him to prevent suffering'; but this principle is *likewise* a prima facie or secondary one. It is not the first or fundamental principle; it cannot be identified with the Principle of Utility itself. The principle that suffering should be prevented is every bit as intuitive, for Hare, as the principle that lives should be prolonged; there is no difference in status between the two principles Hare mentions in the passage under discussion. Both have been selected by critical thinking, and it is in critical thinking itself that we find Hare's version of the Principle of Utility, and not in any of the prima facie principles it selects.

Thus the situation the doctor confronts, according to Hare, is one in which there is a conflict between two prima facie principles, one of which is the principle that lives should be saved whenever possible, and the other of which is the principle that suffering should be prevented. Since this particular doctor has archangelic assistance, he will be able to resolve the conflict between the principles in the way described at the beginning of the present chapter – the way which is, Hare says, 'dangerous' for ordinary mortals. The doctor will be able to set aside both prima facie principles and discover what critical thinking has to say about the case in point. It may say that he ought to withhold treatment; *but it may not*. As we saw above, if his own preference to treat turns out to be the stronger of the preferences involved, then the doctor may – indeed, must – implement it. To put the point in the terms Hare uses when discussing the example: in that event, the principle that life should be prolonged would take priority over the principle that suffering should be prevented. As we have seen, on Hare's account neither of these principles matters in itself; what does matter is that the preferred action should be done, whatever that action may be.

What has emerged quite clearly from this discussion, I suggest, is that if we bring *pure* utilitarian theory to bear on the case Hare describes, *the suffering of the patient can play no special role at all*. We cannot say simply that because the patient will suffer horribly if he is placed under intensive care the doctor should overcome his aversion to leaving this undone; for it is critical thinking which determines what the doctor should do, and as far as that is concerned the doctor's aversion to withholding treatment is of equal importance with the patient's desire to be spared further suffering. It is not open to *pure* utilitarians simply to use the patient's suffering as the basis for a moral condemnation of the doctor's aversion to letting him die. In other words, it is not open to them to argue in the way we said we would expect a utilitarian to argue.

We can now see that for pure utilitarians, the relief of suffering cannot be a moral priority. Hare contrives to suggest otherwise by talking about the suffering of the doctor, and saying that it could outweigh that of the patient. This raises a question about Hare's concept of suffering, to which we must return in due course; for the time being, it is sufficient to repeat that for those impure utilitarians who regard the relief of suffering as a moral ideal, the doctor's suffering – his distress at the thought of withholding treatment – is attributable to his irrational worship of a rule. For this reason, they would not agree that the issue should be decided by a procedure which takes the doctor's preference to treat as given, and does nothing but weigh its intensity against that of the patient's preference not to suffer. The patient ought not to be made to suffer, they would argue, and the doctor should be brought to see that this is so. One does not have to be a utilitarian in order to take this line, of course; but if utilitarians do not take it we may well wonder in what the moral appeal of utilitarianism is supposed to lie.

This point brings us at last to the 'victory' over fanaticism which Hare claims to have achieved. The fanatic, as I said before, appears in Hare's earlier work as someone able to reach different conclusions from the utilitarian, despite the fact that he admits the same facts and follows the same procedure. Where the procedure is critical thinking, however, as it must be on Hare's present account, it is impossible for that to happen. The fanatic must in every case reach the same conclusion as the utilitarian; but this conclusion may be the conclusion that *the fanatic's own antecedent preference should be implemented*, and not the conclusion we would associate with the utilitarian point of view. If it is not, the fanatic will cease to be a fanatic – he will now prescribe universally the course of action to which he was once opposed in virtue of his ideals. If it is, he will cease to *need* to be a fanatic as Hare puts it; he will emerge, not as someone whose ideals dictate a different conclusion from the utilitarian one, but as someone whose preferences are so strong that they have determined what the utilitarian conclusion is. Here, in full, is how Hare himself states the point:

> The fanatic is therefore in a dilemma. Either he has to admit that his own preferences, including those based on his moral convictions, are not enough to outweigh the preferences of the others who will be harmed by implementing them. In that case, if he fully represents to himself the stronger preferences of the others, he will come to have preferences of his own that, were he they, he should not suffer as he is proposing to make or let them suffer. But then he will abandon his fanatical line of action and the universal prescription which requires it. So, on this horn of the dilemma, the fanatic will cease to be a fanatic. Or else he has to claim that his own preferences (together with those of people who think like him) as so strong and unalterable that they will continue to prevail over those of the others whom his actions will cause or allow to suffer. If this claim be granted, then critical thinking will endorse the universal prescription that in such cases the fanatic's preferences should be

implemented. In this case, the fanatic does not *need* to be a fanatic – only a person with fantastically strong preferences. In neither case is critical thinking controverted; nor is utilitarianism. In both, the right solution is the utilitarian one.[28]

In essence, the victory over the fanatic which Hare claims to have won consists in this – that the fanatic and the utilitarian must both come to the same conclusion, the conclusion which counts as the utilitarian conclusion according to pure utilitarian theory.

It seems to me that from any standpoint other than the *pure* utilitarian one, this victory would not be a victory at all; certainly not one it would be worth winning. Let us consider the matter from the standpoint of a certain kind of impure utilitarian, the kind that champions the relief of suffering as a moral ideal or value and for that reason sees fanaticism as an object of *moral* (and not merely *intellectual*) concern.[29]

The fanatic is fanatical in that he is devoted to ideals of a certain sort – ideals which lead him to trample on people's interests or cause people to suffer. The fanatical doctor, for example, makes his patients suffer in the name (probably) of the sanctity of life; the Nazi makes Jews and others suffer in the name of racial purity. The sort of impure utilitarian under discussion sees suffering as an *evil*, and the causing of suffering as morally evil (or at least misguided). It is for that reason he finds the fanatic's ideals morally repugnant, and would welcome a philosophical weapon against them.

I suggest that the weapon Hare has to offer the impure utilitarian will not serve the latter's purpose; from the impure utilitarian's standpoint, the only arm it will strengthen is the fanatic's own. What the impure utilitarian would like, surely, is an account of moral thinking which would rule out ideals of the sort to which the fanatic is devoted – an account which would exclude as moral possibilities actions of the sort the fanatic performs or advocates (such as killing Jews in the name of racial purity, or keeping people alive whatever the cost to them in suffering); but Hare's account does not do that.

Consider the way in which critical thinking would compel the fanatic to 'cease being a fanatic'. (This would happen if the fanatic's antecedent preferences were outweighed by the preferences of those who would suffer if they were implemented; for the fanatic would then acquire the stronger preferences). I suppose that we might speak of *any* procedure which produced this result as having compelled the fanatic to abandon his ideals. Given the character of *this* procedure, however, the fanatic would have had to abandon his ideals only because he *had not managed to be fanatical enough in his devotion to them*. His ideals would have been shown to be morally repugnant – but only because he had not managed to subscribe to them intensely enough; only because he had not managed to feel strongly enough about, for example, the need to exterminate Jews.

What would the fanatic have to do, then, in order not just to hang on to his ideals, but to *make them right*? The answer is: make himself even more of a fanatic than he is at present. If he becomes sufficiently fanatical, it will be impossible (according to Hare) for anyone to call him a fanatic any more, or to call his ideals morally repugnant. Yet the *content* of his ideals, of course, will be wholly unchanged; he will still advocate killing Jews in the name of racial purity, or keeping people alive till the last moment whatever the cost to them in suffering.

So the impure utilitarian described above does not get from Hare a philosophical weapon against certain sorts of ideals; instead he stands to have his *moral* weapons against them taken away from him. The person whose ideals they are, the fanatic, can place his position beyond the reach of moral censure simply by being *very fanatical indeed*. He is not required to argue for his position, or to meet the arguments against it of his opponents. Moral *thinking* is quite unnecessary, on Hare's account of moral thinking.[30]

Hare would reply that the foregoing remarks miss the point entirely. If the fanatic's preferences are strong enough, his own sufferings if they are *not* implemented will be greater than the sufferings of others if they are. Thus if the impure utilitarian cares about *suffering*, he should be satisfied. I shall deal with this reply in a moment (see p.183ff).

At this juncture, it is appropriate to look at the way in which Hare concludes his discussion of the example of the fanatical doctor; for it reveals that not even *he* finds pure utilitarianism credible.

We have seen that Hare allows, as he must, the possibility of victory for the doctor's antecedent preference – the preference to keep the patient alive. Everything depends on the strength of this preference, and it may be very strong indeed, stronger than the preference not to treat which the doctor acquires by putting himself in the patient's shoes. However, Hare goes on to suggest that the preference of the doctor to keep the patient alive in these circumstances is the sort of preference that should be *altered*.[31] So on the one hand he is saying that we are required to 'assign equal weight, strength for strength, to all preferences alike',[32] while on the other he is saying that certain preferences (moral attitudes) are such that they ought to be changed.

But why ought these preferences to be changed? Hare points out that the doctor's preferences *can* be changed; they are 'alterable', he says 'in a way in which the patient's sufferings and consequent preferences are not'.[33] In fact, this is not strictly true. It *is* true, of course, that the patient's *suffering* cannot be altered; but what goes into critical thinking is not the patient's suffering but the patient's *attitude* to his suffering. It is his *preference* not to suffer which figures in critical thinking, and that is the sort of thing that can be altered; for it is possible to see suffering as something one must endure. Even if we set this point aside, it still needs to be explained why the doctor should try to alter his own preferences; and what explanation can Hare give?

Well, he can say, as he does, that the doctor's preference is (in effect) a preference for suffering, in that it is one that brings about or prolongs suffering. However, to say this is to attach importance to something other than the strength or intensity of the preference in question; and it is therefore to go beyond the only factors which are supposed to enter into critical thinking. The suggestion is that the patient's preference is *special* because it is a preference *not to suffer*. But what right has *Hare* to say so? Has he not disqualified himself from saying so by insisting that the content of preferences is of no relevance to moral thinking? It seems to me that he has, and that he cannot change his mind without abandoning his whole account of the sort of thing moral thinking is. Any attempt to give moral priority to the suffering of the patient in this case would contravene something fundamental to pure utilitarianism, namely, the moral irrelevance of what a preference is a preference *for*. As we have seen, a pure utilitarian calculation can take account of nothing except a preference's extent and intensity.

Hare does realise this, of course; and his final comment upon the example of the fanatical doctor is that although victory for the doctor's antecedent preference is *conceivable*, we need not worry about it – for in practice it is not going to happen. Hare does not deny that if putting the patient under intensive care were to emerge from critical thinking as the preferred action, it would then be the right action; he could not deny *that* without giving up his theory. What he denies instead that it would ever *in fact* emerge as the preferred action. It is, he says, 'pretty fantastic' to suppose that it would do so, 'pretty fantastic' to suppose that a medical team's preference to treat would be stronger than the preference of a patient (plus his sympathisers) not to suffer.[34] Since our intuitions are not designed to deal with fantastic cases, it is not surprising that if we imagine such a case critical thinking will give 'counter-intuitive' results – it will pronounce to be right a course of action which seems to most of us to be wrong.

It is surely evident, however, that the case in question is by no means 'pretty fantastic'; if it were, people would not need to argue in the way that Richard Lamerton, for example, argues in the passage I quoted in chapter 2 (see p.32). Lamerton thinks it necessary to urge the point that it is not the duty of a physician to preserve life at any cost; that the right time for a man to die may come before he has breathed the last breath of which he is capable, and that physicians must learn to recognise when that time has come – when it is not in a patient's interests that his life should be prolonged any further. Were Hare right in his opinion that the case of the fanatical doctor is 'fantastic' then, to repeat, Lamerton's arguments would be quite needless; he would be saying what no-one disputes.

I suggest, then, that at this point Hare is refusing to face up to the implications of his own theory. Nor is this the only occasion on which he does so; whenever his theory implies something that he dislikes, Hare tells his readers that it will not come to that. But why should it not? Why, more importantly, does it *matter* that it should not? On Hare's view, let us remember, the results of archangelic thinking *cannot rationally be criticised*. So why do we need the reassurances Hare is so anxious to give us? More to the point, why does *Hare* need them? *We* may be irrational enough to welcome such reassurances, but *he*, surely, is not.

I have said several times that utilitarian thought is associated with the championing of certain values or ideals, and especially with that of *the relief of suffering*. In the case of the fanatical doctor, we would expect a utilitarian to argue that treatment should be withheld from the patient because the latter should not be made to endure suffering he would rather be spared. What I have tried to show is that *pure* utilitarianism, Hare's sort of utilitarianism, eliminates values or ideals, *all* values or ideals, *including this one*. What is right, it says, is what is preferred, whatever that may be; and the action which would minimise suffering in any given case will not necessarily emerge from critical thinking as the action that is preferred. The archangel may pronounce to be right the action which causes suffering, not the action which relieves it.

On Hare's account, therefore, people who are suffering are at the mercy of what other people want; for what people want is the only true or infallible measure of right and wrong. The preferences of the suffering will be taken into account in critical thinking, of course; but there is no guarantee that they will emerge as the ones that should be implemented. Archangelic thinking is as blind to suffering as it is to the content of any aversion or desire, and thus the relief of suffering as a *value* drops out of utilitarianism in its pure form. There goes with it, I suggest, the chief source of the moral appeal which utilitarian theory has exerted upon people from its inception.

At this point, though, we need to return for the last time to Hare's treatment of the case of the fanatical doctor. The reason is that in his discussion of how critical thinking proceeds in this case, there is – as we have seen – a passage which presents the outcome of the procedure as the minimising of suffering in *any* event – even if, that is to say, the victorious preference is the doctor's antecedent preference to keep the patient alive. The significance of this move goes beyond the particular case in question; for it makes it clear that what Hare wishes to say is that critical thinking *as such* is necessarily directed at the minimising of suffering. When one does what is preferred, he wants to say, one does at the same time what will minimise suffering; to do the first *is* to do the second. Thus it is not the case that critical thinking is *blind* to suffering in the way I have said it is. Let us now examine this claim.

We saw above that Hare initially presents the situation faced by the fanatical doctor as one which involves a conflict between two prima facie principles, the principle of prolonging life whenever possible and the principle of relieving or preventing suffering. We saw also that when critical thinking is brought to bear on this conflict, the preferred action may not be the action that would release the patient from his suffering; it may instead be the action that would, by prolonging his life, prolong his suffering at the same time. Nevertheless, even in that event Hare would describe the death-postponing action as the action that will minimise suffering *all told*. If the doctor's preference to treat is strong enough to outweigh the patient's preference to die, he says, then 'in that case even critical thinking will say that the suffering of the two taken together will be minimised by putting the patient under intensive care'.[35]

The picture Hare paints is this: on the one hand there is the suffering of the patient if he is kept alive; on the other there is the suffering of the doctor if the patient is allowed to die. What must be done is whatever will produce the least amount of suffering altogether, whatever will minimise the total amount of suffering involved. This is the goal to be achieved, and it can be achieved only by the doing of whatever is preferred. It is not the case, therefore, that if the doctor's antecedent preference wins he will do what is preferred *as opposed to* what will minimise suffering; in doing what is preferred, he will be doing what minimises suffering; there is no distinction between these two things. Hence, the relief of suffering as an ideal is *not* absent from utilitarianism in its pure form; rather, the relief of suffering is what pure utilitarianism is all about.

I suggest that what must be said in reply to this point is that it *equivocates* upon the notion of suffering. When the relief of suffering is spoken of as an *ideal*, what is meant by suffering is *not* what is meant by suffering when critical thinking is presented as having the relief of suffering as its aim or object. What is meant in the former case are certain specific human ills or evils, both 'natural' and 'social': pain, hunger, disease, poverty and oppression are all prime examples. What is meant in the latter case is the frustration of *any desire or preference at all*, irrespective of its content.

The point is that we do not count as *suffering* – certainly not as suffering which ought to be relieved – the frustration of just *any* desire; but that is what we would have to do were we to regard 'critical thinking' as necessarily directed towards the relief of suffering. Our conception of suffering would have to mirror the blindness of critical thinking to the content of desires or preferences; to suffer, according to such a conception, would be to go without something – anything – one wanted or wished to have. What that something was would be beside the point. I suppose that we might allow this to be a conception of suffering *in a wide sense*; but suffering in *so* wide a sense makes, I suggest, no moral claim on us whatsoever. We would think it a bad joke were someone to draw our attention to – for example – the way in which Nazis 'suffer' on account of the existence of Jews, and suggest that we ought to try and relieve their 'suffering' by providing them with opportunities to satisfy their desires.

Let us go back to what I said in the very first chapter about the relationship between utilitarian theory and moral practice. Utilitarian theory, I said, far from being the measure by which the rationality of moral practice must be assessed, is an aspect of moral practice writ large. Utilitarians pick out one of the forms that moral justification takes and proceed to label it the only rational form; they select one of the many considerations we count as moral in character and proceed to define the notion of moral justification in terms of it. But what is this consideration? What element of our ordinary moral thought is represented in utilitarian theory by the notion of *utility*?

The answer to this question is evident from the way in which Mill himself chose to define the Principle of Utility. 'Utility', he says, 'or the Greatest Happiness Principle, . . . holds that actions are right as they tend to promote happiness, wrong as they tend to produce the reverse of happiness.'[36]

A concern with human *happiness* (or *well-being*) is most certainly a moral value or ideal, and an extremely important one – though not the only one there is. It is the positive side of the moral coin whose negative side was referred to above as the relief of suffering. The roots of utilitarian theory lie in such ideals; and this accounts both for the plausibility of the theory and for its perennial moral appeal. Pure utilitarianism, however, digs up these roots. A concern with human well-being, or with people's happiness, is not the same as a concern to satisfy just any desire which anyone happens to have, as long as he happens to have it intensely enough. It is, I suggest, a concern with *needs*, and with needs whose satisfaction we consider to be more or less essential to the living of a properly human life. This raises all manner of issues, the pursuit of which would require a book to itself; but one point that should be mentioned here, even if it cannot be enlarged upon, is that no account of human well-being or happiness is possible that does not *itself* refer to moral values or ideals. Mill's own account does that, despite his attempts to present it as a purely naturalistic one.[37]

Pure utilitarianism, then, in defining utility in terms of the satisfaction of desires or preferences, any desires or preferences at all, robs the notion of its moral content and disables it as a standard or measure of moral conduct. We need to know what someone desires, for what reasons, and in what circumstances, before we can say whether or not the fact of his desiring that thing has any moral upshot whatsoever. The person in question may be *entitled* to have it, or he may not; it may be *fair* or *just* or *good* or *fitting* that he should have it, or it may not; it may be simply that he *might as well* have it; indeed, it may be that people in general, other things being equal, might as well have what they want. It seems to me, however, that this is hardly sufficient to make utility as defined by Hare into a moral value or ideal.

185

Pure utilitarianism, then, Hare's sort of utilitarianism, in eliminating from the assessment of action all considerations except those of utility defined in preference–satisfaction terms, eliminates moral thinking – all moral thinking, including the sort of moral thinking in which utilitarianism itself is rooted. The utilitarian drive to reduce all rational moral judgement to a single form has culminated in the loss of moral judgement as such.

10

UNMASKING MEDICAL ETHICS

In the first chapter of this book we looked at the conception bioethicists have of the enterprise on which they are engaged. We saw that they present the aim or object of that enterprise as one of resolving the substantive moral issues to which medical practice gives rise; the business of medical ethics, according to them, is to provide *the rational answers* to certain moral questions – the answers, that is, which can be justified from the standpoint of reason or rationality. Implicit in the bioethical account of medical ethics is the attribution to medical ethicists – professional philosophers – of *moral expertise*. Philosophers, the account implies, possess a special competence in relation to moral matters which is analogous to the special competence doctors possess in relation to medical matters. It is for philosophers, therefore, to settle moral disagreements and resolve moral dilemmas; they must uncover the verdict of philosophy itself upon the matters at issue.

I have argued that philosophy as such does not deliver a verdict upon moral issues. When bioethicists purport to tell us what *philosophy* says about abortion, for example, or infanticide, they are telling us only what they, as individuals, say about these issues. Philosophers, I maintain, have no special authority to make moral pronouncements. The conception of rational justification in morality which seems to confer such authority upon them is a radically defective one, and once its defects are brought to light the futility of bioethics is revealed.

'So the philosopher has nothing to contribute to the discussion of moral issues raised by medical practice, or to the education of medical practitioners and other health carers?' It would not be too surprising if someone with little or no knowledge of philosophy were tempted to think that that was an implication of the position for which I have argued. It would be very surprising indeed if any philosopher were tempted to think so. My position is that philosophers do not possess special moral expertise, and that therefore they cannot teach such expertise to others – for example, professional health carers. Morality, I maintain, does not *admit* of special expertise; in so far as it makes sense to talk of moral expertise at all, it is something that people in general possess. People in general, that is to say, know how to make moral judgements; these are judgements of a sort we are all brought up to make, and not ones for which we require a special training or education. This position is hardly a new one in philosophy; it does not imply the irrelevance of philosophical enquiry to the question of how medicine should be understood and practised, and it does not imply either that philosophers can play no useful role in the discussion of substantive moral issues. In this concluding chapter I shall say something about both of these matters; and I shall do so by way of critical comment upon Ian Kennedy's enormously influential book, *The Unmasking of Medicine.*[1]

Kennedy's concern with the subject of medicine is ultimately a practical one. His aim is not to make academic points about the subject, but to effect a radical and far-reaching change in the way medicine is actually practised. Although Kennedy is an academic lawyer and not a professional philosopher, he seeks to bring about this change by conducting an enquiry into medicine which is essentially philosophical in nature. His work shows, therefore, the relevance to medical practice of philosophical reflection and modes of thought, and in so doing it paves the way for a proper account of the contribution philosophers can make to medical education.

Kennedy believes that modern medicine has taken the wrong path, and that in the main it has done so because of the *philosophical* misconceptions which lie at the heart of it. In this I think he is right. It is my view, however, that *medical ethics too* has taken the wrong path, the bioethical path, and for a similar reason. At the heart of medical ethics as it is presently understood and pursued, at least for the most part, is the philosophical misconception that moral expertise is possible, and that philosophers are the people who have it and can impart it to others. It seems to me, furthermore, that Kennedy himself comes close to embracing this very misconception, despite the fact that it is as antithetical to his primary ethical concern as the misconceptions he himself exposes. Thus an incoherence threatens to emerge at the very core of *The Unmasking of Medicine.* This point, like Kennedy's own, is not of merely academic importance; if we wish to achieve the practical objective for which Kennedy argues, it is not only medicine that we must unmask – it is medical ethics also. Let us consider what this objective is.

In his preface to *The Unmasking of Medicine* Kennedy identifies 'the power of the professional' as one of its central themes.[2] His view, as developed in subsequent chapters, can be summarised as follows:

Members of the medical profession – doctors – have power to control our lives through the decisions and judgements they make. That power, however, is not rightfully theirs but ours; we must take it back from them and regain the control over our own lives that we have been led to abdicate. What this means is not that we should make all of those decisions and judgements ourselves, but that we should play a crucial role in setting the standards to which doctors must refer when they make them on our behalf. These standards must be ones which are, in Kennedy's words, 'socially established' or 'agreed'.[3] The reason is that the vast majority of the judgements and decisions in question are not (purely) *medical* but *moral*.

How has it come about, according to Kennedy, that doctors possess power which is not rightfully theirs? How has it come about that they are not expected to account to the rest of us for the moral judgements and decisions they make? The answer, in brief, is that although these judgements and decisions *are* moral, and not (or not exclusively) technical or scientific, they appear to us and to those who make them in the latter guise. They appear to be matters of medical expertise, and thus matters that fall within the sphere of the doctor's unique competence as someone trained in medical science. In reality, doctors are agents of social and political control; yet they seem to us and to themselves to be scientists, engaged in an enterprise which involves nothing more than the application by experts of purely scientific and objective principles. Medicine, which is fundamentally a political activity, masquerades as one which is apolitical and value free; and we will remain its servants rather than its masters until we bring the masquerade to an end.

That is the essence of Kennedy's position; and it will be evident even from my brief account of it that the process of unmasking medicine in which he is engaged is fundamentally a philosophical one. When he analyses what he calls the 'rhetoric' of medicine in the early chapters of his book, Kennedy is doing philosophy. Let us look briefly at the aspects of his analysis which are most relevant to the present discussion; for the details of Kennedy's argument, readers are referred to *The Unmasking of Medicine* itself.

The key to Kennedy's critique of medical thought and practice lies in his rejection of the account given by scientific medicine of the concepts of *health* and *illness*. According to that account, whether or not one is *ill* or *well* is a matter of objective scientific fact. One is ill when one's body is in a state that departs or deviates from a biologically determined norm of proper functioning; and this departure from the norm is attributed, for the most part, to a disease – '. . . some specific entity, which is caused by an attack on or invasion of a part or parts of the body, or by some malfunction of a part, so as to produce circumstances in which someone complains of feeling ill.'[4] So when a person does complain of feeling ill his complaint is well founded if and only if there really is a departure from the norm of the sort just described. If there is, the complainant really is ill, he is really in the objective state for which the term 'illness' stands; and it is for the doctor, the expert on such states, to say whether or not this is so. If the doctor finds that illness is in fact present, his business is to cure it; he must (if he can) restore the complainant, his patient, to that state of normal functioning which is *health*.

It is not difficult to see how the 'medical model' of illness and health invests the doctor with a monopoly of power in these matters, and confers upon him a title to its possession. He holds the power to diagnose illness, and has the right to hold it, because he alone has the special competence or expertise to make the diagnosis. Illness is the doctor's exclusive preserve; and because health is the product of the medical intervention which removes illness, health is his exclusive preserve too. These things are the business of the doctor and not – for example – of his patient, unless the latter happens himself to be medically trained. The business of a patient in this connection is to submit to the judgement of his doctor and obey the orders he gives.

We have seen that according to Kennedy, much of the power which doctors have to control people's lives is power which rightfully belongs to the people whose lives they control. If he is to establish this claim, he must take issue with the medical model of illness and health; and that is what he does. He argues for an understanding of health and illness which is *normativistic* (rather than positivistic) and *social* (rather than medical). Illness, he concedes, does involve a departure or deviation from a norm; but this norm '. . . is a product of social and cultural values and expectations . . .' and not '. . . some static, objectively identifiable fact'.[5] It is, in other words, one which is socially, rather than biologically, determined. Furthermore, any deviation from the norm must be *judged* to be 'illness' (rather than, for example, 'wickedness' or 'evil'). The declaration that someone is ill is not a statement of fact, Kennedy says, but a judgement upon the facts, a *value* judgement; illness is not a technical or scientific term but a part of our moral or ethical vocabulary. 'Each diagnosis of illness', he writes, 'is an ethical decision'.[6]

The doctor, then, has no legitimate title to the power he wields – the *exclusive* power to grant or withhold to his patients the status of illness. The point, to repeat, is not that doctors should stop making the relevant judgements, but that the values doctors refer to in making them should be ones which are accepted by society as a whole. They must be *our* values, and not the values of a single individual, profession or social group:

> . . . since the diagnosis of illness always calls for a judgement it is right for us all to consider when it is properly to be applied and who should set the ground rules for its application. We should consider what limits may properly be placed by us on the power of doctors to manipulate the concept . . . we must make it our business to ensure that the judgements arrived at reflect the considered views of all of us.[7]

It is only if we do this, Kennedy maintains, that the relationship between the doctor and his patient can be one of 'mutual trust and responsibility'.[8]

We saw above that scientific medicine places not only illness but also health within the sphere of the doctor's unique competence or special expertise. 'Health', on this view, designates that state of normal bodily functioning to which the doctor restores the patient when he cures the latter's illness. Health is the product of medical science, and thus the exclusive preserve of those trained in that science: doctors.

Kennedy contends against this that health, like illness, is '. . . an evaluative term redolent with moral, spiritual, political and social overtones . . .'.[9] He proceeds to argue that health is not the product of medicine, but of political, social and economic conditions. Scientific medicine, he says, has concentrated upon 'disease entities' at the expense of such conditions, which political action alone can change. Once again, his point is that we must win back from doctors the control over our health and well-being which properly belongs to us as autonomous individuals and as members of a democratic community. The power and the responsibility for creating a society of healthy people must rest, Kennedy says, not with members of one specific profession, but with society as a whole.

So according to Kennedy, medicine has taken the wrong path, the 'scientific' path; and it follows that it must be put back on the right one. In chapter 3 of his book Kennedy suggests ways in which this might be done, in the form of a 'blueprint for change'.[10]

In my account of his argument, I have tried to bring out the connection between Kennedy's philosophical enquiry into the nature of certain judgements and concepts and his main practical objective of transferring power and responsibility from members of the medical profession to 'the rest of us' – to patients, as individuals and as members of society. As we have seen, Kennedy's argument for the moral necessity of this transfer turns on the *philosophical* distinction between a *scientific* (or *technical*) judgement on the one hand and a *value* judgement on the other. His view, as I understand it, is that whereas scientific judgements must be made by people who possess the appropriate special expertise, value judgements do not require special expertise. People in general are entitled to make value judgements, or to have a say in setting the standards by reference to which others must make them on their behalf. The monopoly of power that doctors presently enjoy over the making of certain judgements – judgements about whether people are *ill* or *well* – depends for its legitimacy on construing such judgements as belonging to the first of the categories mentioned above; in reality, however, they belong to the second. They are not scientific or technical but moral or ethical, and it follows that the doctor must share with his patients the power to make them. So far, I have no criticism to make (here) of Kennedy's position.[11]

My misgivings about his position begin when Kennedy returns in chapter 4 to the business of 'unmasking' the judgements and decisions which doctors commonly make in the course of their professional activities. In this chapter, he is talking, not about decisions concerning health and illness, but about ones which are even less plausibly construed as technical or scientific in nature. Let us look briefly at the kind of decisions he has in mind, and at what he has to say about how they should be made.

Kennedy gives various examples of the sort of decision with which he is concerned at this point in his discussion. Among these examples are decisions about whether or not to treat babies born severely handicapped; decisions about whether or not to let patients die, or even to kill them; decisions about whether or not to tell patients the truth concerning their condition; and decisions about whether or not to grant women abortions, or to admit them to programmes of treatment for infertility. With such examples in mind, Kennedy submits that '. . . the majority of decisions taken by doctors are not technical. They are instead moral and ethical. They are decisions about what ought to be done, in the light of certain values.'[12] Given that this is so, he continues, they are not decisions which only doctors are competent to make. Matters of morality, even in a medical context, are not matters for the doctor and for no one else; he has no special title to decide how they are to be resolved. In making moral decisions, doctors must conform to 'the ethical principles of society' – moral standards set or agreed upon in conjunction with other people.[13] Kennedy finds 'utterly objectionable' the thought that issues like those described above should be presented as ones '. . . for doctors alone to decide upon, so that others intrude at their peril'.[14]

It would seem then, so far at least, that the central point Kennedy is making in the fourth chapter of his book is the same as the point he made – or appeared to be making – in the first. To restate this point in general terms: as far as moral or ethical decisions are concerned, no special expertise is required in order to make them; doctors, for example, are no better qualified to make decisions of this sort than their patients. It follows that we must all have a say in establishing the principles or standards by reference to which such decisions must be made.

However, there are a number of statements in chapter 4 of *The Unmasking of Medicine* which could be read as pointing in a direction not only different from, but also opposed to, the moral egalitarianism expressed in the preceding paragraph. For example, there is the following passage:

> . . . if doctors claim unique competence it must be in something they are uniquely competent to do. Doctors are not uniquely competent to make ethical decisions. *They receive no training to prepare them for such a role. They have no preparation in moral philosophy, they have no special skill in ethical analysis.*[15]

It seems to me that this passage could be interpreted as giving a very different reason from the one mentioned above for saying that the doctor's unique competence does not extend to decisions of the sort Kennedy discusses in the fourth chapter of his book. The point that the doctors' special expertise is *medical* and that these decisions are *moral* would remain the same; what would not remain the same would be the attitude to the idea of *moral expertise* attributed to Kennedy in previous remarks. As I originally presented it, his position was that *no one* possesses moral expertise; or – which amounts to the same thing – that moral expertise, in so far as it exists at all, is something *everyone* possesses. However, what the passage quoted above suggests is that some people *do* possess a special expertise in moral matters; but that doctors are not, as it happens, among them. It implies that special moral expertise exists, but that it is not something in which members of the medical profession happen to have been trained.

It will be evident, I think, that the difference between the two positions just outlined is of major significance. On the second, but not the first, special moral expertise is something that doctors do not possess at the moment *but could come to possess*. They could acquire a competence in the making of moral decisions which, though not unique to them, would be something to which the majority of their patients could lay no claim. Doctors could be taught a 'special skill in ethical analysis' by the people who have it already – professional philosophers.

Now this may not be Kennedy's view, but, as I have said, it is a possible way of reading the passage quoted. What is more, as we have seen, moral philosophers themselves – the ones that dominate medical ethics, at any rate – take very much this sort of line. Moral philosophy, they imply, can make its students better at answering moral questions than other people; better, because more able to provide the rational justification which all moral decisions, beliefs and principles must have. Whether or not Kennedy himself would accept such an account, it is one that has wide currency amongst medical ethicists – the very people he would like to see involved in medical education.[16] It is important, therefore, to consider what implications its acceptance would be likely to have for the objective *The Unmasking of Medicine* sets forth.

This objective, as I said before, is the transfer to the rest of us of the doctor's power (or part thereof) to make ethical decisions; and with it that control over our lives which he is presently allowed to have. The central plank in Kennedy's argument for the transfer, as we have seen, is his claim that ethical decisions do not fall within the sphere of the doctor's unique competence. The doctor has received a special training, to be sure, a training the rest of us lack; but this is *medical* training, training in medical science, and the decisions in question are not medical but moral.

Very well; but there are, apparently, people who have what the doctor does not – 'special skill in ethical analysis' – and presumably these people can teach that skill to others; to the doctor himself, for example. Suppose that the doctor does receive a course of instruction from people of this sort; suppose that he embarks upon a course in 'medical ethics'. What becomes, in these circumstances, of Kennedy's argument for the transfer of the doctor's power to his patients? Will not the doctor be able to say that it no longer applies? Will he not be able to say that he has now *acquired* a special competence to make ethical decisions, one that his patient (the man on the Clapham omnibus) does not possess? Whatever might have been the case once, the doctor will be able to say, he is no longer overreaching the sphere of his unique competence or special expertise when he makes decisions of this sort.

I am suggesting, therefore, that if we think of moral philosophers as the possessors and teachers of moral expertise, their involvement in medical education will serve to *consolidate* the power of the medical profession. It will give the doctor a *title* to that power by enabling him to represent his special competence as extending beyond matters of medical science to value judgements and moral decisions. In this event, the cure Kennedy prescribes will prove worse than the disease.

There is a further point to be made in this connection. As we have seen, Kennedy's argument uncovers a *philosophical misconception* at the centre of modern medicine – namely, the 'medical model' of illness and health. It is primarily this misconception, he says, which accounts for the power doctors have come to possess, power which should be transferred to society as a whole. Kennedy is not blind, however, to the role played by quite other factors in the development of this state of affairs, or at least in its perpetuation. It is a melancholy truth that when people have once acquired power they are most reluctant to give it up; they acquire what is usually termed a *vested interest* in the maintenance of whatever has conferred that power upon them. For this reason, as Kennedy notes, 'the present state of medicine will take some changing'.[17] Whatever its shortcomings, the medical model of illness and health is one that members of the medical profession have good reason to cultivate; besides, 'it flatters the self-esteem of the doctor to see himself as the applied scientist and problem solver spreading health'.[18] It should not need saying – but it does – that to make such comments as these is not to engage in 'doctor bashing'; it is only to recognise that the doctor, like everyone else, has his share of certain common human failings. To repeat: like everyone else – *including, of course, the philosopher*. It flatters *his* self-esteem to see himself as a moral expert, an authority on moral matters called in to advise and assist important people like the doctor.[19]

There is yet a further point. Quite apart from their own personal vanities, philosophers – like doctors – are members of a *profession*, and – again like doctors, perhaps – members of a profession which is in need of help. Philosophy tends to be perceived as the archetypal ivory tower subject, of no *use* at all; it is not surprising, therefore, that it should have fallen from favour in recent years. During the Thatcher administration no fewer than six university departments of philosophy were closed down in the United Kingdom. If we add to this the fact that there is now a method of funding in British universities which gives overwhelming importance to the volume of student recruitment, we can see that philosophers have a vested interest in anything which attracts large numbers of people to philosophy departments. The point is obvious: if philosophers think that what doctors want and expect from them is moral expertise, they have every inducement for seeming to provide it. They have as much reason to cultivate this misconception of 'the power of their craft'[20] as doctors (or pharmaceutical companies[21]) have to cultivate the misconception of health and illness which Kennedy exposes. There is, in my view, a real *danger* here; if not of conscious deception, then at least of self-delusion.

I must emphasise that in making the preceding remarks I am not opposing the participation of philosophers in medical education (or re-education); I am opposing a particular conception of what their participation involves. I am saying that it does not and cannot involve the imparting to health carers of 'moral expertise'; and I am saying also that if it is perceived as involving that, it will serve only to undermine the objective which Kennedy wishes it to further. It will help to *legitimise* the appropriation by the medical profession of power that, as Kennedy says, rightfully belongs to society as a whole.

But if the philosopher cannot offer the health carer moral expertise, what can he offer him? We have seen the beginnings of an answer to this question in our discussion of Kennedy's work; let us return, then, to the point from which our examination of his book began.

We saw above that the central objective of *The Unmasking of*

Medicine is practical rather than academic; Kennedy's aim is not merely to understand medical thought and practice, but to change it. We saw also that he seeks to achieve this aim by exposing the philosophical misunderstandings he perceives at the heart of modern scientific medicine. His claim is that the medical model of illness and health, the model which dominates the way doctors think and act, misconceives or misconceptualises those things; it is *philosophically* inadequate. In presenting and arguing for this thesis, Kennedy shows that it is not necessary to attribute 'moral expertise' to philosophers in order to give philosophy a vital role to play in medical education. What it is necessary to do, in the first instance, is *what he has done*: display the crucial importance for medical practice of a correct philosophical account of how health and illness – and therefore the *production* of health and the *treatment* of illness – should be understood.

Kennedy uses the metaphor of 'unmasking' to describe the process of substituting a correct philosophical account of health and illness for the incorrect account we presently accept. Medicine, he says, appears to us and to those who practise it in a false guise; we must remove the clothes it has borrowed from science and engineering and expose the reality that lies beneath them. Kennedy uses other metaphors too; for example, that of turning medicine aside from the wrong path and putting it back on the right one. A metaphor he does not use, but which would be highly appropriate in this connection, might be drawn from medicine itself. Modern medicine, it might be said, is *sick*. The sickness must be diagnosed, the causes of it established and the patient restored to health. The people responsible for the diagnosis, in this case, are philosophers – or at least, people who use philosophical methods and express philosophical insights. Their responsibility for their patient, however, does not end with diagnosis; it must extend to treatment also. In other words, philosophy, as Kennedy says, should play an important part in the education and re-education of doctors and other health carers. To revert to one of Kennedy's own metaphors: it is philosophical reflection that must not only put medicine back on the right path, but keep it there.

We need to gain a more precise understanding of what this involves; in order to do so, let us look again at Kennedy's account of what is wrong with the path medicine has actually taken.

In the second chapter of *The Unmasking of Medicine* Kennedy sets out to describe the practical and moral implications of the medical model of illness and health, the model that is central to scientific medicine. Many of the points he makes in this chapter concern the preoccupation of medicine with identifying and curing specific diseases, rather than with promoting health and preventing illness; important as these points are, however, they are not the ones I wish to emphasise here. Kennedy argues, as I said before, that health is the product, not of medicine, but of political, social and economic conditions. He argues, moreover, that even as far as the care and treatment of the sick is concerned, medicine has taken the wrong path; and it is upon this aspect of his discussion that I shall concentrate in what follows.

Towards the beginning of chapter 2 Kennedy discusses the image of the doctor created by scientific medicine – the image of the doctor as an engineer or mechanic who applies scientific principles in order to restore his patients' bodies to a state of proper or normal functioning. If the doctor is seen as a mechanic, the patient is seen as a machine and his illness as a mechanical failure. As Kennedy says in a crucial passage in chapter 1, as far as scientific medicine is concerned:

> The Cartesian notion of the body as a machine has remained a central thesis. Like the machine, the body has functioning parts, each of which, with proper taxonomical skill, skill in classifying, has to be listed and its function explained. And, just as the machine will not run for long if a fan belt breaks or a gear cog is stripped, so your body will not function properly if, for example, your kidneys malfunction or are attacked. Humans have been reduced through the application of impeccable scientific skills to ambulatory assemblages of parts.[22]

This process of reductionism, he says in the following chapter, is one to which modern medicine is committed. Human beings are reduced in medical thought to machines, mere collections of functioning parts. They become ill – they 'break down' – when one of their parts malfunctions, usually through the action upon it of a specific disease entity. The proper response to illness, on this account, is to attack this entity; to give attention, not to the sick human being, but to the disease which is responsible for the dysfunctional state his body is in. 'It is this entity . . . which then receives attention, not the person'.[23]

What these and other passages eloquently expose are the *ethical consequences* of modern medical thinking, the moral ill-effects of the way in which medical practitioners are taught to regard and treat their patients. It is not that doctors are given erroneous or inappropriate views about this or that moral issue; it is that their education *dehumanises* and *diminishes* the people with whose health and well-being they are charged. The 'tunnel vision'[24] of scientific medicine is not merely unfortunate; it is ethically disastrous. The human being, 'the sick person in all his wholeness and vulnerability'[25] disappears, and is replaced by a malfunctioning machine; something that can be repaired, but cannot (logically cannot) be healed or cared for (except in the way that a car, for example, can be cared for). It is thus that 'Miss A becomes an x-ray projected on a screen, Baby B becomes a bad case of meningitis, Mr C becomes the pain in the neck at four o'clock'.[26]

The attitude described above – sometimes referred to as that of 'caseness' – is the inevitable product, on Kennedy's account, of scientific medicine as such; it is not something which can be corrected in isolation from a major philosophical shift in medical thought and education – one that would restore to it *the person as a whole*. This is not, of course, the metaphysical entity which bioethicists, for example, have in mind when they speak of the person; it is the person in what I called in chapter 1 the ordinary sense – the individual human being, together with the environment, physical and social, of which he is a part.

The key, then, to the treatment of the sickness from which medicine suffers, to the healing of medicine itself, is the restoration to medical thought and practice of *the human being*, the patient as sick man, woman or child, and not as malfunctioning machine. What is needed, in other words, is not some new discovery, but the *recovery* of what has been lost, what has been pushed out of modern medicine by an over-scientific outlook.

The point that must now be made is this: the recovery of the human being is the recovery, at the same time, of the values which form the framework of his life as a moral being, or member of a moral community. It is this process of ethical recovery, it seems to me, which should be the principal objective of courses in health care ethics;[27] and it is in their ability to contribute to the process that the primary value of philosophers as teachers of such courses must lie. It does *not* lie in their imagined ability to exercise and teach 'moral expertise'.[28]

In connection with the notion of ethical recovery, consider the 'principles' that Kennedy says 'good medical ethics' should incorporate.[29] There appear to be six of them; the principle of beneficence, the principle of (avoiding) maleficence, the principle of respect for

199

autonomy, the principle of truth telling and promise keeping, the principle of respect for the dignity of the individual, and the principle of seeking to do justice or equity among people.

All of the above 'principles', I suggest, are structural features or elements of our everyday moral life; they belong to its framework, or to the scaffolding on which it is built. They are not principles of which one could be *ignorant* unless one were ignorant of moral considerations as such.

Consider the first two: the principles of beneficence and of avoiding maleficence. These, Kennedy says, belong to 'traditional medical ethics' and 'must continue to be respected';[30] doctors must do good to their patients, and not do harm to them. I do not wish to take issue with this at all; indeed, the point I wish to make is that no one *could* take issue with it. What sort of principle would it be that doctors should *not* do good to their patients, or that they should do harm to them? It could not conceivably be a *moral* principle. (Nor, of course, is this a point only about the conduct of doctors to their patients; the principles to which Kennedy refers have universal application). One could not take issue with the principles in question without taking issue with morality itself; and the same goes, I would argue, for the other principles Kennedy lists – tell the truth, keep promises, act justly, and so on.[31]

It does not follow from this, however, that Kennedy need not have bothered to mention these principles, or that he must be mistaken when he says, as he does, that all but the first two are ones 'which present medical ethics ignores or gives scant attention to'.[32] It does not follow, because one can *forget about* or *see as irrelevant* what one is not *ignorant* of; and Kennedy himself has shown how the moral conceptions we take for granted in our ordinary dealings with one another have been expelled from the medical consciousness, the consciousness of the doctor *qua* scientist or engineer. The primary task of health care ethics, as I said before, is to recover or reinstate those moral conceptions – to *remind* health carers of the vital place in their work of familiar values, ones they already acknowledge in other areas of their lives; it is not to give them *new knowledge*.

It is possible, of course, to make it *sound* like new knowledge. This can be done by using an unfamiliar vocabulary – by speaking, as Kennedy does, of *beneficence*, and *maleficence*, rather than (or, in his case, as well as) of *doing good* and *doing harm*; or by speaking of *respecting the autonomy of persons*, rather than of *allowing people to make up their own minds*.[33] In this way the impression is created that we are talking, not about the familiar elements of our everyday moral lives, but about special principles which philosophers or other intellectuals know about, and which must be added to the special scientific principles health carers are taught in the course of their professional training. The point is an important one; for it is thus that concepts which are in reality common or public property come to be represented as the private property of a set of experts, to be used as they prescribe. If moral issues are presented in these terms, they appear as issues for these experts, and not for other people; certainly not for the man on the Clapham omnibus, the ordinary patient, who is even less likely to be familiar with the jargon of medical ethics than with the jargon of medicine itself. As Kennedy himself says on the first page of his book:

> . . . there is a long list of issues which are deeply troubling but which seem effectively to be kept under wraps. One of the most successful ways of doing this is by making the issues and problems appear to be medical, technical ones, not really for the rest of us at all. This can be accomplished by the simple device of translating the issues into medical language . . . The first step on the way to *understanding* modern medicine, looking behind the mask, is to unravel the *rhetoric* of medicine.[34]

Quite so. It is not only medicine, however, which employs a professional rhetoric, and which by so doing contrives to disguise non-technical issues as technical ones; medical ethics employs exactly the same 'simple device'.

I have argued that the principal task faced by medical ethics is one of *ethical recovery*. A framework needs to be put in place for the discussion of the substantive moral issues raised by medical practice; but that framework, to repeat, is one with which we are all familiar; it is not a novel one to which philosophy or some other intellectual pursuit holds the key. In saying this, I am not denying that health care throws up moral *problems*, moral issues over which people disagree and about which any one person may feel uncertain or confused. The ethical recovery I have spoken of will not *solve* those problems, *settle* those issues or *remove* those uncertainties. Nevertheless, it is essential to the perception of them as the sorts of problems and issues that they are – *moral* ones – and to the examination of them *as* moral ones for which courses in health care ethics provide an opportunity.

What is the purpose of the examination of moral issues just referred to? If the position for which I have argued is correct, it is not to discover the answers to moral questions which *philosophy* produces (or underwrites); for there are no such answers to be discovered. Philosophy does not deliver a verdict on moral issues – a verdict on, for example, abortion, surrogacy, genetic engineering or euthanasia. There is no question of identifying by means of philosophical discussion the *uniquely* rational answer to a question like: should we carry out experiments upon living human embryos? There *is* no uniquely rational answer to such a question – which means, of course, not that there is *no* rational answer to it, but that there is *more than one* rational answer; there is more than one answer which can be defended or supported by appropriate moral reasons. A course in health care ethics must identify those reasons; it must uncover both what can be said for an action or practice such as the one mentioned, and what can be said against it. Why is it a moral issue at all for us? How does it connect up with other issues? What values does it put at stake? What are the implications of deciding it in a particular way, or of arguing in a particular way for that decision? These questions, among others, are ones which any health care ethics course should be concerned to address; and in addressing them it may help the people who participate in the course to decide what answers to the moral questions at issue *they* wish to give, or find themselves able to accept.

It should not be forgotten, in this connection, that many of the issues which courses in health care ethics must treat are exceedingly complex. Surrogacy, for example, is not one issue but a cluster of issues, and issues of different sorts at that. It is easy to confuse considerations relevant to one of these issues with considerations relevant to another, or to misunderstand the character of a particular claim or a particular objection; and philosophers can help identify confusions and misunderstandings of this sort. People may make *logical* mistakes in arguing for a certain conclusion, mistakes of the kind which philosophers are trained to identify and expose. People may fail to realise what assumptions they are making in the course of an argument, or fail to think through the implications of what they are saying; and philosophers can help them to do this. Or again, people may fail to distinguish one sort of issue from another – an *empirical* issue from a *conceptual* issue, for instance; and philosophers can help them to make such distinctions. Finally, people may appeal to concepts or ideas – such as 'quality of life' – which are vague, ambiguous or even incoherent; and philosophers can isolate these concepts and subject them to critical scrutiny.

These points are all of them familiar; and they can be summed up in terms that are equally so. The object of the examination with which we are concerned, it might be said, is primarily one of *clarification*: the clarification of issues, types of issue, assumptions, arguments and concepts. In conducting or assisting with this clarification, the philosopher is helping to facilitate the discussion by health carers of the moral issues which arise for them in the course of their work. He does not *resolve* those issues on their behalf; health carers (like other people) must decide for themselves where they stand on moral questions, as individuals and as members of a profession. They must decide as far as they can, that is; disagreements and dilemmas are bound to remain, and health carers (and their patients) will have no option but to live with them.

Philosophers, then, can help to facilitate the discussion of medico-moral issues by health care professionals. This role is hardly of no consequence, even if it is rather less conducive to one's *self*-consequence than the imaginary role which some philosophers seem to covet: the role of moral expert. In fulfilling the former role, philosophers are exercising, not *moral* expertise, but expertise in the carrying out of certain primarily *intellectual* tasks or activities.

It is not only philosophers, of course, who possess the skills necessary to carry out such tasks; philosophers are not *uniquely* well qualified to facilitate the discussion of moral issues. Many lawyers, for example, would do this just as well. Indeed, it might be argued that there are factors which militate against the effective discharge by professional philosophers of the responsibilities the facilitator's role involves. The common perception of philosophy mentioned above – the perception of it as the archetypal ivory tower subject – is not without foundation. Philosophers pursue questions and issues which are abstract and intellectual; and an ivory tower is arguably the most suitable place in which to do that sort of thing. Moral questions and issues, however, are neither abstract nor intellectual; and it follows that habits of thought cultivated in ivory towers are not necessarily the ones most appropriate to the discussion of them. The construction of fanciful scenarios, for instance which is something that many philosophers like to indulge in, is even less helpful to a discussion of moral problems than to a discussion of the philosophical problems which tend to call it forth, such as the problem of personal identity; it is certainly no substitute for genuine moral imagination, a quality conspicuously absent from bioethical writing.

To put the point frankly and in general terms: when philosophers discuss moral issues, they tend to intellectualise them out of all recognition; and they must resist this tendency if they are to facilitate the understanding of such issues which health care professionals are seeking when they embark upon courses in ethics. Self-indulgent displays of intellectual virtuosity, however impressive in their own terms, are inappropriate and unhelpful in this context; what is worse, to conduct a moral discussion as though it were an exercise in mental gymnastics is almost invariably to trivialise the issue at stake.[35]

With the above qualification, therefore, philosophers possess intellectual skills which can be used to help clarify the moral issues raised by the practice of health care and facilitate their discussion. More importantly, philosophy as such (and not merely the philosopher) has a vital role to play in medical education. For it is philosophical enquiry, as we have seen, which uncovers the need in medical practice for a process of ethical recovery; and ethical recovery, I have argued, should be the principal objective of medical ethics in particular and health care ethics in general.

Thus there is no need to present philosophy as something which confers *moral expertise* upon its students in order to give it relevance to the practice of health care; to present it as something which can provide *the right answers* to the moral questions faced by health carers and their patients. Indeed, one of the most important lessons philosophy has to teach in my view is that one cannot speak of the right answers to such questions, in the way that one can speak of the right answers to certain other sorts of questions – mathematical questions, for example, or technical questions. As we have seen in previous chapters, two people may disagree radically about a moral issue without it being the case that one of them is more rational, or more intelligent, or better informed, than the other. This is a philosophical insight; and one, moreover, which it can benefit a person to have – he might be less inclined than before to think that anyone who disagrees with him about a moral matter must be either stupid or wicked. Health carers will not gain such an insight from the writings of bioethicists, who are the new Sophists in the sense explained in chapter 1. The intellectual credentials of the new Sophistry, however, are just as dubious as those of the old.

NOTES

1 INTRODUCTION: UTILITARIANISM AND THE NEW SOPHISTRY

1 Plato, *Gorgias*, 447c, T. Irwin, (trans.), Oxford, The Clarendon Press, 1979, p.13.
2 ibid., 454b, p.21.
3 ibid., 459d, p.27.
4 ibid., 459e–460a, pp.27–8.
5 ibid., 460b, p.28.
6 Thus 'bioethics', as I use the term, stands for a school of thought within medical ethics and not for medical ethics as such. Bioethicists themselves tend to regard 'bioethics' as synonymous with 'medical ethics'; see, for example, Peter Singer's introduction to Singer (ed.), *Applied Ethics*, Oxford, Oxford University Press, 1986.
7 John Harris, *The Value of Life: An Introduction to Medical Ethics*, London, Routledge & Kegan Paul, 1985, p.4.
8 ibid., p.4.
9 ibid., p.4.
10 My position is *not* that *nothing* one thinks about a moral issue is a rational thing to think; nor is it that *anything* one thinks about a moral issue is a rational thing to think. (Indeed, I argue below that there can be circumstances in which it would not *make sense* to deny the applicability of a given moral concept to an action; see chapter 6.)
11 This is a stock example in moral philosophy. The original version was that of William Godwin, in his *Enquiry Concerning Political Justice*, first published in 1793. In Godwin's discussion the trapped people are a famous archbishop and his valet, the father of the rescuer.
12 J.S. Mill, 'Utilitarianism', first published in 1861; reprinted in A. Ryan (ed.), *Utilitarianism and Other Essays*, Harmondsworth, Penguin, 1987, p.272.
13 ibid., p.273.
14 ibid., p.274.
15 ibid., p.296.
16 ibid., p.274.

17 James Rachels, *The End of Life: Euthanasia and Morality*, Oxford, Oxford University Press, 1986, p.148.
18 J.S. Mill, in Ryan (ed.), op. cit., p.278.
19 Generally speaking, impure utilitarians attempt to argue that the values they recognise are *not* independent of utility; for an example, see below, pp.11f.
20 J.S. Mill, in Ryan (ed.), op. cit., pp.295–7.
21 For a discussion in relation to Mill of the distinction between act and rule utilitarianism, see J.O. Urmson, 'The Interpretation of The Moral Philosophy of J.S. Mill', *Philosophical Quarterly*, 3 (1953), pp.33–9; reprinted in P. Foot (ed.), *Theories of Ethics*, Oxford, Oxford University Press, 1967, pp.128–36. For a critique of Urmson's paper, see J.D. Mabbot, 'Interpretations of Mill's "Utilitarianism" ', *Philosophical Quarterly*, 6 (1956), pp.115–20; reprinted in Foot (ed.), op. cit., pp.137–43.
22 J. S. Mill, in Ryan (ed.), op. cit., pp.335–6.
23 ibid., p.336.
24 ibid., p.296.
25 Harris, op. cit., p.192.
26 See Immanuel Kant, *Groundwork of the Metaphysic of Morals*, 1785; reprinted in H.J. Paton, *The Moral Law*, London, Hutchinson, 1948.
27 Harris, op. cit., p.193.
28 See P. Singer, *The Expanding Circle: Ethics and Sociobiology*, Oxford, The Clarendon Press, 1981.
29 P. Singer and H. Kuhse, 'Allocating Health Care Resources and the Problem of the Value of Life', in D. Cockburn (ed.), *Death and The Value of Life* (Trivium 27, 1992) p.9.
30 ibid., p.9.
31 See pp. 43ff and pp. 67ff.
32 R.M. Hare, *Moral Thinking: Its Levels, Method and Point*, Oxford, The Clarendon Press, 1981.

2 'PERSONS': THE FUTILITY OF BIOETHICS

1 Yet, as Gaita has pointed out, bioethicists are children of their time; see Raimond Gaita, *Good and Evil: An Absolute Conception*, London, Macmillan, 1991, p.317.
2 John Harris, *The Value of Life: An Introduction to Medical Ethics*, London, Routledge & Kegan Paul, 1985, Chapter I 'Beings, human beings and persons'.
3 ibid., p.9.
4 ibid., p.18.
5 This is an oversimplification. Infants and pets, unlike pieces of furniture, are sentient; and on the bioethical view sentience is sufficient for a certain degree of moral status. See pp.127f.
6 Michael Tooley, 'Abortion and Infanticide' in P. Singer (ed.), *Applied Ethics*, Oxford, Oxford University Press, 1986, pp.58–9; first published in *Philosophy & Public Affairs*, 2, No.1 (Fall 1972).
7 Harris, op. cit., p.14.

8 This is not a trivial point, for to call something a *belief* is to imply that it needs to be *justified*; See pp.35f and pp.135f.
9 Harris, op. cit., p.15.
10 ibid., p.16.
11 ibid., p.16.
12 ibid., p.16.
13 Value, it seems to me, is necessarily value to *someone*; but it is not necessarily value *for some purpose*. Thus I would not dispute that the value of something can be *intrinsic* as opposed to *instrumental*.
14 Harris, op. cit., p.7.
15 ibid., italics added.
16 Tooley, in Singer (ed.), op. cit., p.59.
17 Harris, op. cit., p.8, italics added.
18 Richard Lamerton, *Care of the Dying*, Harmondsworth, Penguin, 1980, p.125.
19 ibid., p.126.
20 C. Barnard, 'The Need for Euthanasia', in A. B. Downey and B. Smoker (eds), *Voluntary Euthanasia; Experts Debate The Right to Die*, London, Peter Owen, 1986; quoted by G. Fairbairn, 'Responsibility, Respect For Persons and Change', in G. and S. Fairbairn (eds), *Psychology, Ethics and Change*, London, Routledge & Kegan Paul, 1987, p.247.
21 Lamerton, op. cit., p.125.
22 See also pp.129f.
23 I myself gave this answer in an earlier version of the argument of this chapter; see Anne Maclean 'Bioethics and the Value of Life', in D. Cockburn (ed.), *Death and The Value of Life* (Trivium 27, 1992).
24 Ludwig Wittgenstein, *Philosophical Investigations*, IIiv, Oxford, Basil Blackwell, 1958.
25 Ludwig Wittgenstein, *On Certainty*, Oxford, Basil Blackwell, 1969, 204.

3 PEOPLE

1 John Harris, *The Value of Life: An Introduction to Medical Ethics*, London, Routledge & Kegan Paul, 1985, pp.192–5.
2 ibid., p.19.
3 ibid., p.9.
4 Normally, people cannot be opposed to persons. In what follows, 'persons' will sometimes be used (or mentioned) in the ordinary sense and sometimes in Harris's sense; I hope that it will be clear from the context which sense is intended in any given case.
5 The point is the same as that made on p.12, that the Principle of Utility allows us no reason to treat people unequally; the commitment of utilitarians to the denial of special obligations is a *logical* commitment. However, as stated previously, this tends to be combined in utilitarian writings with a *moral* commitment to the equal worth or entitlement of all persons; and that commitment is prominent in the work of Harris. See below, note 7.

6 See also pp.91ff.
7 Harris's insistence on the equal value of all valuable lives leads him to reject this sort of account; see Harris, op. cit., pp.87–110. It is, however, the orthodox utilitarian account (though the recognition of the need for rules creates a complication; see pp.65ff).
8 It must be emphasised that one might take the view a utilitarian takes *about this case* without being committed to the *general theory* of morality which utilitarians put forward; see also pp.85ff.

4 *REASON* AND REASONS

1 Peter Singer, *The Expanding Circle: Ethics and Sociobiology*, Oxford, The Clarendon Press, 1981.
2 ibid., p.100.
3 Singer is inclined to think that a limited amount of group altruism can also be explained in these terms; see ibid., pp.23–53.
4 ibid., p.79.
5 ibid., p.92.
6 ibid., p.92.
7 ibid., p.93.
8 ibid., p.119. Singer argues further that '. . . when we are comparing similar interests . . . the principle of equal consideration of interests demands that we give equal weight to the interest of the human and the mouse'. See below, chapter 8, note 4.
9 ibid., p.93.
10 ibid., p.93.
11 ibid., p.94.
12 ibid., p.93.
13 ibid., p.119.
14 ibid., p.93.
15 ibid., p.90.
16 ibid., p.118, italics added.
17 ibid., p.119, italics added.
18 The character of Mr Spock in the popular television series 'Star Trek' bears witness to this; significantly, Spock is (half) *alien*; see below, pp.66ff.
19 Singer, op. cit. p.113.
20 ibid., p.113.
21 ibid., pp.156ff.
22 ibid., p.167.
23 ibid., p.151.
24 First published in 1726. The page references below are to Herbert Davies (ed.), *The Prose Works of Jonathan Swift*, Vol. 11, Oxford, Basil Blackwell, 1941.
25 ibid., p.251.
26 ibid., p.252.
27 ibid., p.252.
28 Singer, op. cit., pp.151ff.

29 Swift, op. cit., p.256.
30 ibid., p.251.
31 ibid., p.252.
32 ibid., p.258.
33 ibid., p.153.
34 He agrees with Godwin that saving the more useful life would be the 'better' action in this situation; Singer, op. cit., pp.70–1.
35 In the preceding discussion, and in chapter 3 above, only two of these considerations were mentioned: the rescuer's relationship to the charlady and the value of the cancer researcher's work. However, we saw in chapter 1 that there is a third – the equal worth of all human beings.
36 Singer, op. cit., pp.70–1.
37 H.A. Prichard, 'Does Moral Philosophy Rest on a Mistake?', *Mind* (1912).
38 For an example, see D.Z. Phillips and H.O. Mounce, *Moral Practices*, London, Routledge & Kegan Paul, 1969, Appendix I.
39 R.M. Hare, *Moral Thinking: Its Levels, Method and Point*, Oxford, The Clarendon Press, 1981.

5 THE POLICY OF MAXIMISING LIVES

1 John Harris, *The Value of Life: An Introduction to Medical Ethics*, London, Routledge & Kegan Paul, 1985, p.14.
2 ibid., p.9.
3 ibid., pp.18–19.
4 See, e.g., ibid., pp.203–5.
5 ibid., p.21.
6 ibid., p.21.
7 Harris, op. cit., p.5.
8 ibid., p.5.
9 See Raimond Gaita, 'Better One Than Ten', *Philosophical Investigations*, 5, 1982, and 'Fearless Thinkers and Evil Thoughts', in *Good and Evil: An Absolute Conception*, London, Macmillan, 1991.
10 Though also, of course, on the sameness of the means by which it is brought about.
11 J.S. Mill, 'Utilitarianism'; in A. Ryan (ed.), *Utilitarianism and other Essays*, Harmondsworth, Penguin, 1987, pp.289–90.
12 James Rachels, *The End of Life: Euthanasia and Morality*, Oxford, Oxford University Press, 1986, pp.1–2.
13 ibid., p.91.
14 ibid., p.15.
15 ibid., p.15.
16 ibid., p.93.
17 ibid., p.93.
18 ibid., p.94, italics added.
19 ibid., p.93, italics added.
20 ibid., p.93.
21 ibid., p.93.
22 ibid., p.93.

23 ibid., p.92.
24 See pp.109f.
25 Harris, op. cit., p.22.
26 John Harris, 'The Survival Lottery', in P. Singer (ed.), *Applied Ethics*, Oxford, Oxford University Press, 1986; originally published in *Philosophy*, **50**, (1975), pp.81–7.

6 PLAIN MURDER

1 John Harris, 'The Survival Lottery', in P. Singer (ed.), *Applied Ethics*, Oxford, Oxford University Press, 1986; originally published in *Philosophy*, **50** (1975).
2 ibid., p.89. To be strictly accurate, this proposal is not made by Harris himself, but by two of the characters who figure in his paper, *Y* and *Z*; however, this seems to be a device Harris employs to distance himself from the implications of his own account of the value of life. In what follows, I shall ignore for the most part the distinction between Harris and these characters.
3 ibid., p.90.
4 ibid., p.92.
5 ibid., p.88.
6 ibid., p.88.
7 ibid., p.88.
8 ibid., p.94.
9 ibid., p.89.
10 John Harris, *The Value of Life: An Introduction to Medical Ethics*, London, Routledge & Kegan Paul, 1985, p.4.
11 Harris, in Singer (ed.), op. cit., p.94.
12 ibid., p.92.
13 The notion of an innocent threat has been defined as follows: 'An *innocent threat* is someone who innocently is a causal agent in a process such that he would be an aggressor had he chosen to become such an agent' (Robert Nozick, *Anarchy State and Utopia*, Oxford, Basil Blackwell, 1974, p.34). This definition makes it unnecessary for an *actual* aggressor to be involved in the posing of an innocent threat; for that reason I find it unsatisfactory, at least in the context of a discussion of self-defence.
14 See also pp.134ff.

7 THE VALUE OF LIFE

1 James Rachels, *The End of Life: Euthanasia and Morality*, Oxford, Oxford University Press, 1986, p.59.
2 ibid., p.59.
3 ibid., pp.50–1.
4 ibid., p.51.
5 ibid., p.58.
6 ibid., p.57.

7 See Michael Tooley, 'Abortion and Infanticide', in P. Singer (ed.), *Applied Ethics*, Oxford, Oxford University Press, 1986, pp.57–85.

8 Rachels, op. cit., p.5. One's biographical life, Rachels says here, is 'the sum of one's aspirations, decisions, activities, projects and human relationships'.

9 ibid., pp.24–6.

10 ibid., p.58.

11 ibid., p.73.

12 ibid., pp.57–8.

13 ibid., p.58.

14 ibid., p.77.

15 See, e.g., R. Frey, *Rights Killing and Suffering: Moral Vegetarianism and Applied Ethics*, Oxford, Basil Blackwell, 1983, chapter 12.

16 The value meant here, it must be emphasised, is *investment* value, not *aesthetic* value. I am aware that not all collectors are interested *only* – or even *primarily* in the investment value of their collection.

17 Some of these notions are also applicable to our treatment of animals; but this requires separate discussion.

8 HOW TO IGNORE MORAL THINKING

1 R.M. Hare, *Moral Thinking: Its Levels, Method and Point*, Oxford, The Clarendon Press, 1981.

2 James Rachels, *The End of Life: Euthanasia and Morality*, Oxford, Oxford University Press, 1986, p.28.

3 The term is Hare's; see pp.154f.

4 P. Singer, 'All Animals are Equal', in P. Singer (ed.), *Applied Ethics*, Oxford, Oxford University Press, 1986, p.228. It must be stated that Singer's chief concern in this paper, as in many of his other writings, is to argue against 'speciesism': 'I am urging', he writes, 'that we extend to other species the basic principle of equality that most of us recognise should be extended to all members of our own species' (p.216). This requires separate treatment; however, for an indication of what really becomes of this 'basic principle of equality' on the bioethical view, see above, pp.127ff.

5 See John Harris, *The Value of Life: An Introduction to Medical Ethics*, London Routledge & Kegan Paul, 1985, pp.87–110, especially pp.91 and 110.

6 ibid., p.81. Note, however, that in fact he does not rule out the possibility of such causes; the passage continues: 'they would have to be very weighty causes, indeed their weight would almost certainly have to consist in avoidable human suffering both widespread and severe'.

7 The strength of a particular desire for life would be of consequence for Harris, of course, if that desire were in competition with another desire of the same sort; see ibid., p.91.

8 See R.M. Hare *The Language of Morals*, Oxford, Oxford University Press, 1952 (revised 1961).

9 Hare, *Moral Thinking*, p.5.
10 ibid., p.6.
11 ibid., p.4.
12 ibid., p.44.
13 ibid., p.45.
14 ibid., p.40.
15 ibid., p.3.
16 ibid., pp.20ff. I do not discuss the property of 'overridingness' which, Hare says, 'distinguishes *moral* from other evaluative judgements' (ibid., p.24).
17 ibid., p.42.
18 ibid., pp.109ff.
19 ibid., p.111.
20 In what follows, therefore, I speak as though critical thinking *were* logically capable of being carried out.
21 Hare, *Moral Thinking*, p.42. I do not discuss his opposition to 'descriptivism'.
22 ibid., p.42.
23 On the distinction between preferences and moral convictions, see pp.169f.
24 See above, pp.10f; also the discussion of Singer's account of the need for rules on pp.65f. Hare's view seems to be that our present 'moral rules' already have the derivative status Singer would like them to be given.
25 Hare, op. cit., p.44.
26 ibid., pp.49–50.
27 ibid., p.46.
28 ibid., pp.35–43.
29 ibid., pp.28–31.
30 ibid., p.18.
31 ibid., p.185.
32 ibid., p.38.
33 ibid., p.1.

9 VALUES, PREFERENCES AND FANATICISM

1 R.M. Hare, *Moral Thinking: Its Levels, Method and Point*, Oxford, The Clarendon Press, 1981, p.26.
2 ibid., pp.32–3.
3 ibid., pp.51–2.
4 ibid., pp.34–5.
5 ibid., p.30.
6 ibid., p.26.
7 ibid., p.46.
8 ibid., p.91.
9 For a fuller discussion, see Anne Maclean 'What Morality Is', *Philosophy*, 59 (1984); and Julius Kovesi, *Moral Notions*, London, Routledge & Kegan Paul, 1967, chapter 3. Kovesi argues that the reasons for a moral judgement are to be found, not in a universal prescription or general

principle, but in the particular situation which gives rise to the judgement. In his recent book *Moral Reasons* (Oxford, Blackwell, 1993) Jonathan Dancy develops and defends a similar position, which he calls ' particularism'. Moral principles, he argues, are no more than reminders of the kind of importance certain considerations can have in suitable circumstances. My own position is particularistic in Dancy's sense (but *weakly* so; see Dancy, p.103).

10 Hare, op. cit., pp.111–12.

11 ibid., pp.178–9.

12 ibid., pp.185.

13 ibid., p.179.

14 ibid., p.185.

15 ibid., pp.177ff.

16 Yet equality emerges in Singer as a moral ideal; and that, together with his insistence on autonomy, makes his utilitarianism impure. (It is possible, however, that even critical thinking embodies the ghost of a moral conception of equality; in which case not even Hare's utilitarianism would be completely pure.)

17 This is one of Hare's own examples; see *Moral Thinking*, p.170.

18 See R.M. Hare, *Freedom and Reason*, Oxford, Oxford University Press, 1963, chapter 9.

19 Hare, *Moral Thinking*, p.177.

20 ibid., p.177.

21 ibid., p.177.

22 James Rachels, *The End of Life: Euthanasia and Morality*, Oxford, Oxford University Press, 1986.

23 Hare, *Moral Thinking*, p.175.

24 See, for example, J.J.C. Smart, 'Extreme and Restricted Utilitarianism', in P. Foot (ed.), *Theories of Ethics*, London, Oxford University Press, 1967, pp.171–83.

25 Hare, *Moral Thinking*, p.177.

26 ibid., p.180.

27 ibid., p.180.

28 ibid., pp.181–2.

29 This position is an impure utilitarian position, not in admitting values independent of utility (though it *may* do that) but in refusing to define utility in terms of the satisfaction of just *any* desires or preferences; see p.184.

30 It must be emphasised once again that my objection to Hare's account is *not* that critical thinking can yield 'counter-intuitive' conclusions. It is that whatever conclusions it might yield, it does not count as *moral* thinking. In the present instance, one of the points I am trying to bring out is the absurdity of an account of morality which makes the rightness of a point of view depend entirely on how strongly it is held.

31 Hare, *Moral Thinking*, p.180.

32 ibid., p.180.

33 ibid., p.180.

34 ibid., p.181.

35 ibid., p.180.
36 J.S. Mill, 'Utilitarianism'; A. Ryan (ed.), *Utilitarianism and Other Essays*, Harmondsworth, Penguin, 1987, p.278.
37 See, for example, his notorious distinction between 'higher' and 'lower' pleasures (ibid., pp.278ff) and especially his account of education (ibid., pp.302ff).

10 UNMASKING MEDICAL ETHICS

1 Ian Kennedy, *The Unmasking of Medicine: A Searching Look at Health Care Today*, London, George Allen & Unwin Ltd., 1981. The page references that follow are to the Granada edition of 1983.
2 ibid., ix.
3 ibid., p.89 and p.106.
4 ibid., p.20.
5 ibid., p.3.
6 ibid., p.17.
7 ibid., pp.16–17.
8 ibid., p.13.
9 ibid., p.17.
10 ibid., pp.48ff. It needs to be emphasised that Kennedy's objection is not to *science* in medicine but to *scientism* – the treating of non-scientific matters as scientific ones.
11 I would argue, however, that Kennedy's understanding of the fact–value distinction – or at least his use of it in *The Unmasking of Medicine* – is simplistic. More specifically, I would argue that a judgement can be *both* medical *and* moral; see Anne Maclean, ' "The Right Time to Die" and the Concept of Medical Judgement', in G. Hunt (ed.), *Ethical Issues in Nursing*, London, Routledge, 1993.
12 Kennedy, op. cit., p.83.
13 ibid., p.84.
14 ibid., p.88.
15 ibid., p.84 (italics added).
16 ibid., pp.112ff.
17 ibid., p.41.
18 ibid., p.41.
19 Or the lawyer; medical malpractice suits (for example) provide additional opportunities for philosophers to play the flattering role of 'moral expert'.
20 See p.1.
21 Kennedy, op. cit., p.22.
22 ibid., p.20.
23 ibid., p.29.
24 ibid., p.21.
25 ibid., p.21.
26 ibid., p.29.
27 Cf. the view expressed by Dr Geoffrey Hunt that 'progress in health

care now largely requires not medical discovery but *ethical rediscovery*'. ('Project 2000 – Ethics, Ambivalence and Ideology' in Oliver Slevin and Michael Buckingham (eds), *Project 2000 – The Teachers Speak*, Edinburgh, Campion Press, 1992).

28 Unfortunately, however, the recovery of the human being is needed in *philosophy* too – as is amply revealed by the writings of bioethicists.

29 Kennedy, op. cit., pp.121ff.

30 ibid., p.121.

31 It must be emphasised that this does not imply that one could never be morally justified in (for example) telling a lie, or breaking a promise; it implies only that all such acts *require* a moral justification.

32 Kennedy, op. cit., p.121.

33 Kennedy is by no means alone in this. The principal offenders, indeed, are Tom Beauchamp and James Childress, the authors of the most widely used textbook on medical ethics, *Principles of Biomedical Ethics*, New York, Oxford University Press, 1983. That book, it should be noted, takes a view of the relationship between 'ethical theory' and 'particular judgements' that is similar in important respects to the one criticised in the present work.

34 Kennedy, op. cit., p.1.

35 There is a further point. It is one thing to say *within* the ivory tower that – for example – the lives of infants are at our disposal; it is another, in my view, to say such a thing to people who are responsible for the care of infants. This is especially true if one purports to speak with the authority of philosophy itself.

SUGGESTED
FURTHER READING

The following are accessible to beginners:

Anscombe, G.E.M. 'Modern Moral Philosophy', *Philosophy*, 33 (1958) (reprinted in G.E.M. Anscombe, *Ethics Religion and Politics: Collected Philosophical Papers*, Vol.III, Oxford, Basil Blackwell, 1981).
Drury, M.O'C. *The Danger of Words*, London, Routledge, 1973.
Gaita, Raimond *Good and Evil: An Absolute Conception*, London, Macmillan, 1991.
MacIntyre, Alasdair *A Short History of Ethics*, London, Routledge, 1967.
Midgley, Mary *Beast and Man*, Brighton, The Harvester Press, 1979 (Methuen University Paperback).
—— *Heart and Mind: The Varieties of Moral Experience*, Brighton, The Harvester Press, 1981.
Murdoch, Iris *The Sovereignty of Good*, London, Routledge, 1970.
Plato *Gorgias*, Oxford, The Clarendon Press, 1979. *Apology*, in *The Last Days of Socrates*, Harmondsworth, Penguin, 1969.
Williams, Bernard *Morality: An Introduction to Ethics*, Cambridge, Cambridge University Press, 1972.

INDEX